THE CORRINGHAM LIGHT RAILWAY

A New History

Including Kynochs, Kynochtown / Coryton,
and the Oil Industry

with best wishes

Peter Kay

March 2009

By Peter Kay

Dedicated to the late Ivor Gotheridge

CONTENTS

Introduction and Acknowledgements	3
1 Kynochs, the 'Thames Works', and Kynochtown	4
2 The Promotion and Opening of the Corringham Light Railway	21
3 Peace and War: Kynochs and the CLR 1901 - 1921	31
4 The Cory's Years 1921 - 1950	50
5 The Vacuum/Mobil Years 1950 - 1996	65
6 Locomotives and Coaching Stock	76
Postscript: 1996 - 2008	89
Appendix 1: Corringham Light Railway Tickets	90
Appendix 2: Coryton / Shell Haven Bus Services	92
Corrigenda and Addenda to *The Thames Haven Railway*	95
Farewell	96

The CLR idyllic - from the 1949 Southern Counties Touring Society visit.

Lens of Sutton Association

Introduction and Acknowledgments

The Corringham Light Railway was scarcely a typical 1896 Act Light Railway. Its existence as a company was somewhat nominal throughout, for the line was in reality promoted and operated by Kynochs, and subsequently run by their successors Corys and Vacuum/Mobil. Hence the need to cover in full here the industrial activities that brought the railway into being. The line's unusual nature has also served to preserve it in commercial use into the 21st century, long after most of its contemporaries succumbed to nature. Nevertheless, the CLR did possess some of those 'quaint' characteristics that brought enthusiasts out to visit such lines in the 1920s-50s period.

A fair amount has been written about the CLR since the 1950s, notably of course Ivor Gotheridge's short history *The Corringham Light Railway* published by Oakwood Press in 1985. My own researches into the CLR began at the time of writing *The Thames Haven Railway* (published 1999), indeed my original intention had been to include CLR material in that book. I was able to visit Ivor shortly before his death, and then by a curious turn of events I 'inherited' his CLR photographs and notes. I am pleased to dedicate this fuller history to Ivor, for he did more than anyone else to collate information on the line in the post-war years. It would however be wrong to try to cover up the fact that, in his old age, he had unfortunately suffered from some confusion of the mind, and this is evident in places in his book.

Some aspects of the CLR's history are difficult to penetrate. Only the promotion and opening in 1897-1901 is recoverable from the railway historian's normal sources. The company minute book(s) appear to be lost although it is unlikely that they recorded much of interest anyway, at least after 1901 (1). Few timetables are known, and daily activities are little documented. From the average railway enthusiast's viewpoint, the line existed in a very obscure part of the country, and it was little visited by outsiders prior to the 1930s. Many of the 'facts' about the earlier decades would seem to be derived from what later enthusiast visitors were told by staff, in some cases only written down several years after the visit. Published accounts were then embroidered on by subsequent authors. I have accordingly tried to make it very clear where information is hearsay or otherwise unconfirmed.

This book is intended to be read in conjunction with *The Thames Haven Railway*. Together they cover the railway and industrial history of Thames Haven / Shell Haven / Coryton (except that no claim is made to have dealt with the internal details of the oil refineries). *The Thames Haven Railway* is now out of print and will not be reprinted - please feel free to make a photocopy of library copies for your own use if you wish. To assist those who do *not* have it, there is a small amount of repetition here to enable this book to be read in isolation.

I have managed to find more than seventy new photographs of the railway, more indeed than I dared hope for initially; but inevitably a fair number of the views here have been published previously. They have been included for completeness and to enable proper captioning for the first time. Among the railway photographers and photograph collectors who have contributed, I am particularly grateful to Nigel Bowdidge, Ken Butcher, Richard Casserley, Frank Church, Geoff Goslin, Brian Pask, Charles Phillips, John Scott-Morgan, and Chris Turner (and colleagues from the Lens of Sutton Association). I have been unable to trace Brian Hilton who took the photographs on p.61, and would be glad to hear from anyone who has information on this front.

Many 'new' photographs of Kynoch's works are also featured, principally thanks to Thurrock Museum (Jonathan Catton). On this front I am also indebted to Winifred Scott (now Winifred Price) who has kindly allowed the re-use here of some of the more interesting photographs from her 1981 book *Coryton - The History of a Village*, which had a wide circulation locally but has remained unknown to most 'railway' readers (2). Also, ExxonMobil have permitted the reproduction of a number of photographs from the staff magazines *Coryton Broadsheet / Mobil News* (3).

John Butcher, Ken Butcher, Godfrey Croughton, and Brian Pask supplied knowledge and illustrations for the section on CLR tickets. Vic Bradley, Russell Wear, Robin Waywell, Allan C.Baker, and other members of the Industrial Railway Society and the Industrial Locomotive Society, were subjected to prolonged questionings in the course of the production of Chapter 6, in an attempt to avoid the pitfalls of 'duff info' with which the history of industrial locomotives is usually surrounded. Alan Osborne and Peter Clark provided detailed information on the local bus services which killed off the CLR passenger service (4). Assistance on the local history front has been provided by Randal Bingley, author of the Fobbing parish history *Fobbing - Life and Landscape* (Lejins Publishing, 1997); Bill Hammond of Corringham; and Stuart Brand of Corringham who provided photographs from his family's collection (as explained at p.7).

The days when one could interview people who knew the pre-1919 world personally are now over, however I had the pleasure of meeting with Vic Lord (born Kynochtown 1919) and Win England (born Coryton 1926) who, along with Bill Hammond, were personally acquainted with many of those featured in the earlier photographs here, thereby providing us with a direct connection to people who might otherwise be but names from the past.

Once again this book has been put together for the press by Jim Connor, no short task in this case.

Peter Kay, Wivenhoe,
September 2008.

---

1. The minute books of Kynoch Ltd, and the Kynoch Estate Co Ltd, are preserved at the Birmingham City Archives, and were read through; they make partial recompense for the loss of the CLR minutes.
2. The photographs in question are those at p.10 middle left and right, p.12 bottom, p.20 top left and right, pp. 36/37 top, p.37 bottom, p.42 top, p.44 top left and right, p.51 bottom, p.66 top right, p.71, and p.74. It has been necessary to scan them from the published book, hence the quality is not up to present-day standards.
3. These too have had to be scanned from the published magazines and in consequence are not of high quality.
4. Alan Osborne's book *J. W. Campbell & Sons of Pitsea, Essex* (Essex Bus Enthusiasts Group, 2002) gives more details on one of the principal operators, and can be obtained from him price £3.50 (cheque to Essex Bus Enthusiasts Group) at 7 Farley Drive, Seven Kings, IG3 8LT.

Eastward from Ironlatch, 1950. *Brian Hilton, courtesy Charles Phillips*

CHAPTER ONE

KYNOCHS, THE 'THAMES WORKS', AND KYNOCHTOWN

KYNOCH LTD

George Kynoch was born in Peterhead in 1834 and in the 1850s he joined Pursall & Phillips, percussion cap manufacturers of Whittall Street, Birmingham. After a disastrous explosion at this city centre factory in 1859, a new works was built at Witton in 1861/2, in what was then a semi-rural area with plenty of room for expansion. The company soon became 'Kynoch & Co'. By the 1880s it had expanded the Witton works, known as the 'Lion Works', into one of the country's largest ammunition factories. In 1884 a Limited Company, G.Kynoch & Co Ltd, was established, with George Kynoch as Managing Director. However a bad period was then experienced and in 1888 Kynoch was forced out by a shareholders' revolt; he died in South Africa in 1891. Arthur Chamberlain, a leading shareholders' spokesman in this crisis, became Chairman in 1889 and remained in that position, and very much the principal figure in the firm, until his death in 1913. He was the brother of the leading Birmingham and national political figure Joseph Chamberlain, and the two were very close.

In the early 1890s Kynochs expanded into the production of high explosives – gelignite, dynamite, cordite (a new explosive first made commercially available in 1889 and then adopted by the Army) and Kynite (invented by Kynochs themselves, for use in mines where black powder was prohibited). To manage this side of the business, A.T. Cocking, an engineer previously working in the mining industry, joined Kynochs, quickly becoming a leading figure in the company. In 1895 a new factory for cordite and blasting explosives manufacture was built under his supervision at Arklow in Ireland, served by coastal shipping. Shortly afterwards land was bought in Essex for another new factory larger than Arklow (as described further below). Further capital was needed to finance this, and in 1897 the 1884 company was wound up and a new company, Kynoch Ltd, formed in lieu. The Boer War in 1899-1902 brought a boom period for the industry shortly after the Essex works opened, in somewhat incestuous circumstances given that Joseph Chamberlain, as Colonial Secretary in Lord Salisbury's government, was principally responsible for dealings with the Boer leaders in the years of increasing tension from 1896, at the same time as his brother's armaments company was busy expanding its capacity! In fact Lloyd George had already attacked Joseph Chamberlain during an 1895 army ammunition crisis, claiming that he had deliberately managed the crisis (which brought down the Liberal government) so that Kynochs would get more orders. Joseph disposed of his own large shareholding in Kynochs in 1899, but that was scarcely likely to deflect criticism, and Lloyd George returned to the attack in 1900. In the same year a *Punch* cartoon commented 'the more the Empire expands, the more the Chamberlains contract'!

THE 'THAMES WORKS' – OPENING AND EARLY YEARS

Kynochs secured the purchase of Borley House and Shellhaven Farms in Corringham in late 1896 (1). 750 acres were acquired and the necessary government licence was obtained for 200 acres of this to be used as an explosives factory (2). The Thames-side marshes were an ideal site for such a factory, thanks to their remoteness from any centre of population and their easy accessibility to shipping; although the only previous such factory on the Essex side had been the much smaller Miners Safety Explosives Works opened in 1890 (3). When the Kynochs shareholders were told about the purchases at their February 1897 meeting, the point was made that this was 'about the only remaining site on the Thames to which deep water comes'. Although there is no specific contemporary reference, it would seem likely that Kynoch's introduction to Essex (a world away from their previous Birmingham base) was effected by contact with the London solicitor Alexander W. Kerly, who lived at The Gables, Horndon-on-the-Hill, and was a Liberal County Councillor for the Tilbury Division and very much involved in local business affairs generally. Kerly was soon to take on the legal side of the promotion of the Corringham Light Railway, and then became a CLR director.

The local population was welcoming enough, although Kynochs made sure the point was registered by organising a petition in favour (4). In February 1897 the local press reported (5):

'We need hardly say how heartily we welcome Messrs Kynoch & Co into Essex. This celebrated Birmingham firm have acquired the Borley House estate, Corringham, and under a

---

The first edition Ordnance Survey 6in map, surveyed 1865-7, reduced to half the original scale (i.e. three inches to the mile). This shows the area in wholly pre-industrial form. Except for the elevated ground on which the villages of Fobbing and Corringham stand, the whole of this extract consists of reclaimed marshland. The main sea walls have existed in their present form since the seventeenth century at least. The various farmsteads on the marshland were mostly in existence prior to 1600. Several had their own wharves, the ready availability of water transport making up for the lack of roads.

Borley *alias* Borley House Farm had belonged to the Hospital of St Giles in Norwich, and it was the Corporation as the Hospital's trustees who sold it to Kynochs.

Great Ilford (not Ilfords as the OS has it) had no connection with Ilford, the name was a corruption.

Ironlatch was historically Little Ilford, the 'Ironlatch' name being a colloquialism that usurped the proper name.

Oozedam was Ooes in a 1598 document, Ouzey House in 1753, and Ouzeden Farm on the first one inch map.

Oilmill Farm was 'Ye Oylemill' in 1638 and is thought to have been a tidal mill used for crushing crops (not, of course, oil in the petroleum sense). However by the 18th century Oil Mill Fleet had been walled off as seen here.

Shellhaven House is illustrated at *The Thames Haven Railway* p.2.

Reedham appears as Buttons Farm on the 1777 Chapman & Andre map.

Of all these farmsteads, only Oozedam remains active as a farm today.

The marshland here was until the 1880s divided up between several parishes including 'inland' parishes many miles away (the same situation applied on Canvey, Foulness, and some other marsh areas). This could bring great official confusion for the inhabitants of those farms that happened to be part of some far distant parish! However in 1889 a Local Government Order transferred the portions of Laindon, Little Warley and Dunton, and the detached portions Nos 2 and 3 of Fobbing, to the civil parish of Corringham, leaving Kynochs with only one parish authority to deal with for most purposes. (This copy of the map has been overprinted by the OS to show these changes). But Borley Farm still remained within the *ecclesiastical* parish of Fobbing, so Kynochtown's church activities were subservient to Fobbing.

Corringham prior to the 1890s was a tiny village of even less significance than Fobbing (their only claim to fame being their role in the instigation of the Peasants' Revolt in 1381). Except for the area around the church, the Corringham of this map is scarcely relatable to present-day Corringham, which has since 1945 joined up with Stanford-le-Hope to make three miles of estate sprawl. In contrast, Fobbing lasted through the 20th century as a little-changed village.

Fobbing's navigable creek was dammed off (at a point just to the right

4

licence from the Secretary of State, which was approved by the Justices at Grays on Friday [12.2.1897], they propose to erect factories there for the manufacture of sporting and military ammunition. If all goes well, between two and three hundred persons will be engaged in the new works in nine months time, and the factory will eventually find employment for thousands of hands. The inhabitants of Fobbing, Corringham, and Stanford-le-Hope, in public meeting assembled, have recognised the great benefit the new industry will be to them'.

The area, like most of Essex, was suffering badly from the agricultural depression, and the population of Corringham and Fobbing had been falling, although Stanford-le-Hope with its railway connection was doing better.

Cocking was put in charge of the planning and construction of the works. December 1896 saw Kynoch's directors approving £4,311 for the equipping of the Engine House, Accumulator/Hydraulic Plant, Cordite Plant and Guncotton Plant; and also facing up to their responsibilities as landowners with £100 authorised for 'the erection of a sea wall on the villa system'. In January 1897 Arthur Chamberlain and another Kynoch's director, John S. Nettlefold, were taken around the site by Cocking, and 'settled the following matters – the level of the ground, the mode of traction [internal transport?] namely by trams, and the water supply'.

continued at page 8

A sketch of Borley House Farm shortly before the Kynoch's purchase.

Courtesy Marion Paley and Stuart Brand

Oilmill Farm, c1900. The children had no doubt come from Kynochtown, the farm providing a readily-accessible playground. Although not part of their initial purchase, this farm was owned by Kynochs from 1902 to 1912.

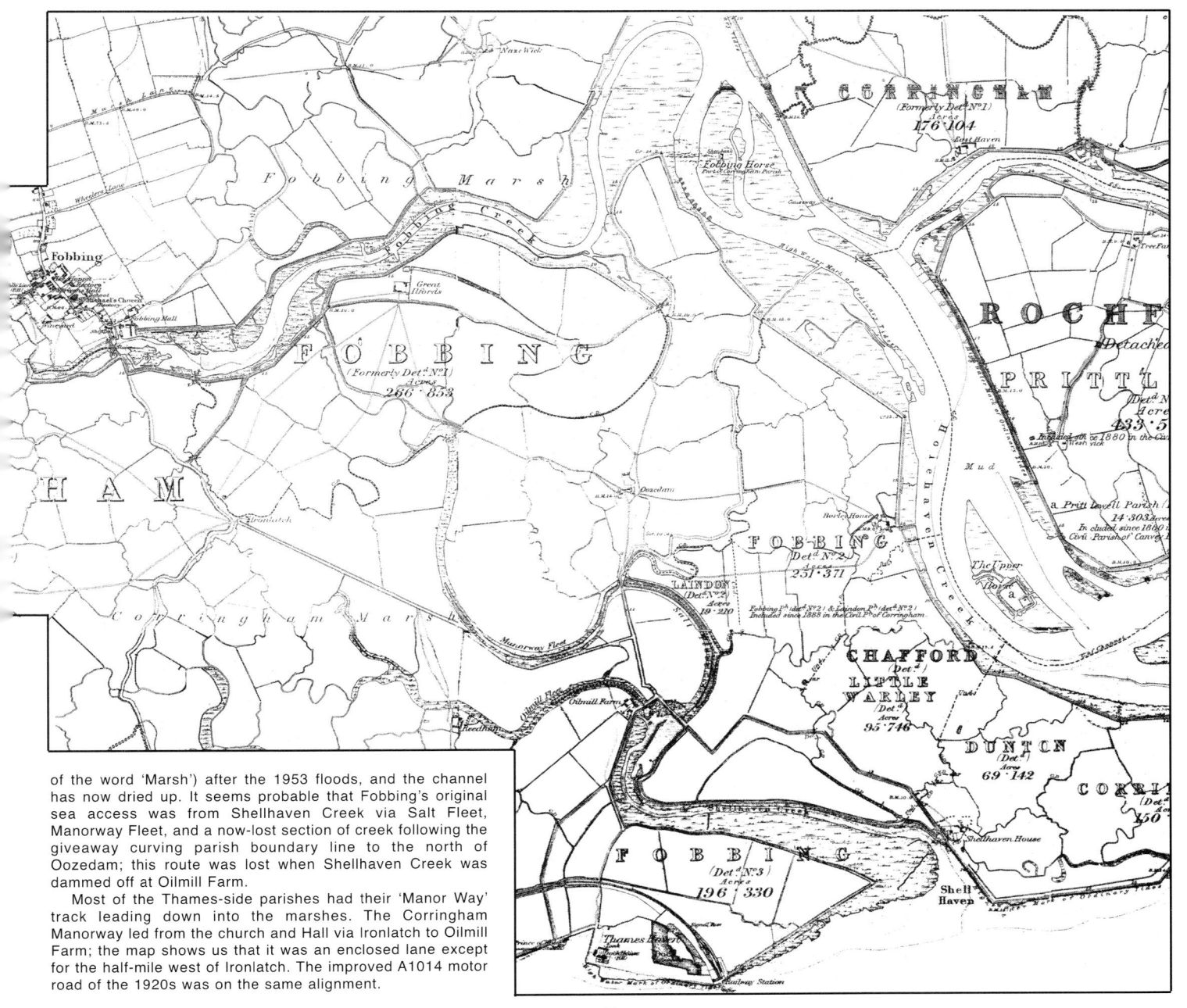

of the word 'Marsh') after the 1953 floods, and the channel has now dried up. It seems probable that Fobbing's original sea access was from Shellhaven Creek via Salt Fleet, Manorway Fleet, and a now-lost section of creek following the giveaway curving parish boundary line to the north of Oozedam; this route was lost when Shellhaven Creek was dammed off at Oilmill Farm.

Most of the Thames-side parishes had their 'Manor Way' track leading down into the marshes. The Corringham Manorway led from the church and Hall via Ironlatch to Oilmill Farm; the map shows us that it was an enclosed lane except for the half-mile west of Ironlatch. The improved A1014 motor road of the 1920s was on the same alignment.

above left
Arthur Chamberlain, Chairman of G. Kynoch & Co Ltd / Kynoch Ltd 1889-1913, and a Director of the Corringham Light Railway. He only ever visited Essex for special occasions. His son Arthur Junior succeeded him in both roles on his death in 1913.

above right
Allan Thomas Cocking, a photograph published in 1910. In his younger days he had sported a large moustache, *cf* the group portrait below.
Born in Rotherham in 1864, Cocking had worked from 1878 to 1889 in the office of C.E. Rhodes (then the President of the Midland Institute of Mining and Civil Engineers). He gained qualifications in physics and chemistry, and became particularly experienced in mining engineering. From 1889 he operated as a Consulting Engineer with offices in Rotherham and London, until joining Kynochs as Technical Manager in 1893, which of course meant a move to Birmingham. In 1896 he went on to the Kynoch's Board as 'Technical Director', and remained a Director until 1920. He was also Chairman and Engineer of the Corringham Light Railway until 1920.

'The Grove', alias 'Grove House', off Wharf Road, Stanford-le-Hope, Cocking's residence from 1897 to 1904. It is likely that the plans for the CLR were prepared here. The 1901 census lists Cocking as 'Ammunition Manufacturer', 37, plus wife Louisa (also from Rotherham), 28, son Allan, 4 (born in Birmingham), and three female servants.
A 1900 profile of Cocking in the *Kynoch Journal*, after describing him as 'quiet, undemonstrative, and amiable', continued
'A glance into his pretty house at Stanford-le-Hope shows at once that the owner is a man of an extremely artistic nature. The walls are lined with beautiful pictures, several of which are the work of Mr Cocking himself'.
The Grove must have been owned or leased by Kynochs, as when Cocking left in 1904 they let the Works Superintendent Col Frend have it. The house still exists but has been converted into flats, and the large grounds have been built over.

This photograph from Morris Paley's albums has no original caption, but was almost certainly taken at Borley House in the summer of 1897 to record the staff working on the construction of the Thames factory. The central figure with bow tie and boater is Cocking. Standing at either end of the group, with pillbox hats marked PATROL, are the men responsible for site security. They continued in post after the works opened (see photo p.10).

Courtesy Marion Paley and Stuart Brand

6

Morris John Paley came to Essex from Witton as a very young man in the initial construction phase in 1897, and stayed here until the end in 1919. In 1906 he married Louisa Brand of Stanford-le-Hope, where they lived in Scratton Road. Her father Lewis Brand was a builder in Stanford, and gained a good amount of work from Kynochs.

Paley returned to Witton after closure here. His photograph albums now belong to his daughter-in-law Marion Paley, and several views from them are featured here.

right

This plan is dated 26.3.97 and is therefore contemporary with the start of construction work. The distances between buildings are shown.

Most if not all of the buildings and magazines shown here were indeed built (and most were still in use in 1919, *cf* the OS map at p.38). However a good number of extra buildings were also provided in the original construction period, which ran on into the Boer War expansions. The non-consecutive numbering of the buildings here would also suggest that what is shown here was from the start regarded only as an 'initial phase'.

It is noticeable that there was originally a considerable gap between the 'Danger Area' buildings and the other buildings alongside the east-west roadway. The cordite buildings are concentrated in the central area (3-6, 9-10, 16-17, 21, 23). There are four 'drying houses' but no 'stoves'.

The tramway system is shown, with some sections seemingly as double track. (It is not clear whether any section was actually built double). The 'main line' sections shown here all remained in use until 1919 (but a lot of additional track was added subsequently).

Courtesy Marion Paley and Stuart Brand

1	Dining Room for women
2	Dining Room for men
3/4	Cordite cutting
5/6	Cordite blending and packing
9/10	Cordite drying houses
13/15	Guncotton
13A	Tanks
17/18	Cordite drying houses
21	Main cordite range
23/25	Magazines
28	Nitro Glycerine making
33	Waste water tank
34/41	Nitro Glycerine purifying
37	Acid
43/44	Air compressor
45	Tanks
46	Glycerine store
47	Acetone store
49/56	Dynamite making
53	Magazine
60-65	Cartridge huts
78-82	Magazines
91	Laboratory & Foreman's office
93	Laboratory magazine

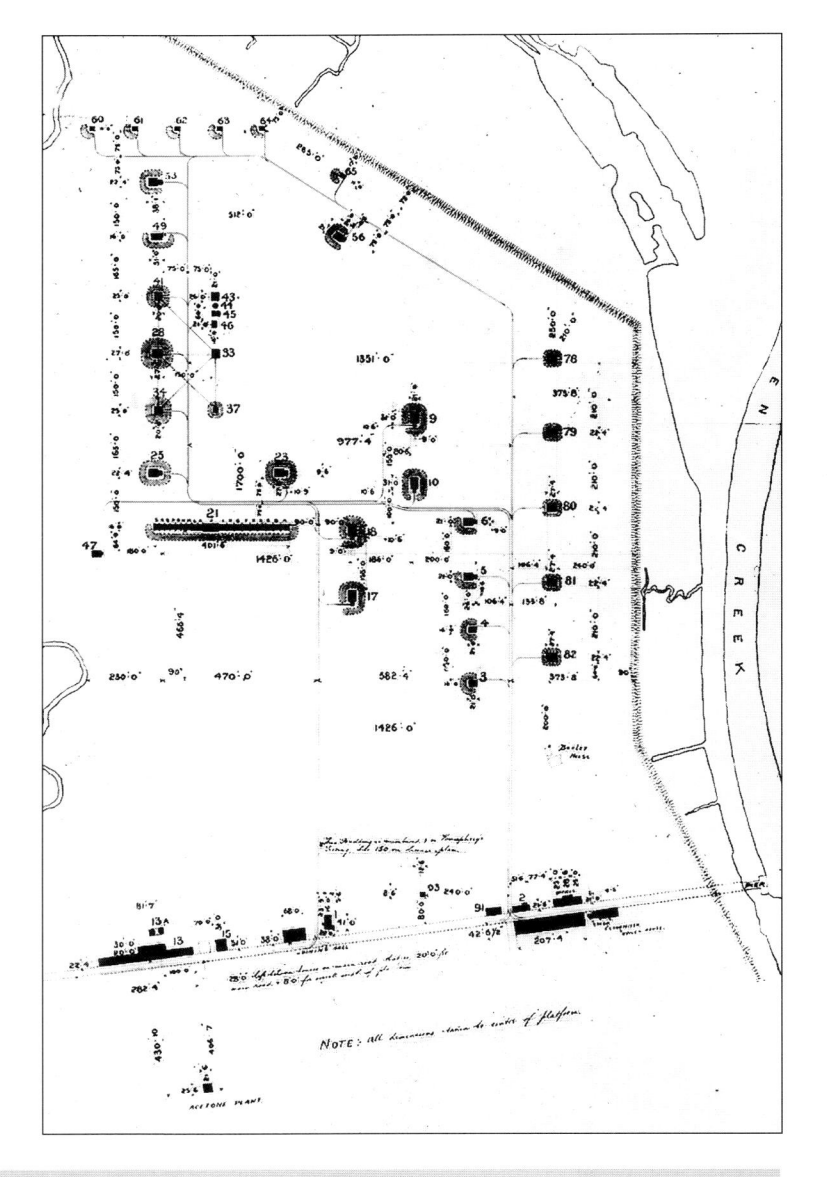

The Thames works under construction in 1898: a view north from the main cordite range, showing the north-western part of the works, with the three Nitroglycerine buildings (34, 28, 41) at left, and the water tanks (45) conspicuous at right. The trestling for the tramway 'main line' here is already completed; it is eight boards wide (as at p.45), but if what we are looking at here is a line of wooden 'rails' on it, they are a temporary way to a narrower gauge than that adopted. The 'diagonal' trestle-ways are completed as per the 1897 plan (but what was their purpose?). There are also several high-level trestled routes between buildings.

Courtesy Marion Paley and Stuart Brand

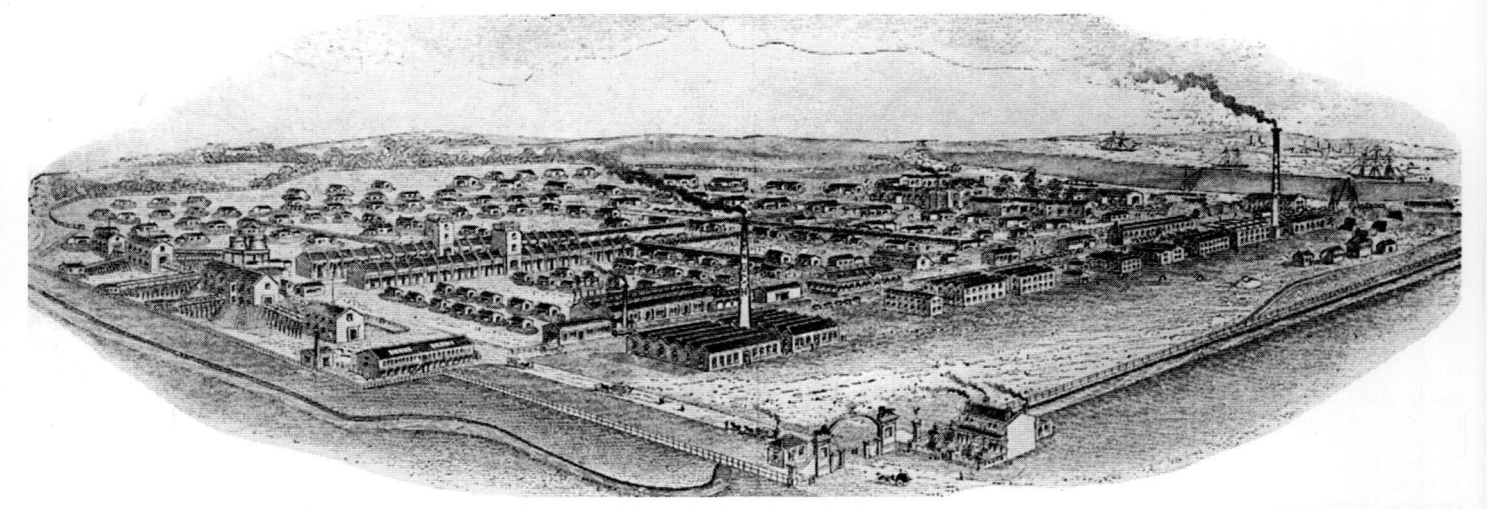

This artist's impression of the 'Thames Works' was one of a set illustrating all the Kynoch's works. Its earliest known appearance was in November 1899, when it was stated 'The Kynoch Thames Factory when the work now in hand is completed will have an appearance similar to [this] sketch'. Unfortunately there must be considerable doubt over the accuracy of much of what is depicted, and many presumably-intended buildings are shown that were never actually built. For example, the considerable range of buildings at left, to the north of the correctly-shown offices building, never existed, as all this area is still shown as undeveloped marsh, outside of the works area, as late as the 1919 OS map. The power station is correctly shown but many of the other sizeable brick buildings shown along the south side of the east-west spine road probably never existed. The fence around the works did exist, although not all on the alignments shown here. Note that the southern boundary fence runs due east from the works entrance gates – this may well have been the case originally. The entrance gates area is well depicted. The CLR has yet to be constructed.

Construction seems to have begun in March 1897, the press noting on 2nd April that (5)

'the new Ammunition Works at Borley House near Thames Haven are in progress, and about two hundred mechanics and labourers are employed upon them. Messrs Kynoch are transforming a desert into a veritable beehive. A truck tramway is being constructed, and the marshes are covered with stacks of timber. All the surplus labourers from Barking to South Benfleet are employed at the works. All the houses in Fobbing, Corringham, Stanford-le-Hope and the marshes are full of lodgers, and things look very prosperous. It is also rumoured that a new Brass Works is to be started, and that a thousand houses are to be constructed on the Fobbing marshes' (a decided exaggeration – see below!).

The contractors were Messrs Hickling, Bradbeer, and J. McCulloch (6). McCulloch at least had worked previously for Kynochs at Arklow.

Whilst most construction materials would one imagines have been brought in by sea, construction was not without difficulties. 'It was a formidable task to get there in winter, and many are the memories of broken axles, carts abandoned to be dug out of the clay at a more convenient season, and pedestrians labouring to extricate their sunken feet from the sticky mire' (7). Similarly J.H. Freeman was later to record that 'during the construction of the works, pieces of plant had to be dragged across the marshes, as there were no roads, by teams of horses. The large Lancashire boilers took something like six weeks to get from Corringham' (8).

No exact 'opening date' has been traced, but production started some time in autumn 1897. It was only in early September that the contract for electric lighting was given to Chamberlain & Hookham (9), so clearly opening was still some weeks off then. On 28th October Capt. Thompson of the Home Office 'inspected the Thames Works and expressed himself as in every way satisfied with all the arrangements'. This one imagines was a formality performed just before opening. The accounts of the great Thames flood of 29th November 1897, when the whole site was submerged in 'three feet of water', prove that the works was in action by then. It was recalled that 'the workpeople had to stay in the buildings all night and were rescued by rafts the following day' (7). Fortunately the buildings had been designed with such flooding in mind and the event was not a disaster.

A little internal ceremony took place on 27th January 1898 when Arthur Chamberlain visited the works and 'the cordite machinery started making cordite for the first time in our presence'. Three months later the opening of the factory was celebrated by a dinner for the local Kynochs officers and their guests at the Railway Hotel, Stanford-le-Hope, on the evening of Saturday 23rd April 1898, where 'one of the choicest public meals ever served in the town' was consumed. Cocking took the chair and made the principal speech. In the intervals between speeches many of the attendees contributed songs, whilst Mr Val Mason played on the pianoforte (10).

A report to Kynoch's shareholders in April 1898 noted that 'the departments at present opened are those for the manufacture of Gun-Cotton, High Explosives, and the Kynoch Smokeless Sporting Powder'. This rather obfuscated the point that *cordite manufacture* was the principal intended, and actual, purpose of this factory. Cocking reported in June 1898 that work to the sum of £10,285 had still to be done to complete the initial plans.

The new works was christened 'The Thames' by Kynochs. This name, no doubt invented in Birmingham, must have seemed odd to locals, and did not catch on in local usage, where 'Kynochs' would have sufficed. By 1905 the 'Thames' name was disappearing from Kynoch's own usage as well, replaced by 'the Kynochtown Works' (11).

With the Boer War getting the new works off to a good start, the local press was able to report in January 1900 that (12)

'Kynoch's works are at present busy in the execution of orders for cordite for ammunition purposes for South Africa for the British government. Every department is in full swing and working day and night'.

Through the war years the Kynoch's Board minutes regularly report expansions of the facilities:

16.10.1899 - Proposed plant for making Nitric Acid.

29.1.1900 - Insurance on the Thames Works to be increased from £22,265 to £27,965.

- Plans submitted for the principal parts of the new Gun Cotton factory.

26.2.1900 - Approved £6,000 for 'erecting a complete Black Gunpowder Plant at the Thames'.

18.2.1901 - Further sum of £650 for the erection of the Glycerine Refinery Plant.

- £2,000 for plant for manufacture of Muriatic Acid.

7.10.1901 - Agreed to erect a phosphate manure plant to produce 60 tons a week, using the nitre cake produced in the manufacture of nitric acid.

6.1.1902 - Approved £1,200 for 'a new range of buildings for Smokeless Powder at Thames'. (Smokeless powder had however been made here from the start, *vide* above).

- Approved £1,100 for 'new black powder mill at Thames'.

3.2.1902 - Approved £100 for improvements in the chemical works at Thames.

After 1902/3, however, references to expansion largely cease until 1915.

Cocking retained overall responsibility for the works after completion, and from 1897 to 1904 he lived locally at The Grove, Stanford-le-Hope (p.6). Twice a month he paid a two-day visit to Birmingham for Kynoch's Board meetings. He was also responsible for the Arklow factory, but he could only make occasional visits there. His day-to-day responsibilities at the Thames Works were reduced in August 1901 when Col Frend was appointed as 'Superintendent' under him, 'to be responsible to the Board for everything to do with the factory'. Under Frend was William Charles Sealy who had been Manager of Kynoch's Worsborough Dale works from 1897 until coming here in 1900 to assist Cocking. It was Sealy who lived in the Manager's House at Kynochtown.

A new laboratory was set up here in 1901 for Cocking to engage in technical research for Kynochs.

In February 1904 Cocking told the Kynoch's Board that 'a great amount of travelling and inconvenience and general strain upon his health was occasioned in consequence of his living at Stanford-le-Hope'. He was given permission to move to London, so long as he retained overall charge here. (In fact he moved back to Birmingham some time after this). However 'management difficulties' were being experienced as Cocking's hold on the reins here loosened. In 1902 Sealy was given notice after 'repeated rejections of black powder'; however he survived this and was still in post and in occupation of the Manager's House through the war years. Not so lucky was Col Frend who, after being formally congratulated by Arthur Chamberlain in late 1901 for 'his good work and the progress made at the Thames Works since his appointment as Superintendent', found himself ordered to fall on his sword in 1905 'in consequence of the unsatisfactory condition of the factory'. It has to be said that it is clear from the Kynoch's Board minutes that 'rejections' and management sackings were all too often occurring at the other factories as well!

Frend's disappearance in 1905 brought promotion to 'Works Manager' for 26-year-old Wilfrid Helcke who had been here in a junior management position since 1897/8 (see 1901 census p.17). He retained this post until closure (13), his salary of £200 a year in 1905 increasing to £425 by 1912. Sealy, although 30 years Helcke's senior, seems to have been below him after 1905.

Several of the other staff here in the early years had previously been at Arklow. The works office was headed initially by George F. Willis who was a longstanding Kynoch's employee from Witton (14). He was subsequently also made Secretary of the Kynoch Estate Co and the Corringham Light Railway Co.

The best description of the works in its early years is to be found in an article in the *Essex Review* in 1907 (15). The author visited the factory and was shown round by Helcke.

'And now as to the Kynoch Factory, that great spreading range of mysterious, low-pitched buildings, which lies to the left of Kynochtown, and entrance to which can only be obtained through the great gates, impressive in their size, and guarded by the Kynoch Lions carved in stone. From the moment of entry the visitor cannot help feeling that he is in unwonted and possibly perilous surroundings. The searching query with which he is met by the patrol at the gates, as to whether he has any matches or other combustibles upon him, serves to impress his mind at once with the magnitude of the explosive forces which exist on every side, forces which are merely hidden, but could in no way be confined within the lightly constructed buildings which, in the main, make up the factory. And in the second place the remarkable stillness of the place is profoundly impressive. The workers are there, all around us, varying in number, when the factory is in full operation, from three or four hundred up to six hundred; but the various buildings are so detached, and the whole factory covers such an extensive area, that the silence of the place is only broken by the plaintive cry of the marsh birds, or the sighing of the wind, which, whatever the season of the

An early view, definitely pre-1907, of the northern half of the works (the Danger Area). The viewpoint (from the power station) is marked on the 1919 OS map at p.38. At right is Borley House and its ancillary farm buildings, which lasted into the 1920s, part of them having been used as a works stores. It was reported that 'the stock includes everything from a pin to an anchor, from a pair of galoshes to a suit of clothes, with a helmet to complete the outfit if needed'. The piles of miscellaneous materials at bottom may also be part of the 'stores' area. Most of the works buildings here can be readily identified on the 1919 OS, however a good number of further buildings were also erected subsequent to this photograph. The Cordite Range referred to in the 1907 article is the east-west range with the central tower seen in the distance here (the later range seen at p.36 middle had not yet been erected at this date). The two north-south 'main lines' of the narrow gauge tramway system stand out well here. For further general views of the works see p.37.

below
The main office block. This corrugated-iron-clad building was one of several acquired by Kynochs that had reportedly first been erected in Hyde Park to accommodate troops during the 1887 (1897?) Jubilee celebrations. Note the raised entrances as a flood precaution. The works telephone exchange was also housed here, hence the many wires on the end wall.

above
A view within the Danger Area – see map p.38 for the viewpoint - where many of the buildings were surrounded by artificial mounds to deflect blast should any explosion occur. This photograph gives us one of the best insights on the construction of the elevated sections of the narrow gauge tramways, and is one of the few available views of the tramway rolling stock. The elevated sections were also used by staff walking between buildings in the boggier parts of the site, although there does not seem to be much room for them to have got past a loaded truck! The trucks were pushed by hand.

Ivor Gotheridge collection

above
One of the many magazines, showing the blast-deflecting earth mounds which surrounded them except at the entrance.

left
An early view of the works entrance gates, which were probably erected in 1898. A 'Patrol' man, now supplied with a more policeman-like uniform in addition to the hat, stands on guard. The lions on the gate pillars were in imitation of one that stood over the entrance to the Witton works. (The Essex factory was also referred to colloquially as 'The Lion Works' in some early press reports, but this did not stick). The upper notice reads 'Bicycles are not to be ridden through the factory between the hours of … pm and … am' (presumably the times were filled in according to the hours of darkness). Subsequently this restriction was deemed insufficient and more forceful notices were posted banning cycling and motor cycles in the works except for permit holders, 'owing to the danger to pedestrians and to explosive transport arising from the reckless riding of bicycles throughout the factory'. A 5mph speed limit for motor vehicles was also imposed.

The gate pillars were demolished around the time of the closure of this entrance by Mobil in 1969. The lions were preserved, initially on the roof of the Bulk Terminal enquiry office, later on the lawn by the new No.2 gate.

Ivor Gotheridge collection

year may be, seems ever to blow over these lowlands. The silence and the space exercise an undeniably solemnizing effect on the visitor unused to the place – an impression that would probably be lessened as the result of more familiar acquaintance with it – and prepare him for that extreme caution and implicit obedience to directions which must be observed by any who are fortunate enough to be permitted to examine closely the various departments of which the factory is made up'.

'Kynochtown factory is occupied in the manufacture of ammunition, chemicals, and every variety of explosives.............. [It] is divided into two distinct areas – the danger area, and [the area] containing the chemical portion of the works and sundry workshops offices etc. A main road, which leads to the landing stage in Holehaven Creek, constitutes the [southern] boundary of the danger zone, which is divided into sections, devoted respectively to the manufacture of gun-cotton, black gunpowder, smokeless powder, cordite, nitro-glycerine, and .303 cartridges. In either section there is much that is of the utmost interest to see, and a great deal that can be, to some extent at least, appreciated even by the layman who is so unlearned that he may not know a moderant from a solvent, or distinguish Troisdorf from Plastomenite powder. In a brief and entirely non-technical paper like this only a general impression can be given. And just as on entering the factory its intense silence strikes the mind, so, on closer examination, the admirable discipline of the place becomes a marked feature. Take, for example, our visit to the cordite range – a long line of low houses, with the square tower of the accumulator rising in the midst. Before entering any of the houses, or, indeed, being permitted to step across a certain line along the gangway which runs outside them, rubber overshoes have to be put on, in order to avoid the danger of friction being set up by the contact of ordinary walking shoes or boots with the floor within'.

In each stage or process and in every separate house, there is apparent that subdued air of discipline which, more, perhaps, than aught else, convinces the visitor of the underlying sense of danger, and necessity for absolute care, with which even the most thoughtless employee is impressed while engaged on his or her work. For at Kynochtown, and in kindred factories, the workpeople are of either sex. Probably of the whole something like ten per cent are women or girls, whose deft touch and quickness of hand render them specially fitted to deal with such branches as the blending of the cordite and other stages in the process of its manufacture. Passing from room to room, one sees the lines of women and girls quietly and busily employed, all uniformly clothed in scarlet dresses, the colour denoting that they are employed within the danger zone, and emphasizing the necessity for the utmost care on the part of the wearer. Moreover the company, rightly and wisely, strengthens this sense of responsibility by the infliction of the severest penalties on any employee detected transgressing rules which are essential for the safety of the whole place. There is danger everywhere, from the drying of the gun-cotton onward, and the immunity from serious disaster which has happily attended Kynochtown since its commencement is the best testimony as to the care with which the regulations have been observed. The comparatively recent disaster at Woolwich, which caused damage to houses in Corringham, many miles distant across the river, serves as on object lesson in this direction'.

Further details of cordite manufacture are included with the photographs at pp.12-13.

Kynoch's time here was never to be darkened by 'disaster', but there were of course occasional incidents to be reported to the Board – 'the Cordite Packing House burnt down and a ton of cordite detroyed' in June 1899, 'a fire in the Guncotton Factory' in October 1899, and so on.

The works relied principally on shipping for transport of goods in and out. The plans for the pier in Holehaven Creek were approved by the Commissioners of the Fobbing Levels in January 1898, and Cocking reported it completed in July 1899. (There must have been some temporary wharf facility in 1897-8). Kynoch's own coasters the SS *Kynoch* and SS *Anglesey* called here as necessary on their circular voyages to and from Arklow. The principal shipping import was coal for the Engine House which we can assume came from the northeast. Manufactured explosives for the government were taken upriver by Kynoch's own barges to Woolwich. Cocking had bought a 'steam barge' for £400 in January 1898, followed by the sailing barges *Hearts of Oak* (110 tons) and *Lily* (70 tons) in September, and a fourth not named in 1899.

continued at page 15

above
When Cocking was given permission to build a new Laboratory in 1901, he clearly decided that he deserved something better than the usual run of wooden huts, and came up with this solid little example of GER-esque 'Domestic Revival' style. It was located on the south side of the main east-west roadway. For the interior see p.43.
Thurrock Museum

right
Kynoch's smaller barge *Lily*. The 'advertising' on the sails may also have helped generate greater respect from other vessels in the Thames!
Courtesy Marion Paley and Stuart Brand

left
This poor photograph is the only available view of the activity at Kynoch's pier in the early years; we are looking down Holehaven Creek towards the Thames.

THE MANUFACTURE OF CORDITE

The photographs here, all except the first dating from 1917/18, illustrate the various stages in the manufacture of cordite. The 1907 *Essex Review* article described the operations as follows:

'Cordite is the smokeless powder which has been used by the British service these sixteen years past, and is composed of nitro-glycerine and gun-cotton gelatinised by means of a solvent, to which a certain proportion of a mineral hydrocarbon is added as a moderant. The principal stages in its manufacture consist of drying the gun-cotton, mixing it with nitro-glycerine; incorporating, pressing and reeling, or cutting; drying and blending; and packing'.

'As to the appearance of cordite, after the earlier stage, in which it is paste, it is passed through machines from which it emerges in strands of varying size which are cut to the required length. The blending follows after it is dried, and the nicety of this operation may be inferred from the fact that some sixty separate strands, of varying thicknesses, go to make up one cartridge. The size of the strand may vary from the thickness of a single hair to a quite considerable diameter. The packing of cordite is done into wooden boxes, holding 50lbs or more, according to the cordite. Alongside of all these processes, or succeeding them, there are, of course, tests – the moisture test, the heat test for stability, and so on, some carried out in the laboratories by accomplished chemists, and others on the ranges, where the actual velocities and pressures have to come within certain defined limits'.

top
An interior view of the 'Gun-Cotton Dipping House', c1900. This was the first stage in cordite manufacture, where dry gun-cotton was placed in pans and nitro-glycerine poured onto it, and mixed with it by hand until a 'paste' was formed. A reporter visiting in 1900 noted
'here were observed men working harmlessly in an atmosphere impregnated with gases, which were a source of irritation to the 'green' hand. The stuff is stored away in utensils not unlike cooking pots, and these are placed in water for, as our guide said, they sometimes go off, and then there is every chance of being suffocated, or scalded with acid'.

middle
'Incorporating', the next operation, involved adding mineral jelly and acetone solvent to the 'paste'. It was done in a power-driven kneading machine, and took several hours. The paste emerged as a stiffer 'dough'. The length of the Incorporating Ranges, and the numbering of the machines seen here, show that a large number of machines were required for this.

Thurrock Museum

bottom
The next stage was 'pressing'. The 'extrusion cylinders' were filled with the cordite dough. At the bottom of the cylinder were several perforated plates or 'dies' through which either a single or multiple long 'cords' of cordite were expressed.

In the case of cannon cordite, several large diameter cords were produced together, and these had to be cut by hand to the required lengths and laid out evenly on the wooden trays as seen here.

Rifle cordite however was produced as a single .0375in diameter continuous cord, which was wound onto a metal reel until about 1 lb in weight was on the reel. (Not illustrated, but see p.13 middle photo).

The uniform for most of the women working in buildings in the 'Danger Area' was (as here) khaki with red borders and a red vertical stripe.

top

The trays or reels were then taken to drying stoves where at 100 degrees the cordite would take between two days and eight weeks to dry, depending on its diameter. In the course of this the acetone was driven off.

This view shows a range of three Cordite Stoves which cannot be located on the 1919 OS. The appearance of the brickwork suggests that they were newly-built when photographed here in 1917/18, and perhaps they were demolished early as well. They would have been provided to supplement the previous range of five stoves noted on the OS (p.38).

This photograph also shows good detail of the narrow-gauge tracks. These have iron rails on the made up ground at left but wooden (?) 'rails' on the elevated timber sections outside the building. A proper point lever has been provided to work the point on the iron-railed section (but it would seem from photographs that points on the wooden-railed sections were just kicked over).

Thurrock Museum

middle

On emerging from the stoves, the cordite had to be 'blended'. For cannon cordite this was simply done by hand mixing of lengths from different batches (not illustrated). Rifle cordite, in contrast, was 'reeled' as seen here in long continuous lengths, cords from up to 60 of the original single-strand reels being fed together to create a multi-strand 'rope' on the larger reel on the machine at left. This machine bears the markings of 'Easton & Anderson Branch Pulsometer Engineering Co Ltd London & Reading 1915'.

Thurrock Museum

bottom

'Packing Cannon Cordite'. Here we see the large wooden boxes referred to in the *Essex Review* article. The man at left is weighing boxes before despatch.

The final stage in the production process, the 'filling' of cartridges, was done in the government factory at Woolwich.

Thurrock Museum

above
A general view of Kynochtown village from the Manorway / Fleet Street corner. The two main terraces (Nos 1-6 and 7-18 plus shop) and the Institute appear at right, and the works entrance is in the distance at left. This and the bottom photograph are actually pre-1914 views, recaptioned in the 1920s by the postcard publisher.
Padgett collection, Southend Museums service

left
Looking across the south end of the Salt Fleet to the shop and the Institute, c1925. In looking at these pleasant scenes, one should bear in mind that the village was raw and treeless in its first years.
Ivor Gotheridge collection

below
The 'best' houses in Kynochtown, the detached Manager's house of 1899 and the four 'Villas' of 1901/2. None of these were in the original plan (see opposite).
The Manager's house was originally known as 'Glendarvel', then became 'Kynoch Villa', 'Coryton House' in the 1920s, and 'Cory House' from the 1930s. W.C. Sealy occupied it in the Kynoch's years, followed by J.H. Freeman throughout the Cory period, and Mr Bartholomew the Mobil Refinery Manager in the 1950s. Other staff lived there in the last years up to demolition in 1970.
Padgett collection, Southend Museums Service

The barges also brought in acid, some at least of it from the chemical factories on the Lea marshes, as we read of one Kynoch's barge catching fire at Hackney Wick in 1900 when laden with acid. A pressman visiting Kynochtown in 1900 noted 'men busy unloading great tanks of acid' at the pier. In 1902 authorisation was given for facilities to enable acid to be piped from the pier to the works.

Kynoch's use of rail transport is discussed later (p.31).

So far as road transport is concerned, this clearly was not a priority when the site was chosen, as the Manorway, the only road access, was at this time scarcely usable for wheeled vehicles, at least in wet periods (cf the comments earlier) (16). Unlike most businesses, Kynoch's were not likely to find any *local* customers for their products, and therefore had no need for road delivery vehicles. Nevertheless, it does seem that once the works was in operation, Kynochs found themselves and their local suppliers having to make daily vehicular use of the Manorway. In April 1898 they signed an agreement which Cocking had made with the Orsett RDC for it to be 'made up' (meaning gravel, not tarmac, at this date) on the basis of Kynochs contributing half the £300 cost. It would seem that this work was done, as the Manorway was being used by motor vehicles prior to 1914 (17). Kynochs themselves owned several motor vehicles by the war years.

Another problem in 1897 was that the only access from the Manorway to the works was by rough paths across a field belonging to Oozedam Farm (see OS map p.5). The Borley House property had some ill-defined right to use these for agricultural purposes, but Col Whitmore the owner of Oozedam did not take kindly to Kynochs workmen tramping in large numbers. Early in 1898 he obtained a writ against Kynochs who had to pay £15 damages plus costs. However this problem was resolved that same year by the construction of the new road 'Fleet Street' from further down on the Manorway to the permanent works entrance at the 'lion gates'.

A Kynoch's employee from Birmingham who visited in 1900, shortly before the CLR opened, found himself conveyed from Stanford-le-Hope station to the isolated works by 'Tom the driver and Tom the horse' who, he reported, were 'familiar visitors' there, and 'brought in the gossip of the countryside' to the villagers (18).

'KYNOCHTOWN' AND OTHER KYNOCH'S HOUSING

The several hundred employees (quoted as 500 in the evidence given at the Light Railway Commissioners' inquiry at Southend in January 1899) had no housing available to them in the immediate vicinity of the works at the time of opening. Like the staff at the existing London & Thames Haven Oil Wharves (LATHOL) site, they would have had to come in daily by walking or cycling along the unofficial path beside the track of the Thames Haven branch railway from Stanford-le-Hope, or via the Manorway track from Corringham.

Kynochs had built a small number of staff houses at the Arklow plant, and it soon became clear that a more substantial 'works village' would be needed at the 'Thames Factory'. Kynochs therefore started work on a number of houses near the works, which may have originally been intended to be known as 'The Thames', like the works, but which had become 'Kynochtown' by the end of 1898 (19). 34 houses were erected in the original construction period in 1898/9 – one pair by the works gates, a large detached residence for the Manager, two terraces of six bungalows in Church Avenue, and terraces of twelve (plus shop) and six houses in Fleet Street. This work was done by the main company Kynoch Ltd (20). The total was increased to 38 in 1901/2, when two pairs of semi-detached 'Villas' were built next to the Manager's house (21). After that no more houses were built until after 1945.

A fair number of houses had been occupied by the end of 1898.
continued at page 18

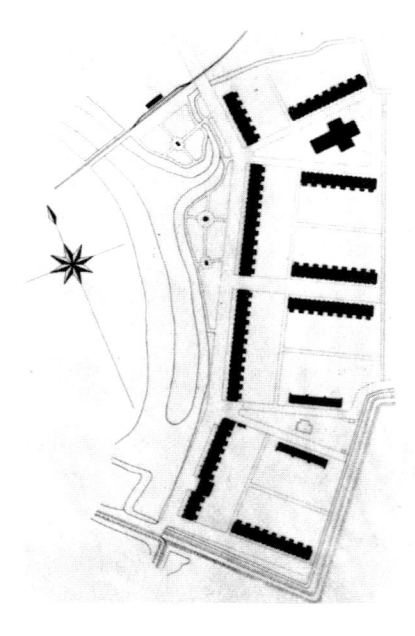

This plan was reproduced in the programme for the ceremony of November 1899 (the cover of which appears below), and is our only extant evidence showing how large Kynochtown was originally intended to be. (However, the full scheme was effectively already abandoned by this date). 179 houses are shown here, including 79 in Fleet Street. The two houses actually built by the 'lion gates' are revealed to have been planned as the northernmost two of an intended terrace of twelve. Seven further never-built terraces of 16 - 24 houses are shown. The large cross-shaped building is presumably the originally-proposed church.
Courtesy Marion Paley and Stuart Brand

KYNOCH LIMITED.

KYNOCHTOWN SCHOOLS
Foundation Stone Laid
NOVEMBER 18th, 1899,
BY
MISS KATE CHAMBERLAIN.

below
The School and the bungalows on the south side of Church Avenue. The street was referred to as 'School Avenue' in 1899, when it had still been intended to erect a church elsewhere, but was already 'Church Avenue' in the 1901 census. This suggests a 'plan B' to build a church *here*, but that did not happen either: instead church services were held in the School or the Institute at different periods.

The plans for the school were drawn up by Cocking, and approved by the Kynochs Board in September 1899. £500 was contributed by Kynoch Ltd and £100 'privately subscribed by the directors'. Not content with laying the foundation stone in November 1899, Kate Chamberlain returned on Saturday 26th May 1900 for the ceremonial 'opening' of the school. This was effected by means of a 'golden key' handed to her by Cocking. The Fobbing and Corringham clergy attended and 'Brother Booth's Sunday School children' led the hymn-singing. (Booth was a lay-reader who took the services here, riding out every Sunday morning from Stanford on a tall white horse).

Arthur and Joseph Chamberlain had a longstanding interest in improved education for the working class. The running costs of the 'Kynochtown Voluntary School' were subsidised by Kynochs. From time to time Cocking (and later J.H. Freeman) would visit to 'inspect'. The classroom on this side housed 24 infants, and that on the east side 40 juniors, which proved sufficient, even after children from the Shell houses started coming here.

On 15th August 1900, the Master Edwin Broad wrote in his Logbook (30) 'Commenced duties as Master of the new school with an attendance of 40 scholars. I found the children in a very backward state – some of them not having attended a school for more than two years'.

Broad kept away from getting too closely involved in village politics by living in Stanford-le-Hope (p.17). Assisted by a succession of ladies as Infant Teacher, he was to reign here with an iron rod until 1927. Originally, children who passed the scholarship exam at 11 moved on to Palmers High School, Grays, the others staying here until leaving at 14. But by the 1930s all the over-11s went elsewhere. The school closed in summer 1940, when the village was evacuated. After the village was repopulated the Kynochtown children attended the Herd Lane school in Corringham. The building was later converted into a house, 'School Bungalow', inhabited in the 1950s by Mobil's Foreman Gardener 'Joe' Pepper.

The Institute when new. It was was formally opened by Arthur Chamberlain on a visit on 31st March 1903. Originally the 'Kynoch Institute and Reading Rooms', it had by 1910, when it gained a licence, become the 'Kynochtown Working Men's Club and Institute'. Wilfrid Helcke the Kynoch's Manager was Chairman of the committee which ran it, with one of the 'men' as Secretary. The Institute also provided the venue for all other social events in the village. It became the 'Cory Institute' in the 1920s, and lasted until 1970.
Courtesy Marion Paley and Stuart Brand

Officers and men pose to mark the completion of the Institute, circa March 1903. We can guess that the bowlered figure in the central position of honour is Col. Frend, with the rounder figure of Manager William Sealy, then 53, next left, followed by his young wife Jennie, 26, and her sister Mabel Wood, 21. The bearded man to the right of Frend also appears in the photo at p.6, but no identification suggests itself.
Courtesy Marion Paley and Stuart Brand

1901 CENSUS - KYNOCHTOWN

Children are only named if over 14 and working for Kynochs. Boarders are only named if occupation appears connected with Kynochs.

TOTAL POPULATION – 184 (in 32 houses and one 'hut')
  comprised of 120 adults (40 of whom are boarders)
  and 64 children under 14.

The most striking feature is the cosmopolitan nature of the village population. Only 7 of the 32 male 'heads of household' were born in Essex. (Of course, locally-born staff would be more likely than outsiders to be living in other nearby villages). Neighbours in Church Avenue hail from Stowmarket, Peckham, Roumania, and Tunbridge Wells via India. Only a third of the married couples come from the same vicinity as each other.

As might be expected in a new community, there are few older people – William Fry living with his daughter is the only inhabitant over 60.

Almost all the male heads of household are definite or probable Kynoch's employees. None of the wives work (most having young children). Eleven older children work for Kynochs. The 40 boarders are (with the exception of cook Maria) all young men; only 13 are definite Kynoch's workers but many of those noted as 'General Labourer' may have been too. A total of 60 – 80 Kynoch's employees live in the village, i.e. 15% of the total workforce at maximum.

Those coming from Birmingham, Worsborough Dale, or Waltham Abbey / Cheshunt had probably come here from the explosives industry in those places.

Two 'Patrol' men live by the works entrance, a third elsewhere in the village (and a fourth in Digby Road).

FLEET STREET

No. 1 Eva Kennedy Widow 20 born Inworth; two children; Edith Whipps (sister) 15 Cordite Sorter born Latchingdon; Alfred Wilson (boarder) 21 Labourer Explosives Factory; George Broughton (boarder) 32 Labourer Explosives Factory.

No.2 George Johnson 33 Stoker stationary boiler born Surrey; Alice (wife) 33 born Surrey; two children.

No.3 William Collett 49 Patrol born Haverhill; Margaret (wife) 36 born Portsmouth; Edith (daughter) 16 Cordite Packer born Aden; six other children.

No.4 John B. Hayter 38 Stoker born Portsmouth; Mary (wife) 38 born Surrey; four children; William Fry (father in law) 78 Retired Platelayer born Surrey.

No.5 James Bassett 51 Carpenter born Hendon; Annie (wife) 45 born Sussex; Charles (son) 18 Cordite Maker; Alfred (son) 14 Labourer Explosives Factory; three other children; Alfred Amos (boarder) 21 Stoker stationary boiler; George Blanchard (boarder) 17 Cordite Maker; one other boarder.

No.6 Robert Jones (?) 42 House Painter born Scotland; Laura (wife) 38 born Norfolk.

No.7 Thomas Record 47 Carpenter Foreman Explosives Factory born Birmingham; Ruth (wife) 47 born Birmingham; nine children (all except the last born Birmingham).

No.8 Alfred Porter 43 Foreman Explosives Factory born Fobbing; n/k (wife) 45 born Beds; Edward Everett (boarder) 25 Cordite Maker; four other boarders.

No. 9 unoccupied.

No.10 Alfred H. Bodeker (?) 40 Foreman, Gun Cotton Department born London; Charlotte (wife) 29 born Kent; two children; two boarders.

No.11 C. Stanley Heaven 26 (single) Electrician Foreman born Birmingham; Maria J. Cottee (?) (boarder, widow) 53 Cook, Restaurant born Kent.

No.12 William Jiggens 33 Housekeeper, Explosives Factory born Stanford-le-Hope; Ellen (wife) 30 born Orsett; five children; one boarder.

No.13 unoccupied.

No.14 Robert Gibson 43 Foreman Chemical Plumber born Scotland; Maggie (wife) 42 born Ireland; William (son) 21 Freestone Mason; James (son) 17 Chemical Plumber; one other child; two boarders.

No.15 John J. Findlay 43 Cordite Maker Foreman born Waltham Abbey; Frances (wife) 46 born Waltham Abbey; one child.

No.16 John Foster 45 Stationary Engine Driver born Scotland; Emily (wife) 40 born Surrey; four boarders.

No.17 Ernest Weavers 30 General Labourer born Southminster; Florence (wife) 28 born Rochford; five children; two boarders.

No.18 Robert Stevenson 39 Foreman Cordite Maker born Scotland; Margaret (wife) 29 born Scotland; one child; John Henderson (boarder) 24 Foreman Cordite Packer born Scotland; Louis Rushford (boarder) 24 Foreman Blast Powder Maker born Worsborough Dale.

Shop William Hawkins 59 Grocer's Foreman born Wilts; Maria (wife) 46 born Kent.

CHURCH AVENUE

No.1 Thomas Johnstone 27 Stationary Engine Driver born Northumberland; Elizabeth (wife) 23 born Bermondsey.

No.2 Albert Harvey 24 Guncotton Nitrator born Basildon.

No.3 Lewis Parsons 25 Machine Fitter Explosives Factory born Norfolk; Martha (wife) 26 born Canning Town; three children.

No.4 Charles Cuthbert 38 Wood Sawyer born Stowmarket; Amy (wife) 42 born Stowmarket; six children.

No.5 Frederick G. Morgan 45 Guncotton Nitrator born Peckham; Mary (wife) 47 born Somerset.

No.6 Isaac Fishman (?) 40 Carpenter born Roumania (foreigner); Sophie (wife) 30 born Roumania (foreigner); three children; Louis .... (boarder) 30 Carpenter born Russia (foreigner); Louis Parmutt (?) (boarder) 27 Carpenter born Russia (foreigner).

No.7 Edward J. Wheatley 47 General Labourer born Tunbridge Wells; Sophia (wife) 46 born Greenwich; Margaret (daughter) 17 Cordite Blender born India; Maud (daughter) 15 Waitress Restaurant born India; Gertrude (daughter) 15 Cordite Blender born India; two other children; one boarder.

No.8 Alfred Smith 40 Plumber born London; Esther (wife) 30 born Feering; one child; two boarders.

No. 9 Walter Whipps (?) 57 Labourer Acid Mixer born Inworth; Mary (wife) 55 born Feering; Emma (daughter) 23 Cordite Blender; one niece.

No.10 George J. Heather (?) 30 Guncotton .... born Guildford; John ...... (boarder) 20 Pattern Maker Explosives Factory born Scotland.

No.11 William Newman 23 Cordite Maker born Surrey; Mary (wife) 20 born Scotland; one child; William Binder (boarder) 24 Guncotton ....; Arthur Curtis (boarder) 25 Cordite .... Foreman born Cheshunt; one other boarder.

No.12 Arthur E. Walshon (?) 38 Cordite Maker Foreman born London; Annie (wife) 25 born London; two children; Henry W. Smith (boarder) 17 Black Powder ....; four other boarders.

FLEET STREET

'Glendarval' William C. Sealy 51 Manager Explosives Works born Tonbridge; Jennie (wife) 24 born Lancs; one child; Mabel Wood (sister-in-law) 19 born Lancs; Robert Wood (brother-in-law) Laboratory Scientist   born Lancs.

(House by works gates) George Carman 42 Patrol born Dorset; Mary (wife) 39 born Ireland; Josephine (daughter) 16 Gelignite Packer; Beatrice (daughter) 14 Gelignite Packer; four other children; one boarder.

(House by works gates) Dominick J. Brewster 33 Stationary Engine Driver born West Tilbury; Anne (wife) 42 born Tillingham; one child; one nephew; James G. Pryse (boarder) 20 Fitter Explosives Factory born Birmingham; Alfred A. Holmes (boarder) 31 Fitter Explosives Factory born Birmingham.

'The Iron Huts' (assumed near gates) Henry W. Willis (?) 49 Patrol born Tonbridge; Alice (wife) 49 born Woolwich.

1901 CENSUS - KYNOCH'S WORKERS IN FOBBING, CORRINGHAM, AND STANFORD-LE-HOPE

The census reveals 12 definite/probable employees living in Fobbing; 6 at Thames Haven; 63 in Corringham (mostly in Digby Road / Fobbing Road) ; and 57 in Stanford-le-Hope. A fair number of others listed as General Labourer etc may also have worked for Kynochs.

We can already see in 1901 that Corringham is being turned into a community of industrial workers, whilst Fobbing is much less influenced by change. Twelve of the 28 houses occupied in Digby Road at this date have definite Kynoch's employees as Head of Household. In one of two 'Kynoch's Cottages' (not identifiable) somewhere off Fobbing Road are Alfred Bee 'Commercial Clerk' and Annie Bee 'Lodge House', presiding over eleven girls working for Kynochs, eight of them from Birmingham.

Some incomers chose to live in the more metropolitan Stanford-le-Hope. In addition to Cocking at The Grove (p.6), his junior manager Wilfrid Helcke (22) lived with wife Florence (25) and eleven-month-old Eric at 1 The Woodlands, Fairview Avenue. Kynochtown schoolmaster Edwin Broad (36, born Cornwall) was at Stanley Villas, Rectory Road - well out of sight of his pupils! - with wife Isabella (29), five-month-old Elizabeth, and his mother Elizabeth (76) 'Retired Schoolmistress'.

POPULATION GROWTH 1871 – 1931

Figures are for civil parishes. The 1881, 1891, and 1901 figures have been checked in the original census returns. Different figures appeared in some Directories etc and have been copied by subsequent authors. The 1911 / 1921 / 1931 figures are taken from Kelly's Directories.

	1871	1881	1891	1901	1911	1921	1931
Fobbing	448	429	357	412	423	607	734
Corringham	268	273	257	817	693	1278	1897
Stanford-le-Hope	699	827	1093	1750	2545	3379	4311

The Kynochtown shop / Post Office, which was built and opened in 1899 along with the village houses. (A temporary shop was operated in an iron building in the works in 1898/9). In June 1898 another separate Limited Company, 'The Thames Stores Ltd', had been formed to manage this shop. This company was controlled by Kynochs and like the CLR had the Kynochs chief clerk G.F.Willis as its first Secretary. The company was wound up in 1922 after Kynochs sold out, after which Cory's owned the shop. In the 1920s directories J.H. Freeman, the Cory's Manager, also appears as 'Grocer, Coryton Stores'.

The shop's headed notepaper in the 1900s read 'General Store, Shop and Warehouse Keepers, and Licensed Victuallers, Factors and Wholesale and Retail Dealers in all kinds of Articles, Apparatus, and Appliances'. It remained open until the end of the village in 1970.

Digby Road, the heart of Kynoch's Corringham community. The south end terraces 1-6 and 30-35 were smaller houses built to a quite different design to the two longer terraces. The back gardens of Grove Terrace and Digby Villas protruded somewhat oddly into the roadway.

Courtesy Bill Hammond

The farm house at Herd Farm. After Kynochs purchased the farm in 1898 it was continued as a working farm, Isaac Bush at 23s 6d per week 'and a lad at 12s' being appointed to run it, 'the horses and cart not needed for the farm to be put to building work'. Grazing land was let to another local farmer, Lilley. Bush lived in one of the new Kynochs cottages in Herd Lane and the first occupant of the farm house after Kynoch's purchase was the Estate Co / CLR Secretary George F. Willis, wife Jane, and their brood of nine children. Subsequently James W. Ramsay his successor as CLR Secretary lived here, until 1909. Then in summer 1915 the house was altered for occupation by the ladies running the girls' colony. The house was demolished in 1959 in preparation for the building of the new Pegasus Club facilities.

This is the south front of the house. The colony ladies lived in proper style, having (left to right) a conservatory, drawing room, dining room, and breakfast room. The house boasted nine bedrooms, so Willis' children had more space each than most of their contemporaries!

On 24th February 1899 the Southend paper's Vange correspondent bemoaned the fact that

'some of the inhabitants are beginning to migrate to Borley-on-Sea (Kynock's – [*sic*] - Town, near Thames Haven). As the houses get finished they are at once taken, and Vange is losing what Borley is gaining. The Lion Works are gradually reducing the population of this district'.

On 18th November 1899 the new village was officially named 'Kynochtown' by Arthur Chamberlain's daughter, Miss Kate Chamberlain. She had come to lay the foundation stone for the village school, which opened in 1900 (p.15). The final facility was the large 'Institute' opened in 1903.

The 38 houses of Kynochtown were however nowhere near what was required to house the number of workers in question. It is evident from the plan at p.15 that Kynochs had started on Kynochtown with the intention of it being a much larger community, but this had then been overtaken by the idea of building on the 'healthy uplands' instead, in connection with the idea of the Corringham Light Railway which was being firmed up in summer 1898. It is also clear that Kynochs were expecting local speculative builders to provide large numbers of new houses in the nearby villages. The June 1898 Kynoch's shareholders meeting was told that 'the Board look to private local enterprise to erect at least 500 additional cottages. If this is not quickly forthcoming, the Board have it in mind to start a subsidiary company with that special object'. In fact it did not take long for them to decide that local enterprise was *not* going to come up with the goods. In July 1898 the Board approved the formation of a separate company, The Kynoch Estate Co Ltd (22), to build and manage more workers' housing. The company was registered on 3rd January 1899, with Arthur Chamberlain, Cocking, and Kerly as the Directors, and G.F. Willis, abstracted from his post of Kynoch's chief clerk here, as Secretary. Most business was actually transacted at 'committee meetings' held at frequent intervals in Stanford-le-Hope, which Chamberlain did not attend. J. Adams of Southend was appointed as the Estate Co's architect.

As soon as the company was registered, it had transferred to it several properties which had been acquired by Kynoch Ltd (in practice, by Cocking) in November – December 1898, *viz*

The 'Corringham Building Estate', a large field (field 158 on map p.40) on the north side of Fobbing Road, adjacent to the site for the CLR Corringham station.

Herd Farm, Corringham.

The 'Stanford Estate', a smaller area of land in the centre of Stanford-le-Hope.

The 'Canvey Estate', alias Brookhouse Farm (for which see next section).

This land had not all been bought purely for workers' housing, but also because it was envisaged that a profit could be made by a rise in the value of land locally as the works brought increased population.

The Corringham Building Estate was regarded as the first priority for staff housing development, partly because of its mutual relationship with the Light Railway project (the plans for which had just been deposited). In January 1899 plans were submitted to Orsett RDC for 53 houses here, producing objections that 'the system of drainage might pollute the marshes, if not satisfactory'. These were assuaged by an 'undertaking' from Kerly. Local builder J. Ballard did the site preparation work in March, and by June fourteen houses were under construction. In the event, the Estate Co soon decided to sell or lease plots to local builders (including Ballard), for them to build under their own aegis, as well. By the time everybody's enthusiasm had waned in 1901, 51 houses had been built here in total, as shown on the 1919 OS map at p.40 (23). Ten were in Fobbing Road, the rest in new roads named 'Wingfield Road' and 'Digby Road' after the vendor of the field Digby Hanmer Wingfield (of the Wingfield Baker family of Orsett Hall, Lords of the Manor of Corringham). The 'Wingfield Road' name however did not stick, and this road is now known as 'Hill Terrace' after its houses.

All this land was passed on to Cory's and Mobil, and as late as 1959 the Coryton staff magazine was advertising that 'a few plots of building land are still available for sale to employees at Recreation Avenue and Fobbing Road, Corringham'.

At Herd Farm the only housing actually built was two cottages in Herd

above

The Kynoch Estate Co's speculative block on the corner of The Green and Central Road in Stanford-le-Hope was an early piece of London-suburban intrusion on the village centre. It was built on the site of the old village smithy, and indeed a replacement smithy was built behind it. Designed by the Estate Co's architect J. Adams, the building contract was let to H.R. Rous in June 1899 at £2,000. The larger of the two shop units was let on a 21 year lease to the London & Provincial Bank in May 1900.

right

The Hotel Kynoch, from a 1908 advertisement. It was situated on the Canvey river front some 800 yards east of the Lobster Smack (grid reference 779821). The name HOTEL KYNOCH 1900 was featured on a large panel on the far side of the building. The roof terrace was provided to enable guests to view passing shipping. The elevated walkway led to the sea wall.

The first recorded Manager(ess) was Mrs Annie L. Bee who we came across previously in the 1901 census (p.17) running a Kynochs lodging house in Corringham. She was replaced c1909 by James Went (who also acted as Secretary of the CLR, the Institute and the Thames Stores Ltd). Around 1915 he moved down the front to become landlord of the Lobster Smack, where he presided until the 1930s. Douglas Hemus and Edward Hibbert Smith were the subsequent Hotel managers under Kynochs.

After Kynochs sold it in 1922, it continued as a hotel until the mid-1930s, and served as an army billet during the war. It then became offices for London & Coastal Oil Wharves, until demolished c1960.

Lane, in summer 1899. In April 1901 it was resolved 'to prepare a plan of the upper part of Herd Farm, and peg out roads and building plots'; but nothing came of this.

However a brickworks was established on one of the fields between the farmhouse and the CLR-to-be (see OS map p.40) (24). This brickworks was run directly by the Estate Co, both to manufacture bricks for their own work and for buildings at the works, and for general sale. In summer 1899 improvements were made in the form of two kilns and a 90ft chimney. To combat a lack of management expertise in this field, J.J. Curry of Grays was appointed as 'adviser to the Company on brickmaking' at £50 a year, and he quickly had changes put in hand (25). The brickworks was still active in 1910 but is marked as disused on the 1919 OS map. Next to the brickworks a small ballast pit was opened up, and this was the source of gravel ballast for the CLR (26). Later the girls' colony was built nearby in 1915 (p.41). The Herd Farm land too was passed on to Cory's and Mobil and the areas referred to are now the Pegasus Club sports field.

The only work ever done on the Stanford-le-Hope land was the erection of a large shops/offices block in the centre of the village (photo above), a purely speculative development. After the Estate Co's first meeting in January 1899, nothing more was ever heard of any further building here.

In September 1901 it was decided that the Estate Co had served its purpose, and the necessary steps were taken for it to be taken over by the main company Kynoch Ltd, all the lands being transferred back also. Willis was appointed as liquidator and the formal winding up was in April 1902. The Estate Co had, one suspects, become distracted by the peripheral activities entered into to make use of the land acquired. Kynochs generally were prone to diversifying into other fields (e.g. soap and candle making at Witton), and this would have made it easy for Cocking to establish little side-empires here. The Estate Co had secured the building of only 53 staff houses in total (plus 6 on Canvey) to add to the 38 houses built by Kynoch Ltd at Kynochtown. The 1901 census (p.17) suggests that about 130 Kynoch's workers lived in these 91 houses, leaving say 370 to find other housing. (It is however unlikely that there had ever really been a need for as many as 500 new houses).

CANVEY ISLAND SCHEMES

The Estate Co also had transferred to it the 240 acres of land at Brickhouse Farm on the southwest side of Canvey Island which Kynochs had bought in 1898 (27). On this land the Estate Co built the Hotel Kynoch in 1899/1900. The Hotel was to prove an expensive investment. Adams' initial estimate was £2,500 but £7,000 had been spent by the end of 1900, and opening was delayed until 1903. The Estate Co also fell out with Adams over this, ending in a court case. The Hotel was purportedly needed for accommodating 'important visitors' to the works, but in reality more of the visitors were political friends or cultivatees of the Chamberlains who came here for shooting weekends! A 'steam launch' was acquired in 1902 to operate a ferry from the works jetty to the Lobster Smack public house on Canvey. Brickhouse Farm itself continued to operate as a farm under a Bailiff appointed by Kynochs. Six cottages were built nearby in 1899, one assumes for farm workers (28).

Cocking, who was something of a yachting enthusiast, also had ideas of the company developing the west end of Canvey Island as a 'seaside pleasure resort'. In 1906 an agreement was made with a Mr Smetham Lee under which his syndicate was to build a pier and promenade, and Kynochs sell off plots for bungalows. Lee also expressed an interest in buying the Hotel; but in 1907 he pulled out of the whole scheme. The majority of the Kynoch Ltd Board had by this time become sceptical of Cocking's enthusiasm for Canvey – when Lee pulled out they resolved that 'the Board are tired of granting options for the development of this property', and in 1908 the farm and the Hotel were put up for sale at auction, only to find no bidders. Cocking's ideas should be seen in the context of other attempts at this period to develop the island. Henry Woods had proposed a 'Hotel Hollandais' and pier in 1895, but got nowhere. The sea walls had then been raised after the 1897 floods and the perceived new immunity from flooding further encouraged ideas of building. In 1899 Frederick Hester, a Southend estate agent, bought a large part of Canvey, and a 'monorail' horse tram operated by him began running in 1901 to Leigh Beck. In 1904 work began on a 3ft 6in gauge electric tramway to replace the monorail, but this was abandoned on Hester's bankruptcy in 1905 (29). In the event the development of Canvey took place on a more informal bungaloid basis.

Kynoch's land on Canvey was eventually sold at auction in April 1922. The purchaser, at £29,000, was Sir John Bethell the MP for East Ham North, who was actually a cover for the Port of London Authority, to whom the land was conveyed in 1926. They wanted to prevent other parties from promoting rival port facilities here.

```
                    CONTRACTORS TO THE WAR OFFICE AND ADMIRALTY
Telephone No.: 23 Sandford
Telegrams:
  "Kynoch, Kynochtown"              KYNOCH Limited
Head Offices:
  Lion Works, Witton, Birmingham
  London Office:  G/MJP/25.          KYNOCHTOWN
    12 Orange Street, Leicester Square, W.C.
  Passenger Station: Stanford-le-Hope ] L.T. &   STANFORD-LE-HOPE, ESSEX
  Goods Station: Thames Haven        ]  S.R.
FACTORY FOR                                       Aug. 3/15.
KYNOCH SMOKELESS SPORTING POWDER
CORDITE, NITRO EXPLOSIVES
BLACK GUNPOWDER AND CHEMICALS

            Messrs. L.E. Brand & Sons,
                    Stanford-le-Hope.
```

above left Kynoch's Shand Mason fire engine - Edgar Bird driving, Arthur Ockendon standing. The building behind, which looks like another 'Hyde Park' building, is the foreman's office on the main roadway. Kynoch's Board minutes approved the purchase of a 'fire engine for Thames' in 1901. It lasted into the Cory years. Edgar Bird became the local policeman in the interwar years.

above right Edgar Bird also drove Kynoch's left-hand-drive Ambulance, pictured here with a company motor car outside their garage. The location is at the junction of the road from the 'lion gates' with the main east-west works roadway, just to the east of the office block.

left Kynoch's headed letter paper for the Kynochtown works. This batch was printed in 1915 long after the 'Thames' name was given up. Note though that the local stations are still listed as 'LT&SR' three years after the Midland took over.

Courtesy Stuart Brand

---

1. The first reference to these purchases is in Kynoch's Board minutes 6.7.1896 where it was reported that '230 acres bordering on the Thames' had been offered at £2,000, which it was agreed to acquire at that price (Shellhaven Farm??). The signing and sealing of the agreement to purchase Shellhaven Farm was authorised by Kynoch's 'Office Committee' on 9.11.1896. After the usual legal delays, the sealing of the conveyances for both Borley House Farm and Shellhaven Farm was approved by Office Committee 28.6.1897; but the company had been in possession since late 1896.
2. The area covered by the factory on the 1919 OS map is indeed very close to 200 acres.
3. For the Miners Safety Explosives works see *The Thames Haven Railway* p.42.
4. See Essex Record Office T/Z 25/41, the recollections of a Corringham resident who remembered her father being given 'the task of securing signatures from local people in favour of the proposed explosive works'.
5. Unidentified cutting in Essex Record Office T/P 181/4/3.
6. Only known of from their presence at the April 1898 dinner, and a reference in the Kynochs minutes to the accidental death of one of McCulloch's men.
7. *Kynoch Journal*, Vol.3 No.15 pp. 49-53.
8. From Freeman's 1933 talk (see p. 48, footnote 7). As Freeman did not come to Kynochtown until 1910 this is second-hand.
9. Chamberlain & Hookham, electrical engineers, of 4 New Bartholomew St, Birmingham, was a company owned by the Chamberlains and another Kynoch's director George Hookham.
10. *Grays & Tilbury Gazette* 30.4.1898.
11. The name 'The Thames' was decided upon at the time of buying the land. Kynoch Ltd's headed letter paper was already showing 'Thames' in the list of factories by March 1897. Cocking in his speech at the April 1898 dinner refers repeatedly to 'The Thames'. When The Thames Stores Ltd company was registered in June 1898 two of the subscribers gave their place of residence as 'The Thames' (this being before the 'Kynochtown' name had been finalised for the village) – and of course this company's name is itself significant. The Kynoch's Board minutes refer exclusively to 'The Thames', 'Thames', or 'The Thames Works' in the first years. But after Kynochtown village was built it naturally started to create a perception of the works being 'at Kynochtown'. Odd references in the minutes to the works as 'Kynochtown' can be found from 1901, and by 1905 this nomenclature had become the norm. Compare also the 1907 *Essex Review* article whose author does not seem to have had the 'Thames' name mentioned to him. However as late as 1915 the drawing office here was still stamping its drawings 'Kynoch Ltd Thames Drawing Office'.
12. *Grays & Tilbury Gazette* 13.1.1900.
13. Helcke and Sealy are both still listed in the 1917 Kelly's Directory. J.H. Freeman became Manager vice both of them in 1919.
14. Willis was born in Colchester in 1863 but his time at Witton is attested by the fact that his wife was from Birmingham and his children of 1887-95 vintage were born in Birmingham.
15. A. Clifton Kelway, *Kynochtown: A Great Explosives Factory on the Essex Marshes*, in *Essex Review* July 1907, Vol.XVI No.63.
16. Compare also the recollections of W.G. Styles (in *Panorama* No.29) who was in the 1890s taken via the Manorway from Corringham 'in a tumbril cart with two horses' to start work as ploughboy at Borley House, and recalled that 'the clay was up to the horses' bellies and the bottom of the cart was drawn along like a sleigh'.
17. *Grays & Tilbury Gazette* 12.9.1914, report on a collision between a motor car and a horse van on the Manorway; both vehicles were making for Thames Haven.
18. *Kynoch Journal* Vol.2 No.7 p.23.
19. An early public use of the 'Kynochtown' name was by Counsel for the promoters at the Light Railway Commissioners' public inquiry at Southend on 25.1.1899. The name was sometimes given as 'Kynoch Town' in the first years, *cf* 'Kynoch-Town' in the drawing at p.26 which probably dates from November 1898.
20. The Kynoch Ltd minute books are curiously quiet about the building of Kynochtown, but do refer to the subsequent building of the school in 1900 and the first Villas in 1901, proving that the village remained owned by and the responsibility of Kynoch Ltd throughout. Much of the work was in any case done *before* the Kynoch Estate Co Ltd was set up in January 1899. It was intended, when the formation of the Estate Co was mooted in summer 1898, that it would take over the completion and management of Kynochtown, but this did not happen, and indeed the minutes of the Estate Co make no reference at all to anything regarding Kynochtown. The 1901 census shows indisputably that there were 34 houses at that date. Dorothy Taylor in *Under Five Flags – The Story of Kynochs Works Witton Birmingham 1862-1962* (1962), the official history of the company, refers to 52 houses. This erroneous figure was no doubt obtained by her from a rather jokey piece on Kynochtown in the October-November 1900 issue of the *Kynoch Journal*.
21. The first pair were authorised by the Kynoch Ltd Board 18.2.1901 at £800; both pairs are present on the June 1902 plan in the Oilmill and Reedham Farms auction advertisement at Essex Record Office D/SF 41.
22. The minute book of this company is at the Birmingham City Archives, and the Companies House records are at National Archives BT31/8284/60159.
23. Property plans of 1921 and 1950, prepared in connection with the sales to Cory's and Vacuum, show Kynoch's / Cory's as owning Nos 1-18, 19-23, and 30-35 Digby Road, the two Digby Villas in Fobbing Road, and the six houses in Hill Terrace, a total of 37 houses. Other parties unnamed own 24-29 Digby Road, Grove Terrace, and Baden Villas, totalling 14 houses. It seems likely that this represents the 1901 situation, however some references in the Estate Co's minutes seem to conflict with this. The Digby Road houses were numbered from the start on the present system. No.19 Digby Road, whilst visually two ordinary terraced houses, was from the start a single property, a social club for Kynoch's employees. This has been demolished, the other houses are all still standing in 2008.
    It is most likely a complete coincidence that the 51 houses actually built here plus the two in Herd Lane total 53 houses, i.e. the number applied for to the RDC in January 1899.
24. There was no brickworks here on the 1895 OS map, however it was already functioning by January 1899, only a few weeks after Kynochs purchased the farm.
25. Another brickfield, owned by Kynoch Ltd, and situated between the works and Kynochtown village, was probably the source of the bricks for the earlier Kynochs buildings. The Estate Co was originally intending to take over this brickfield as well, but they regarded it as inefficient compared to the Corringham brickworks, and possibly never actually took it on. There is no sign of this brickfield on the 1919 OS map.
26. The Estate Co minutes of 11.1.1901 note that Kynoch Ltd had mistakenly been charged only 1s per yard for the ballast instead of the 2s 6d intended.
27. Kynoch Ltd Board minutes 24.10.1898, 21.11.1898. It was originally intended to buy Tree Farm as well.
28. The farmhouse was at grid reference 780829. The cottages were on the north side of the track from Haven Road to the farm, and are now demolished.
29. See article by J.H.Price in *Modern Tramway* May 1968.
30. Essex Record Office E/ML7.

Chapter Two

THE PROMOTION AND OPENING OF THE CORRINGHAM LIGHT RAILWAY

Whilst relying on shipping for most of their transport needs here up to 1914, Kynochs nevertheless clearly also saw rail communication as necessary, and this was another plus point for the Borley House / Shellhaven site which was but a short distance from the London Tilbury & Southend Railway's Thames Haven branch. The LT&SR minutes first refer to Kynochs on 28th January 1897 when it was reported to the Board that 'application is to be made by Messrs G. Kynoch & Co for permission to erect an Explosives factory at Hole Haven'. For reasons not stated it was decided to oppose the Kynochs plans; given that the Thames Haven branch had just lost most of its previous business with the end of cattle and sheep importing (1), one might have thought that the LT&SR would have been keen to see any new traffic. However, a few days later the LT&SR Managing Director Arthur Stride had a meeting with A.T. Cocking and came to an agreement on the matter, on the promise of 'a considerable traffic'. At the next LT&SR Board meeting on 11th February 1897 it was noted that the company had withdrawn its opposition to Kynochs, as also had the London & North Western Railway which (for reasons explained at *The Thames Haven Railway* pp. 33 and 37) actually owned more land here at this period than the LT&SR did.

The LT&SR may well have been assuming in 1897 that Kynochs would simply build a short private siding from Thames Haven to the works, even if this was not specifically discussed. They would certainly not have been expecting Kynochs to build a whole 'railway' of their own! The larger ideas of the Light Railway as built emerged during 1898 in connection with the proposals for extensive housing development at Corringham, for which a passenger service would be provided.

THE LIGHT RAILWAY ORDER

Application was made in November 1898 for a Light Railway Order, under the Light Railways Act 1896, to authorise the construction of the 'Corringham Light Railway'. The application was in the names of Arthur Chamberlain and A. T. Cocking. Cocking was the man principally involved as he was also the Engineer to the line (and became the company Chairman on incorporation in 1899). The estimated cost was given as £5,473. 10s 2d, a very low sum. The legal work was done by A. W. Kerly's firm Kerly Son & Verden.

The plans and sections, submitted to the Board of Trade and Essex County Council on 30th November 1898 (2), showed three 'railways' (see plans p.24):

Railway No.1, 5 furlongs 2.3 chains [= 1151 yds] from a separate CLR Thames Haven terminus in the field just north of Dock House level crossing, to the northwestern junction of the triangle (18).

Railway No.2, 4 furlongs 5.6 chains [= 1003 yds] from Kynochtown station to the southern junction of the triangle.

Railway No.3, 1 mile 4 furlongs 9 chains [= 1 mile 1078 yds] from Corringham station to the northeastern junction of the triangle.

The total length of these railways being 2 miles 1472 yds.

In addition the plans showed a c165 yds long junction line linking Railway No.1 to the LT&SR line at Dock House crossing. (The spur to an 'independent terminus' was a common procedure in railway promotion, in case of any difficulties occurring with the other company over a junction or use of a station).

It was never explained what purpose the south to northwest side of the triangle was meant to serve.

It is fairly clear that no consultation had been engaged in with the LT&SR on the details of the line prior to the application being submitted. Stride (who had probably had no dealings with Kynochs since February 1897), informed the LT&SR Board on 1st December 1898 that he had received a letter regarding the CLR from Kerly Son & Verden, but they had not included a copy of the plans, so Stride had to buy a set. Cocking may have assumed (correctly) that the LT&SR would have no major objections, especially now that the Thames Haven branch was a one train a day goods line.

The Book of Reference accompanying the plans shows that the majority of the land needed for the line belonged to Anne Kent of Herd Farm, and Henry Charles Long and Herbert Clarence Long, the major Corringham landowners, at Reedham Farm and Oilmill Farm. Otherwise there was only a fraction of LT&SR land at the junction, and a small area already owned by Kynochs on which Kynochtown station was to be built (3). No difficulties seem to have arisen with the land acquisition.

Also submitted with the plans was a Draft Light Railway Order prepared by Kerly Son & Verden, the practice being for the applicants to submit such a draft setting out the powers they desired, and for the Board of Trade to amend it should they wish any changes.

On 25th January 1899 the Light Railway Commissioners' public inquiry was held at Southend by the Earl of Jersey and Col Boughey. It was reported in the local press that

'Mr A.T. Cocking the Managing Director of Kynoch's Explosives Works gave evidence in support of the application, and said the line would take the workpeople from the marshland to the upland to reside, which would be a boon to them. Mr Morley Hill (County Councillor) supported the scheme. He knew the advantages of living on gravel soil at Corringham, instead of living in the dreadful marshes'.

It was also noted that currently Kynochs had to 'send part of their goods by cart and put them on the rail at Thames Haven station'.

Light Railway Commissioners.—November, 1898.
Corringham Light Railway.

NOTICE is hereby given, that application is about to be made by Arthur Chamberlain and Allan Thomas Cocking for an Order authorizing the following light railways in the parish of Corringham, in the county of Essex, namely :—

Railway No. 1, commencing at the point where the footpath from Thames Haven to Oilmill Farm crosses the Thames Haven branch of the London, Tilbury, and Southend Railway, and immediately north of that railway and west of that footpath, and terminating at a point 240 yards north-north-east of Reedham Farm-buildings.

Railway No. 2, commencing at the Bawley Farm at a point 366 yards north-east of the point where the footpath from Thames Haven joins the Manorway-road, and terminating at a point 186 yards east of Reedham Farm-buildings.

Railway No. 3, commencing at the disused gravel pit on the south-east side of the main road from Corringham to Fobbing, about 260 yards in a westerly direction from the point where the boundary of the parishes of Corringham and Fobbing crosses that road, and terminating by a junction with Railway No. 2 between Manorway-road and Oilmill Farm.

Dated this 28th day of November, 1898.
KERLY, SON, and VERDEN, 14 Great Winchester-street, London, E.C., Solicitors.
SHARPE, PARKER, PRITCHARDS, and BARHAM, 9 Bridge-street, Westminster, Parliamentary Agents.
g 194

The public Notice of Application for the Light Railway Order.

The only concerned parties present at the inquiry were lawyers for the LT&SR and the Rural District Council. The LT&SR expressed concern over the details of the junction. Rather oddly the CLR's representative replied that they 'did not desire a physical junction……..they intended to bring trucks to the line where the goods could be transhipped, or they might run direct on to the line and be taken straight away'. He also stated that no running powers would be sought. Possibly he was trying to convey that the CLR would leave wagons on their own line short of the junction (as was actually done).

After the inquiry an internal report (4) on the CLR was prepared by the Commissioners:

'This is a proposal for a short line from the villages of Corringham and Fobbing which are close together, across the marshes to the banks of the Thames at Thames Haven, where it connects with the Thames Haven branch of the London, Tilbury and Southend Railway. (It is not clear whether this Thames Haven branch is a passenger line or only a goods line). The proposed line from Corringham to Thames Haven is about 2 miles in length and from a point on this line about half a mile from Thames Haven it is proposed to make a branch about half a mile long to Kynochtown which is stated to be a new village in the Marshes where new factories employing 500 people have just been started. The object of the line is to convey goods and coal between the Factories and the existing line at Thames Haven, and to convey workmen to and from the villages which are situated at the edge of the marsh on slightly higher ground'.

'Two gentlemen are named as the promoters, one of whom, Mr Cocking, is the Engineer of the line'.

'The line is perfectly flat with the exception of a slight fall of about 27 feet in a quarter of a mile from Corringham to the level of the Marshes. The line is generally straight, the few curves are laid out with a radius of 10 chains (660 feet)'.

'A good deal of drainage is crossed, which it is intended to carry under the line in 12 inch Cast Iron pipes. Only £175 is allowed in the estimates for culverts and drains, and it seems probable that this is not nearly enough'.

'The line is estimated to cost £5,474 or only £1,927 per mile. This seems to be much too low an estimate. The permanent way is estimated at only £1,086 per mile for 50lb rail. Though the rail is a light one, it can hardly be properly laid and ballasted for this sum. The amount allowed for sidings and stations is very small and the small estimate for drainage has been referred to above. If the line is constructed for £7,000 or only £2,500 per mile it will be cheaply done allowing only a 50lb rail'.

'Only two public roads are crossed, one on the main line between Corringham and Thames Haven and one on the Kynochtown branch. Both are crossed on the level, and there is no need for gates at either'.

'It seems a question whether this line across the marshes need be fenced at all. The draft Order incorporates the sections of the Railways Clauses Act 1845 which require fencing'.

'By the draft Order it is not proposed to require continuous brakes. I certainly think this is a case where we might represent to the Board of Trade that they can be of no possible use'.

'The draft Order proposes a capital of £9,000 with power to borrow £3,000. Total £12,000 or about £4,225 per mile. This is perhaps not excessive, if as I anticipate, the line will cost about £2,500 per mile to construct'.

'3 years for the purchase of land and 5 years for construction seems too long to allow in the case of this short line. And the power to have seven Directors seems also unnecessary'.

'Clause 27 of the draft Order proposes to allow 14 Tons load on a 50lb Rail. 10 Tons is the proper load for a 50lb rail'.

The criticisms raised here of the costings resulted in Cocking preparing a revised estimate, totalling £7,529. 16s 4d. This was forwarded to the Commissioners on 9th February.

In April 1899 the Light Railway Commissioners submitted their formal report to the Board of Trade, recommending that the application be granted, together with the Draft Order as modified by them.

Col Marindin, one of the Board of Trade Inspecting Officers, then made a report on the Draft Order, dated 26th May 1899. He was under the impression (not really justified) that 'it would seem likely that the line will be worked by the LT&SR Co', and noted that provision had been made in the Draft Order authorising this. He was a little concerned that the Commissioners had not seen fit to include a power enabling the Board of Trade to impose the use of continuous brakes, albeit the line was mostly flat for practical purposes. He concluded that there should be such a power included, whilst noting that 'all the London, Tilbury & Southend stock would be fitted already with continuous brakes'.

The Board of Trade officers considered that the proposed maximum fares, at 3d per mile First, 2d Second, and 1d Third, although in line with the average for such Orders, might be reduced to the much lower levels of the LT&SR. The proposed maxima for goods traffic were already based on LT&SR rates. (However the passenger maxima were *not* reduced, in the event).

The side-remark by the Commissioners about it being unclear whether the LT&SR Thames Haven branch was a passenger or goods line, would have been made in the context of the possibility of through passenger working. In fact the branch had lost its last regular passenger service in 1880, but subsequent new signalling work at Thames Haven Junction in 1885 and Thames Haven station in 1889 had been done to passenger standards. However the collapse of traffic after 1895 was starting to give an impression of a rustic goods siding.

Similarly the question of fares matching LT&SR rates would not have been seen as so relevant if there had not been the possibility of through working.

On 15th June 1899 Sir Courtenay Boyle, the Permanent Secretary of the Board of Trade, presided over a formal meeting in Whitehall to consider the confirmation of the Draft Order. Cocking, Kerly the Kynochs Solicitor, and Pritchard their Parliamentary Agent, appeared for the promoters, but no objectors presented themselves, so the proceedings were brief. It was decided that there would be powers included to enforce continuous brakes at a later stage if seen fit.

<u>The Corringham Light Railway Order 1899</u> was then confirmed, dated 10th July 1899. Many of the provisions were of course standard. The most significant sections were:

4 Arthur Chamberlain, Allan Thomas Cocking 'and others' to be 'united into a company'.

6 The number of Directors to be 3, 4 or 5.

7 Directors must possess £250 in shares.

9 Chamberlain and Cocking 'and one to be nominated by them' to be the first Directors. [Alexander Kerly was appointed].

10 Authorisation of Railways 1, 2 and 3.

11 Railways to be 4ft 8½in gauge.

13 Powers of compulsory purchase to expire two years after the date of the Order.

19 The works to be completed within three years from the date of the Order unless an extension of time is applied for.

25 Protection Clause for the Commissioners of Fobbing Level regarding ditches and bridges. (The Commissioners had objected to having *all* the ditches crossed by embankments with small culvert pipes, and the CLR had given an undertaking at the Southend inquiry that 'the five largest' would have bridges).

26 Protection Clause for Henry Charles Long and Herbert Clarence Long, confirming their agreement dated 23.2.1899 with the promoters, requiring the making of 'sidings, stopping place (and) accommodation works' at Reedham Farm [see p.29].

28 The railways not to be opened for passenger traffic without the usual one month's notice to the Board of Trade.

29 Not to run any train at more than 25mph, and not to use any engine carriage or truck with a greater weight than 12 tons on any pair of wheels, or 14 tons if 60lb rails are provided.

30 The Board of Trade may at any time impose a requirement for continuous brakes on passenger trains.

32 The company and the LT&SR may enter into agreements

for the 'maintenance and management' of the railways, their 'use or working', 'supply of stock', or 'employment of officers and servants'.

39 Maximum charges for passengers to be 3d per mile First Class, 2d Second Class, 1d Third Class.

43 The authorised capital of the company to be £9,000 in £1 shares.

47 The company may borrow up to £3,000.

Schedule - Rails to weigh at least 56lb. No turntables need be provided but tender engines not to run tender-first at more than 15mph. Stations shall be provided with platforms 'to the satisfaction of the Board of Trade', but there shall be 'no obligation on the company to provide shelter or conveniences at any station or stopping place'. [Yet at the Southend inquiry the Rural District Council had been promised that there would be conveniences, and they *were* provided in the event].

As noted earlier, G.F. Willis was appointed as the CLR Company Secretary on incorporation.

A CLR prospectus was printed in December 1899, and distributed (it would appear) solely to shareholders in Kynoch Ltd. The resulting applications, from some twenty persons, amounted to only £2,975. In January 1900 it was agreed that the Kynoch Ltd company would itself guarantee the residue of £6,025. The allotment to the ordinary shareholders was made on 12th March 1900, and the residue was allotted to Kynoch Ltd and associates on 12th April (see table p.30).

Whilst the CLR was legally a fully separate company, in practice, with the majority of the shares held by Kynoch Ltd and its associates, it had no real independent existence, any more than the Kynoch Estate Co Ltd and the Thames Stores Ltd companies did; it existed purely to do what Kynochs wished of it. For the same reason it was to be largely ignored throughout its life by the wider 'railway' world.

A significant point about the CLR was that it was engineered and operated entirely by men with no previous railway experience.

CONSTRUCTION AND OPENING

Until the CLR company was formally constituted after the granting of the Order, 'CLR' matters were dealt with by Cocking and Kerly (the CLR directors-to-be) at their Kynoch Estate Co committee meetings. The Estate Co also paid for the costs of obtaining the Order, including the parliamentary expenses (£1,375 was transferred from CLR funds later to recompense for this). At the 15th April 1899 Estate Co meeting it was agreed that 'the construction of the railway should be commenced by fencing one side of the line, the fence to be posts and wire, the posts to be made out of the materials of the old buildings on Herd Farm'.

There are no known references to the CLR construction work subsequently. It was an extremely easy job, as the majority of the route was laid at existing ground level, the main work being the installation of culvert pipes for the many ditches on the marshes. Indeed the railway was a lesser job than the previous building of the works and the housing; one of the contractors for the works may have been given the job? The out-turn cost of the railway was given as £13,960. 13s 4d – Legal and surveying £438, Parliamentary costs £1,022, land £3,282, and construction £9,217 (5). This was a lot more than Cocking's £5,474 and £7,529 estimates.

In the closing weeks of 1900, the CLR had taken delivery of a second-hand Kitson locomotive, and two carriages from Kerr Stuart, putting it in a position to open the line. A second loco was already under order from Kerr Stuart.

Light Railways had to be inspected by the Board of Trade before opening for passenger traffic, in the same way as other new railways. On 13th November 1900 George Willis the CLR company Secretary wrote to the Board informing them that Railways 2 and 3 would 'soon be ready for opening'. The Board accepted this as the 'first notice' required by law, and appointed Col Yorke to inspect the line when ready; but a few days later Lt Col Von Donop was given the job instead. Willis sent in the 'second notice' on 21st December together with the standard forms

Cover page of the confirmed Order as published by HMSO.

giving details of the line's construction, and gave notice that it would be ready for inspection from 23rd January 1901. However he subsequently had to report 'delays from bad weather' and request postponement of the inspection until after 5th February.

Included with the forms sent to the Board on 21st December 1900 was a second set of the CLR deposited plans and elevations (6) with alterations shown in red at those points where the line had been built on slightly different alignments to the 'centre line' of the plans. All sidings are also shown, so these amended plans give us a complete picture of the CLR – or to be precise, the Corringham to Kynochtown section of the CLR – as actually built in 1900. Railway No. 1 is shown as 'not completed', although it must have been pretty well completed given that it opened to goods traffic only 11 days later! – the expression may rather have signified that this part of the line was not being put up for inspection (because it was only to be opened for goods traffic, not passengers).

Also, the south to northeast side of the triangle is shown as 'at present not laid'.

The alterations from the original plans are illustrated at p.24.

The gradients had also been altered. On the original plans the majority of the line had been on very slight gradients, but the line as built was deemed to be 'level' apart from the 22 chains at 1 in 55 (which had been 1 in 56 on the original plans) on the approach to Corringham station.

Also submitted on 21st December were scale drawings (reproduced at p.26) of Corringham and Kynochtown stations, two underbridges, a 'general section of railway over ditches', and a section of the 60lb rail used. These drawings actually dated from 1898.

Von Donop in the event made his inspection on or about Monday 11th February 1901 (7). Strictly speaking he was inspecting the 36 chains of Railway No.2 from Kynochtown station to the triangle northeastern junction, and the whole of Railway No. 3 from that point to Corringham. He noted in passing that the

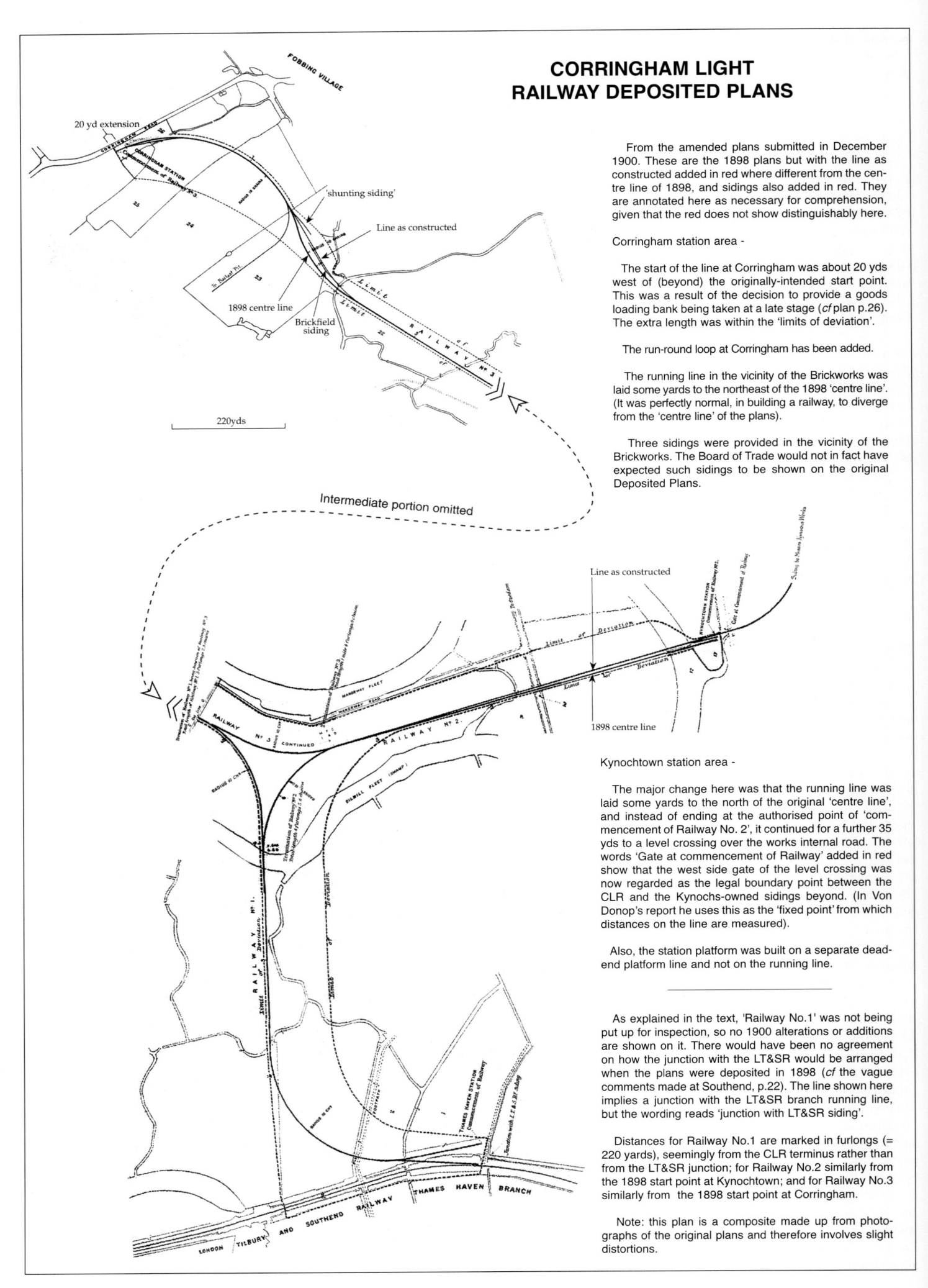

CORRINGHAM LIGHT RAILWAY DEPOSITED PLANS

From the amended plans submitted in December 1900. These are the 1898 plans but with the line as constructed added in red where different from the centre line of 1898, and sidings also added in red. They are annotated here as necessary for comprehension, given that the red does not show distinguishably here.

Corringham station area -

The start of the line at Corringham was about 20 yds west of (beyond) the originally-intended start point. This was a result of the decision to provide a goods loading bank being taken at a late stage (*cf* plan p.26). The extra length was within the 'limits of deviation'.

The run-round loop at Corringham has been added.

The running line in the vicinity of the Brickworks was laid some yards to the northeast of the 1898 'centre line'. (It was perfectly normal, in building a railway, to diverge from the 'centre line' of the plans).

Three sidings were provided in the vicinity of the Brickworks. The Board of Trade would not in fact have expected such sidings to be shown on the original Deposited Plans.

Kynochtown station area -

The major change here was that the running line was laid some yards to the north of the original 'centre line', and instead of ending at the authorised point of 'commencement of Railway No. 2', it continued for a further 35 yds to a level crossing over the works internal road. The words 'Gate at commencement of Railway' added in red show that the west side gate of the level crossing was now regarded as the legal boundary point between the CLR and the Kynochs-owned sidings beyond. (In Von Donop's report he uses this as the 'fixed point' from which distances on the line are measured).

Also, the station platform was built on a separate dead-end platform line and not on the running line.

As explained in the text, 'Railway No.1' was not being put up for inspection, so no 1900 alterations or additions are shown on it. There would have been no agreement on how the junction with the LT&SR would be arranged when the plans were deposited in 1898 (*cf* the vague comments made at Southend, p.22). The line shown here implies a junction with the LT&SR branch running line, but the wording reads 'junction with LT&SR siding'.

Distances for Railway No.1 are marked in furlongs (= 220 yards), seemingly from the CLR terminus rather than from the LT&SR junction; for Railway No.2 similarly from the 1898 start point at Kynochtown; and for Railway No.3 similarly from the 1898 start point at Corringham.

Note: this plan is a composite made up from photographs of the original plans and therefore involves slight distortions.

section of Railway No.2 from the northeastern to the southern triangle junction was 'not yet completed' (confirming the CLR statement in December above); but confirmed that the northwest to south curve was completed.

The line was laid with 60lb flat bottom rails in 30ft lengths. Each 30ft length had seven half-round sleepers and three rectangular-section sleepers (one at each end and one in the middle). The sleepers were 9in by 4 1/2in by 9ft, creosoted. The rails were fixed to tie plates with 3/4in fang bolts and 5/8in dog spikes. The ballast was 'mostly gravel – in some cases broken bricks have been used for a bottom, in others burnt clay'. The line was single throughout but land had been acquired for a second track should it ever be necessary. It was fenced throughout, with seven-wire fencing (despite the Order not requiring fencing). The two level crossings on public roads (the Manorway) had gates (again not required by the Order). There were 12 occupation crossings in addition. The cuttings and embankments nowhere exceeded 4ft in height.

There were no signals (8); the line was to be worked on the 'One Engine In Steam' system, with a 'train staff' carried by the driver as his authority to be on the line.

Five 'junctions' existed on the single line:
- Ballast Pit Siding, near Corringham.
- 'Shunting Siding' adjacent to last – it is not evident what purpose this siding served, and it was noted that 'this siding will probably be dispensed with shortly'.
- Kynoch Estate Co's Brickfield Siding.
- Junction with Railway No. 1 (i.e. the triangle NW junction).
- Connection at Kynochtown station between the platform line and the line into the works.

Corringham station had a platform 150ft long (excluding ramps), 2ft 9in high, and 6ft 6in wide. 'It is provided with shelter and suitable accommodation for both sexes, but both the platform and the station buildings are in a very incomplete state. It is provided with a loop to enable the engine to run round'.

Kynochtown station platform was 100ft long, 2ft 9in high, and 6ft 6in wide. 'There are also some station buildings in course of erection, but both these and the road approach are in a very incomplete state'.

Von Donop did not comment on the station platforms being, rather oddly, of different lengths; or on the point that station buildings and lavatories were being provided although the Order had not required them.

There were two underbridges, one of 10ft span at 'Manorway Fleet', and another of 7ft span near the Brickfield Siding. At all other points where ditches were crossed, 18in earthenware pipes set in concrete were provided in the low embankments. Von Donop decided not to inspect the two bridges in February because he had already decided to reject the line on other grounds. He noted instead

'The two underbridges will be reported on after the next inspection when it is understood that the actual engine which it is intended to use on this line will be available for that purpose. At present there is only a very light engine available'.

(A reference to the fact that the larger Kerr Stuart loco was not yet delivered; it arrived in March).

In rejecting the line, Von Donop's requirements included
- All points to be locked by a key on the train staff (9).
- All sidings to be provided with trap points, including the connection to Railway No. 1 at the northwestern end of the triangle, 'so long as it is used as a goods line'.
- The station platforms and buildings to be completed, and lamps and nameboards provided.

The Board of Trade accordingly wrote to the CLR on 13th February stating that passenger opening must be postponed until a reinspection was made.

In the mean time, the whole of the CLR (other than the so far unlaid northeastern to southern side of the triangle) had been opened to goods traffic – which required no outside permission – on (probably) 1st January 1901 (10). On 3rd January the LT&SR senior officers were shown over the line: Willis the CLR Secretary told the press that this visit had been arranged for them 'to inspect and improve the connection between their line at Thames

---

WAS THE 'SEPARATE TERMINUS' LINE AT THAMES HAVEN ACTUALLY LAID? EXACTLY WHERE WAS THE ORIGINAL JUNCTION WITH THE LT&SR?

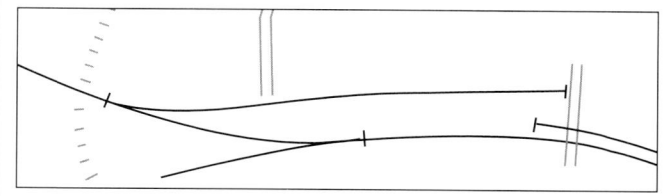

This plan is redrawn from the map in the Reedham and Oilmill farms auction notice of June 1902, the only plan of this area available for the period immediately after the opening of the CLR. Of course one may well wonder whether a map of this sort is necessarily an accurate depiction of the track layout; but the surveyor has not just copied the CLR Deposited Plans, as they show the junctions at different points. Does this plan constitute evidence that the CLR did build the 'separate terminus' spur line? The 1919 OS map seems to back it up insofar as it shows the CLR north side fence arranged for this alignment. At right the LT&SR down side siding is shown ending a few yards to the west of Dock House LC, as on the 1895 OS (*The Thames Haven Railway* p.30). But did the CLR line *really* ever run into the LT&SR running line as shown here? We have no proper railway plan until that of 1915 (p.48, ref.1) where the CLR is shown as running (as it did subsequently) into the LT&SR down siding, not the running line.

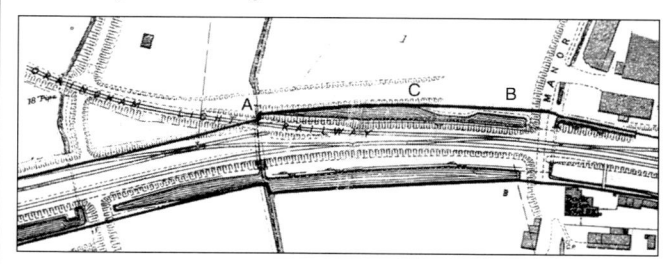

Further evidence that the 'separate terminus' spur line may indeed have been laid comes from this 1920 Midland Railway 2 chain survey (reduced to half the original size), showing an 'embankment' on the alignment of the spur much more clearly than the OS maps do.

This plan also confirms the precise position of the CLR/LT&SR *property* boundary (the thick line at A). (The 1895 OS map shows that the LT&SR north side fence was already on the same alignment as shown here, before the CLR was built). The CLR/LT&SR *maintenance* boundary was at B in 1915 - i.e. the point where the LT&SR down siding had ended in pre-CLR days - but after the additional crossover west of Dock House LC was put in by the Midland in 1916 the maintenance boundary was moved to C.

Haven and this company'. This may indicate that some *ad hoc* connection was still in use at the time of goods opening, and was replaced by a 'permanent' connection soon afterwards. A 1930s LMS report (11) gives 16th January 1901 as the date when the 'connection was effected' at Thames Haven. Such a date for a 'permanent' connection would fit well with the 3rd January LT&SR officers' visit. But we do not know exactly where either of these connections were (see plans above). Because the CLR was a statutory railway company, there was no 'Private Siding Agreement' for the junction with the LT&SR at Thames Haven. (This slightly puzzled the LMS in the 1930s as they could not see why what to them was just a glorified works siding did not have a PSA like all the other sidings off the Thames Haven branch!). Nor is there any record of any financial argument over the making of the CLR connection. As no signalling was required, it probably involved no significant cost on the LT&SR's part.

We must assume that the northeast to south curve of the triangle was laid and brought into use shortly after February 1901. The northeastern connection, as an additional connection on a passenger line, should have been inspected by Von Donop on his second visit, but there is no specific reference to this.

The CLR was now caught out for engaging in dubious activities on the passenger front. The local press had already reported on 11th January 1901 that

'This railway is........at present being used privately for the conveyance of the clerks and staff from Corringham to the explosive works, an engine and American cars being engaged in the work'. [A reference to the appearance of the Kerr Stuart coaches].

The Board of Trade clearly had not noticed this hint of improper passenger operation prior to their approval, but the CLR did not escape for long, as on 19th February an anonymous correspondent

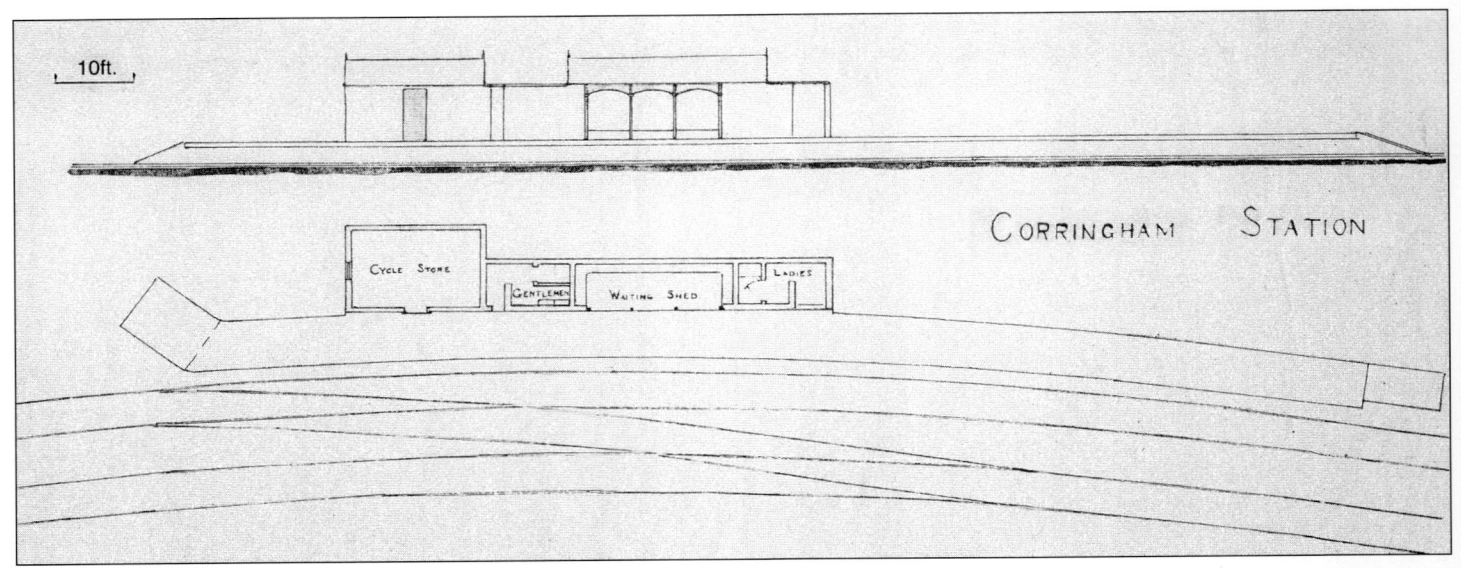

1898 Elevation and Plan for Corringham station, submitted to the Board of Trade in December 1900. The main building was actually built with a longer gabled roof covering more of the Gents, and the run-round loop was built without the spur siding. The goods loading bank is not shown here, confirming that it was a late idea; there was in consequence no platform ramp at this end as built. The platform ramp at the east end was indeed slightly narrower than the platform itself, as it was not corbelled out.

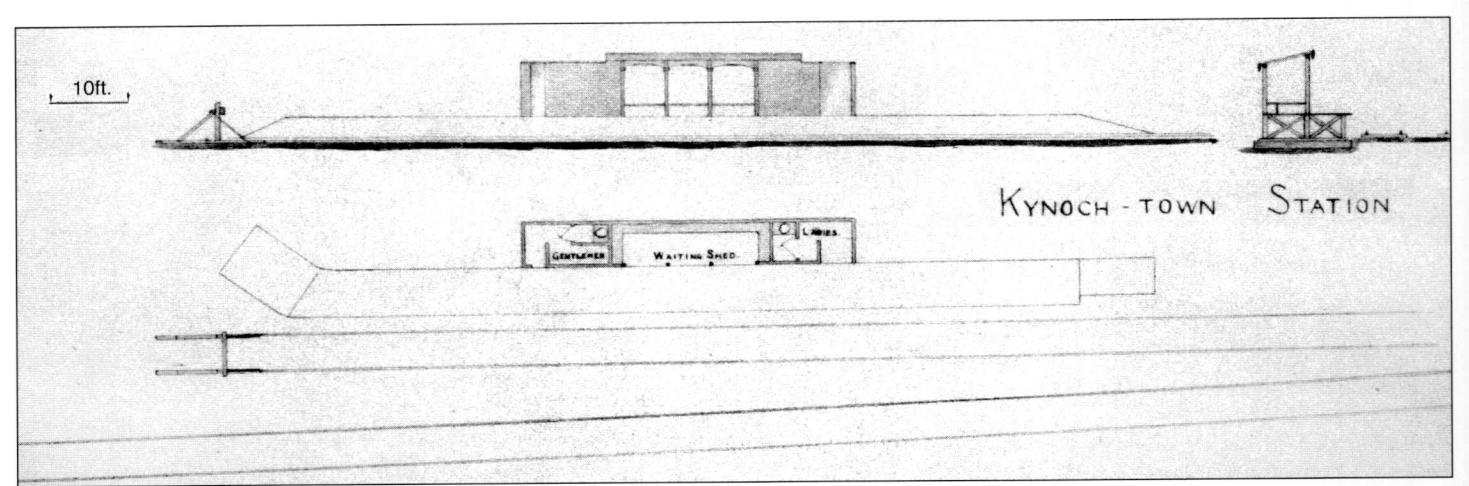

1898 Elevation and Plan for Kynochtown station. Note the hyphenated name. The (internal) measurements of the building are identical to Corringham. As at Corringham the drawing shows one platform ramp to be built at an angle, for reasons not evident.

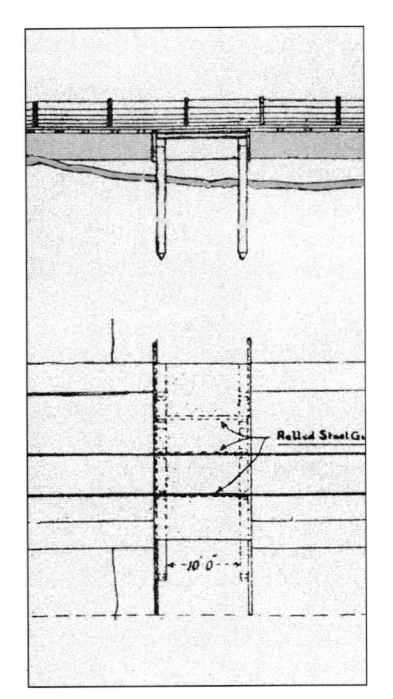

Elevation and Plan of the 'Manorway Fleet' underbridge (in fact, the bridge over the Salt Fleet at Kynochtown station). The 12in square piles support timber cross-beams which carry longitudinal steel girders.

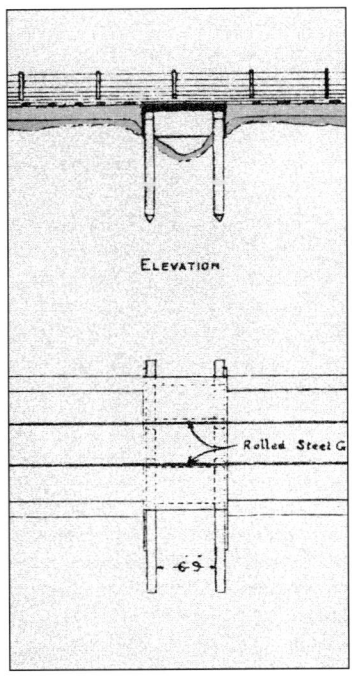

The similarly-built 'Bridge over ditch near Corringham Brickfield' (see OS map p.40 for the location, immediately southeast of the Brickworks). Per scale the span should be 7ft 9ins.

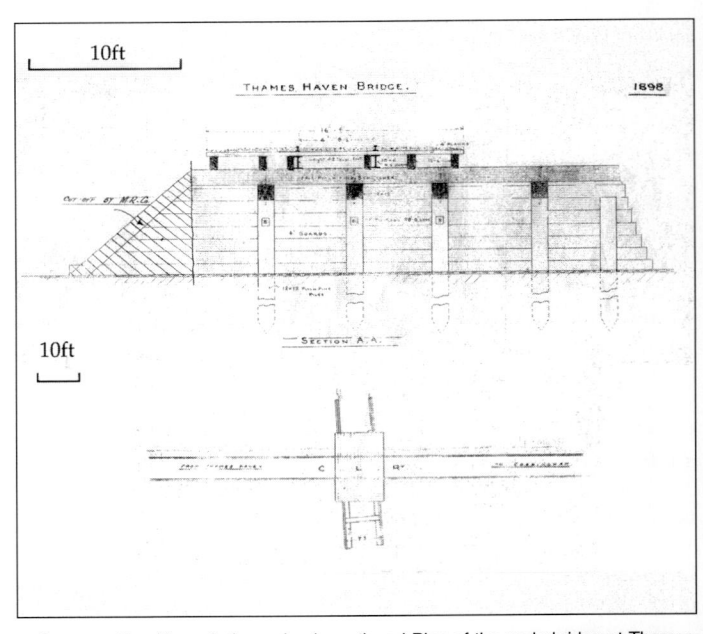

Cross-section (through the embankment) and Plan of the underbridge at Thames Haven, over the ditch running N-S in the centre of the 2 chain survey at p.25. The piles and cross-beams are both noted as 12in by 12in pitch pine. The track is carried on a 16ft 9in transverse-planked platform on the cross-beams. The drawing was made by the CLR in 1898 and altered in 1918 when the Midland Railway cut out the south slope of the embankment to fit in the headshunt for Reedham Sidings. The Elevation, which is omitted due to poor quality, confirms that the span of this bridge was only 5ft. No drawings are known of the other bridge on Railway No.1, over the Oil Mill Fleet immediately south of the triangle south junction.

wrote to the Board directly

' Sir – Corringham Light Railway – You may be interested to learn that in spite of the fact that the line has not been passed by your Department, passengers are being daily carried, and have been now for several months'.

The Board of Trade did write to Willis about this, and in his reply of 5th March he evaded answering specifically as to whether passenger trains had already been operated, merely noting that 'your instructions will be fully complied with until the Inspecting Officer has made his final inspection and recommends the opening of the line for traffic'.

He did not, as he might have done, attempt the argument that the passengers were all staff and not 'public' – although this might not have washed legally given that Kynochs and the CLR were separate companies.

It can be assumed that the reports were true and that the CLR had indeed commenced passenger traffic improperly some time in the last weeks of 1900. Unless they pushed their luck, it must also be imagined that the service then had to be suspended from March until June. (So, as is so often the case, research reveals that the date always quoted hitherto for 'opening' of this line is not the real commencement of service date at all!).

Correspondence with the Board of Trade resumed on 6th May 1901 with Willis writing to say that the line would be ready for reinspection from 29th May. It would seem that Von Donop actually came the week after that, as his report is dated 4th June. He noted that all his previous requirements had now been carried out except that there were still no lamps erected at the stations. He now also wanted 'a railing at the east end of Kynoch Town station'. The underbridges were tested with the new Kerr Stuart loco and 'proved themselves stiff'. The 'trap points on the siding leading from Kynoch Town station to Kynoch's works' had not been placed in the usual position close to the points. The CLR claimed that this could not conveniently be done, and promised instead that 'no wagons will be allowed to stand between the siding and the junction', whatever that meant.

On 5th June the Board of Trade gave formal notice that the line from Corringham to Kynochtown could now be opened for passenger traffic, provided that the lamps and railing were installed.

The formal 'opening' celebrations took place on Saturday 22nd June 1901 (12). The *Grays & Tilbury Gazette* reported:

'The Corringham Light Railway between that place and Kynoch Town was formally opened by Mr Austen [sic] Chamberlain (who was accompanied by Mrs R. Chamberlain) on Saturday, and is now ready for traffic according to a Timetable which the company have issued. Its chief purpose at present is in conveying workmen, officials, and visitors to the works, and the former are conveyed to and from their houses each day for 6d a week'. [For the actual fares see Appendix 1]. 'On Saturday tea was provided for the children. There were sports in the afternoon and the day was closed with a ride in the train for parents and children'.

It was actually the Kynoch's Chairman Arthur Chamberlain who attended. Austen Chamberlain, Joseph Chamberlain's eldest son, was a well-known national figure by this date, much more than Arthur, who the reporter had probably not come across previously. And Austen had no wife until 1906.

The Kynochtown Schoolmaster Edwin Broad gave a fuller guest-list in the school logbook:

'Mr and Miss Chamberlain' [i.e. Arthur and Kate], ' Mr and Mrs Cocking, Rev and Mrs Moir, Dr and Mrs Basden, Colonel and Mrs Frend, Mr and Mrs Kerly, and others who were visiting Kynochtown in connection with the opening of the Corringham Light Railway, visited the school in the afternoon'.

It cannot be taken for granted that the ordinary passenger service only resumed after 22nd June; the CLR would have been legally entitled to start (resume!) the passenger service as soon as the lamps and railing were erected.

It was only on 17th September that Willis informed the Board of Trade that all requirements had now been complied with.

There was also the question of the usual 'undertaking' as to the method of working of the single line. This was belatedly submitted by Willis on 3rd October, correctly signed by himself as company Secretary and Cocking as company Chairman. It stated that 'Mode II' of the Board of Trade Requirements for the working of railways would be adopted, i.e. One Engine in Steam with Train Staff. As the company owned two locomotives, this meant that if both were in steam simultaneously, one would have to be confined to the works sidings east of the Kynochtown station level crossing. (There is no evidence that a staff was actually carried in later years).

The sidings within the works, which were not part of the CLR, were also laid in 1900/1. However we have no plan of them until the 1919 OS map. Shunting within the works was done by the 'CLR' locos and the cost recharged to Kynochs for bookkeeping purposes.

In June 1903 Willis informed the Board of Trade that it was intended to put in an additional siding for Kynochs Brickfield, further SE than the existing siding; but nothing came of this.

THE LT&SR AND THE CLR 1901-1902

In January 1901 there was a flurry of speculation in the *Grays & Tilbury Gazette* regarding a rumour that the LT&SR was going to take over the CLR company. Willis the CLR Secretary claimed that 'no negotiations for purchase have been proceeding between the two companies'. This may have been strictly true but (as the paper's editor commented) if so, why had the LT&SR included a clause empowering it to take over the CLR in its 1901 parliamentary Bill ? Willis did not respond to that.

The preamble to the LT&SR Bill stated that the CLR had 'suggested' that the LT&SR might take it over. The provision was included, as s.33, in the LT&SR's 1901 Act as passed (13).

Far from the LT&SR *taking over* the CLR, it was in fact already clear by early 1901 that (at least so far as the immediate situation went) they were not even going to *work* the line as had been provided for in the Light Railway Order. As noted above, the CLR had two locos of their own on site by the end of March 1901. Indeed, it is difficult to see how the LT&SR could have worked the line, as it had no locos suitable for the lightly-laid track.

Nevertheless on 29th May 1902 the LT&SR takeover idea was aired again, with Stride giving the LT&SR Board a report on the subject. He had in fact recently made an inspection of the CLR from this viewpoint. The Directors resolved to inspect the CLR line themselves before making a decision on the matter. But there is no evidence that they did, and the idea of an LT&SR takeover was never mentioned again.

In contrast, the idea of CLR passenger trains running to/from Thames Haven, and/or through LT&SR passenger trains via Thames Haven, was seriously discussed for the first time in the late summer of 1902. This resulted in Willis writing to the Board of Trade on 7th October 1902 advising that Railway No.1, 'hitherto used as a siding for goods traffic only', had now been completed in readiness for passenger traffic, explaining:

'We beg to inform you that it is intended to use this railway in conjunction with the Thames Haven branch of the London Tilbury & Southend Railway, and it is proposed to erect a joint platform at the point where our railway joins the LT&S railway at Thames Haven Junction'. [He meant near Dock House crossing]. 'Under these circumstances, we have not erected a station or platform at the terminus of our No.1 Railway as shown on sheet No.1 of the Corringham Light Railway plans'. (This comment is perhaps a further hint that the independent terminus *line* itself *had* been laid).

If the 1889-built signal box at Thames Haven was no longer working the points there (14), having an interchange platform at the CLR junction would avoid the cost of having to interlock the points at the terminus again, which would have been necessary for passenger trains to follow the possible alternative option of running to and from Thames Haven station.

On 16th October Willis gave notice to the Board of Trade of 'our

Kynochtown station, undated but probably summer 1901 given the complete lack of any vegetation growth. The two original coaches and the first LT&SR coach (acquired by late 1901 – see p.87) are at the platform line stops. The loco shed has yet to be built.

The platform and building here were entirely of timber, no doubt because this was new-made ground on marshland. The same Waiting Shed plus Gents and Ladies facilities were provided as at Corringham, but the building here had a lean-to roof. There was no requirement for a cycle shed at this end of the line.

The sleepers are ballasted over as per the normal practice of the day.

The layout here was clearly decided on the assumption that no passenger train would ever be much longer than the original carriages. Given that a run-round loop was provided at Corringham, why not here? The platform could easily have been built some yards further west, with an extra connection to the running line at the east end. What *did* happen when a passenger train arrived at Corringham pre-1915? Either the carriages would have had to be moved by tow-roping, or the whole train run round the triangle (not very likely). The CLR cannot have been intending to *propel* passenger trains one way or it would not have bothered with the loop at Corringham. And why did Von Donop not comment on this peculiarity?

The passenger entrance gate is seen, open, immediately to the right of the nearer lamp. The railings seen between the LT&SR coach and the station building are for the ramp up from the gate to the platform.

The entrance to Kynochtown station from the far side of the Salt Fleet in the 1900s. Access to the platform was via the ramp to the right of the building. (During the 1914-18 war further entrances had to be provided). The Kitson loco is ready with one of the Kerr Stuart coaches for the next departure. The length of the platform building shows up better here than in the usual foreshortened views. The light-coloured works buildings in the background are also seen at the left hand side of the photograph at p.36 top.

The two houses here by the works entrance, Nos 78 and 79 Fleet Street, were no doubt built for the 'Patrol' men as gatekeepers, although in the 1901 census only one was actually so occupied. See also the plan at p.15 top. *Thurrock Museum*

Corringham station soon after opening. The station site here was a disused brick-pit and therefore provided good enough ground for the platform and buildings to be built of brick.

There is a low-sided wagon (not a coal wagon) at the end of the line, alongside the loading bank section of the platform, which was an afterthought. It was in earlier years continuous with the passenger section of the platform, but some visual confusion arises from the passenger section being corbelled out at the top. The sheet draped over the edge of the loading bank makes for extra confusion. In later years there was a gap between the two sections of platform. There are two platform lamps, as at Kynochtown, and the nameboards are to the same design.

In the background are (left to right) Grove Terrace, Digby Villas, and Nos 35 to 30 Digby Road, all part of the 'Corringham Building Estate'.

intention to open Railway No.1 for passenger traffic on November 18th'. (He seems to have forgotten that he should also have given notice re the triangle southern to northeastern junctions section of Railway No.2). However he then asked for this to be postponed.

Meanwhile Stride had told the LT&SR Board on 2nd October of his proposals

'for a train service between Stanford, Thames Haven, and over the Corringham Light Railway, involving the construction of a temporary platform at May's Crossing on the Thames Haven branch, and the expenditure of a small sum upon the platforms at Thames Haven station to adopt them for the traffic'.

Although said within days of Willis' remarks above, this clearly envisages a quite different scheme, with through running of trains, reversing at Thames Haven station. Mayes Crossing is on the road from Stanford-le-Hope to Mucking Creek, at grid reference 691816 (where a Halt did later exist, as described at *The Thames Haven Railway* Chapter 9). Stride was clearly referring to a service starting from there and not from Stanford-le-Hope station via an inconvenient reversal at Thames Haven Junction. Mayes Crossing would be convenient enough for those living in Stanford-le-Hope itself, but not very good for those coming from elsewhere by the LT&SR. Why was the platform at Mayes Crossing referred to as 'temporary' ? – perhaps because it could be taken down again if the service proved a failure?

From October 1902 on, the LT&SR's monthly Engineer's expenditure reports do show the spending of significant amounts of money on 'May's Crossing Station, Thames Haven Branch', which clearly indicates that some work was done. However nothing more was reported at Board level, and the scheme must have been abandoned after a few weeks work. If one were to speculate why the LT&SR got cold feet, it may be that reports were coming through of reduced staffing levels at Kynochs following the end of the Boer War?

The CLR did not become aware of the LT&SR's backsliding until February 1903. On 12th January they told the Board of Trade of 'our intention to open on Friday February 13th' (i.e. open Railway No.1 for passenger traffic). Details of the line were submitted – unfortunately they are now missing from the file (15). There were no stations and only two bridges, the underbridges for Oil Mill Fleet and a ditch near Thames Haven.

It was arranged that Von Donop would make his inspection on 10th February. The CLR then wrote to suggest that he came on the 10.15 from Fenchurch St 'and we will arrange a conveyance to take you from Stanford-le-Hope station to Corringham station, where a train will be waiting'. But on 3rd February they had to write again saying that

'since writing we have seen the representative of the London Tilbury & Southend Railway and we are informed that the work they are engaged upon at (sic) their Thames Haven branch will not be ready by the date arranged for your visit to our line………..under the circumstances we thought you might prefer to wait until the LT&S Railway portion of the work is ready'.

This letter also re-iterated the CLR's previous interpretation of what was intended, i.e. that passengers would be exchanged at a platform near Dock House crossing – 'the arrangement is that our passenger trains shall meet their train near Thames Haven'.

Then on 5th February the CLR withdrew their formal notice of opening – and nothing more was ever heard. 'Railway No. 1' remained goods-only.

The CLR's statement that their side of the work had been completed may imply that they had completed a short platform on their line near Dock House crossing – but there is no other evidence of this.

At least one (non-public) passenger train did run subsequently over this section of the CLR. On 26th June 1903 a party of gentlemen, all leading figures in the world of shooting, visited Kynochtown 'to witness the manufacture of smokeless sporting powder'. They travelled by a special train from Fenchurch Street to Thames Haven 'and on arriving at Thames Haven changed to the Corringham Light Railway and were conveyed by the engine 'Cordite' to Kynochtown' (16). We can assume that they transferred at the old Thames Haven station island platform.

MANORWAY SIDING PLANS

When Von Donop inspected Railways 2 and 3, no comment had been made about the absence of the 'sidings' and 'stopping place' near the Manorway that were required under s.26 of the Light Railway Order. No copy of the actual February 1899 agreement with the Longs (the owners of Oilmill and Reedham farms) is known, however the location of the agreed siding is shown on the June 1902 sale notice for these farms (17) and has been marked here on the OS map at p.41.

The Longs soon decided that further pressure was desirable, and their Land Agent F. Kemp-Smith wrote to the Light Railway Commissioners, who merely advised them (in June 1901) to approach the CLR and failing that the Board of Trade. In March 1902 Kemp-Smith wrote to the Board saying that he could obtain 'no definite answer' from the CLR, 'and shall be glad to know whether you can inform me whether the public will be able to obtain the public siding, otherwise the Light Railway becomes a private undertaking practically for the sole benefit of the factory'. The Board replied that they had no powers to enforce the construction of the siding, and that nobody else did either. This conclusion would seem to make the whole idea of including protection clauses in Light Railway Orders quite pointless.

Note the reference to this being a public siding rather than a private siding for the Longs. Presumably it was intended that neighbouring farmers would use it. 'Stopping Place' would normally mean a passenger halt, but it is difficult to see the purpose of having a halt here.

The question then became academic in June 1902 when Kynochs purchased both farms from the Longs at auction for £4,500. Reedham Farm was subsequently sold to the London & Thames Haven Oil Wharves company (LATHOL) in 1909 for £7,000 so that they could expand their site northwards, and Oilmill Farm was disposed of for £7,000 in 1912 – so this was one piece of side-activity that Kynochs did profit from! The agreement regarding the siding was formally 'discharged' prior to the sale to LATHOL.

The CLR did however come to handle a small amount of public goods traffic at Corringham.

PAYING FOR CONSTRUCTION

As noted earlier, £13,960 had been spent on the construction of the line, and an additional £1,912 on 'working stock' (i.e. the locomotives, carriages, and wagons) – total £15,872. The authorised and issued capital however was only £12,000 (£9,000 in shares and £3,000 in debentures). It is to be assumed that Kynoch Ltd had borne the excess.

In May 1904, seeking to regularise this situation, the CLR sent a 'memorial' to the Board of Trade requesting an increase in their authorised capital and borrowing. It was stated that the costs of building the line had been in excess because of 'high land prices awarded and a rise in the cost of materials and labour'. (This was no doubt deemed to sound better than 'unrealistically low estimates' !). The CLR also stated that they needed extra funds for 'additional rolling stock'; it is difficult to envisage what they may have been thinking of, and no extra stock was acquired for ten years after this, in the event. An Extraordinary General Meeting of the company – probably just the directors, in reality – was held at the Witton works on 4th July 1904 to approve formally the application for £5,000 in additional shares and £1,666 in additional debentures. The Corringham Light Railway Certificate 1905 was then issued by the Board of Trade on 6th April 1905.

£3,000 of additional shares were issued immediately after this, almost all to existing CLR shareholders (table p.30). The company's borrowing fluctuated in subsequent years as some of the original debentures were paid off, whilst new debentures were issued. The CLR company's financial performance is discussed at p.31.

1. See *The Thames Haven Railway* p.28.
2. Essex Record Office C/PP 2/79, National Archives MT54/132.
3. In 1914 it was discovered that this land at Kynochtown station had never been conveyed from Kynoch Ltd to the CLR. The conveyance was then made in May 1914.
4. Undated and unsigned report in National Archives MT58/49. It must have been written prior to the receipt of Cocking's amended estimates which he sent in on 9th February.
5. Figures from the annual accounts for 1903, in National Archives MT6 1338/6. These are the first annual accounts known to survive. It is likely that a very small amount of extra work had been done in 1901-3.
6. In National Archives MT54/132, along with the original set.
7. Date of report; he would not have visited on a Sunday but it is possible he had come on the Saturday. National Archives MT6 1600/1 has this report and much subsequent CLR / BoT correspondence from 1901-3, as referred to here.
8. This is reconfirmed ('no signals') by J.H. Freeman's 1933 talk (see p.48, footnote 7). But *cf* the photograph at p34 !
9. Willis had told Von Donop on 16.1.1901 that 'in constructing the line we have been under the impression that it was not necessary to use locked points .... we are not clear that it is compulsory to use these on Light Railways'.
10. Date given, presumably by the CLR, to the *Locomotive Magazine* (15.6.1905 pp.96-98) and the *Railway Magazine* (June 1913 p.498).
11. National Archives RAIL 1007/280.
12. Wrongly given as 29th June in the June 1913 *Railway Magazine* article and *Bradshaw's Manual*, and so copied by many subsequent authors including Gotheridge. The *Grays & Tilbury Gazette* article is in the 29th June issue and, whilst it says only 'Saturday', it could not be reporting events of that same day. However the School Logbook entry is conclusive evidence. Also Chamberlain told the Kynochs Board on 24th June that he had 'visited the Thames Factory and was present at the opening of the Corringham Light Railway'. The earliest published article, in the *Locomotive Magazine* 1905, correctly gives the 22nd June date.
13. The committee evidence relating to this Bill is lost so we have no knowledge of what was stated in Parliament.
14. See *The Thames Haven Railway* p.72.
15. The CLR's letter states that there are 'seven facing points' on Railway No.1, but also that there are 'four junctions and sidings'. The most likely explanation of this is that the four junctions are Railway No.1 with Railway No.3, Railway No.1 with Railway No.2, the connection to the 'independent terminus' siding, and the connection with the LT&SR. If the first three had trap points (as per Von Donop's requirements in 1901) that would make seven facing points.
16. *Kynoch Journal* Vol.4 No.23 (June-July 1903) p.99.
17. Essex Record Office D/SF 41.
18. It seems clear from the Deposited Plans (and the Notice of Application) that Railway No.1 was originally conceived of as commencing at the 'independent terminus'. However the Light Railway Order s.10 describes it as 'commencing by a junction with the London Tilbury and Southend Railway', and gives the length as 5 furlongs 2.8 chains.

CORRINGHAM LIGHT RAILWAY COMPANY SHAREHOLDERS

	Allocated 12.3.1900	Allocated 30.6.1905
Edward Bucklow, Morayshire	1 - 40	9001 - 9020
Arthur Chamberlain (?) *	41 - 590	9021 - 9645
not known	591 - 690	- - -
Jane Kerr Davies, Birmingham	691 - 990	9646 - 9845
Charles Emanuel, Birmingham	991 - 1090	9846 - 9895
James Gillman, Norwich (?) *	1091 - 1240	9896 - 9995
Thomas C. Icke, Birmingham	1241 - 1340	9996 - 10045
A. W. Kerly	1341 - 1590	- - -
William & Matilda McLandsborough	1591 - 1715	10046 - 10170
Thomas C. Mackenzie, Birmingham	1716 - 1915	10171 - 10270
John Page, Ringmer, Sussex	1916 - 2015	10271 - 10310
John Paton, Osterley (?) *	2016 - 2115	10311 - 10410
not known	2116 - 2215	- - -
Edwin, Edwin & Thos Slingsby, Boston	2216 - 2365	10501 - 10600
Alice Woodhall, Birmingham	2366 - 2615	10601 - 10700
A. T. Cocking **	2616 - 2685	- - -
not known	2686 - 2875	- - -
Peter Roberts, St Asaph	- - -	10411 - 10450
James Robinson, Harrogate (?) *	2876 - 2975	10451 - 10500
	Allocated 12.4.1900	
Kynoch Ltd	2976 - 5975	- - -
Arthur & Herbert Chamberlain ***	5976 - 6158	11701 - 12000
Kynoch Estate Co Ltd ****	6159 - 6258	- - -
Chamberlain & Hookham *****	6259 - 9000	10701 - 11700

* Original ownership of 1900 shares not recorded, but deduced from the fact that subsequent transfers of these shares took place on the same date as the transfer of other shares definitely belonging to this person.
** Cocking should have held at least another 180 shares to qualify as a Director. 2686-2875 were possibly the rest of his initial holding.
*** Original shares transferred 1902 to Mrs Gertrude Bowen, to whom the 1905 shares were issued.
**** Transferred to Kynoch Ltd 1902.
***** For whom see footnote 9, p.20.

It will be seen that most of the original 1900 shareholders also took up the new shares in 1905, and that with a couple of exceptions the share certificates were made out in 1905 in the same order as in 1900. Cocking (?) and Kerly only took up a minimum allocation in 1900 and did not subscribe at all in 1905, whereas Chamberlain made a significant personal investment.

By 1919 several of the original individual shareholders had died and their holdings had passed to their heirs, being split up in some cases. 250 of the shares originally taken by Kynoch Ltd were transferred to Arthur Chamberlain Junior in 1914 to qualify him as a Director (the transfer of his father's shares under his will did not take place until 8.2.1916).

The unknown holder of 2116-2215 would by elimination seem to be the one shareholder who refused to sell in 1919.

SOURCES: CLR share certificates (incomplete set) and 1919 letters to shareholders, Birmingham City Archives MS1422/34/2/11/2.

CLR Share Certificate No.1, issued to Edward Bucklow on 12th March 1900. The CLR did not waste money on specially-printed certificates!

CORRINGHAM LIGHT RAILWAY COMPANY

DIRECTORS

Allan Thomas Cocking (Chairman)	1899-1920
Arthur Chamberlain	1899-1913
Alexander William Kerly	1899-1921
Arthur Chamberlain Jnr	1913-1921
Sir Clifford J. Cory (Chairman)	1921-1935+
Henry A. Griffin	1921-1935+
S.M. Jones	1921-1935+
J.P. Johns	1921-1935+
T.L. Griffiths	1921-c1930
G.H. Robinson	c1930-1935+

The names of the Directors for the Vacuum/Mobil period are not known, it is to be assumed that selected Vacuum/Mobil company Directors were allocated CLR Directorships.

SECRETARIES

George F. Willis	1899-1903
James W. Ramsay	1903-1908
James Went	1908-c1910
Percy J. Gorman	c1910-1914
Herbert Reeve	1914-1921
John Henry Freeman	1921-1952

The last four at least were styled 'Secretary and Superintendent'. The names of the Secretaries for the Vacuum/Mobil period are not known, the post would have been fulfilled by a senior officer in the Vacuum/Mobil Company Secretary's office.

CORRINGHAM LIGHT RAILWAY FINANCIAL RESULTS
(for those years for which information is available)

	1903	1906	1911	1912	1913
Gross Receipts Passenger	£1,390. 11s 0d	nk	nk	nk	£ 353. 0s 7½d
Goods	£ 1,057. 5s 1d	nk	nk	nk	£1,920. 17s 5d
TOTAL	£2,447. 16s 1d	£2,063. 12s 8d	£2,125. 18s 2d	£2,471. 0s 10d	£2,325. 16s 10½d
Working Costs	£1,521. 13s 7d	£ 867. 8s 1d	£ 873. 13s 9½d	£1,240. 4s 8d	£1,059. 10s 4½d
Net Income	£ 926. 2s 6d	£1,196. 4s 7d	£1,252. 4s 4½d	£1,230. 16s 2d	£1,266. 6s 6d
Sum c/f from previous year	£183. 5s 2d	£136. 14s 10½d	£ 45. 15s 3½d	£43. 8s 4d	£59. 13s 2d
Total for distribution	£1,109. 7s 8d	£1,332. 19s 5½d	£1,297. 19s 8d	£1,274. 4s 6d	£1,325. 19s 8d
Directors' Fees	£37. 10s 0d	£ 37. 10s 0d	£ 37. 10s 0d	£ 37. 10s 0d	£ 35. 0s 0d
To Depreciation Account	£187. 15s 5d	£185. 16s 6d	£185. 1s 4d	£185. 1s 4d	£ 185. 1s 4d
Debentures Interest	£120. 0s 0d	£132. 13s 3d	£132. 0s 0d	£92. 0s 0d	£92. 0s 0d
Dividend on Ordinary Shares	£675. 0s 0d	£900. 0s 0d	£900. 0s 0d	£900. 0s 0d	£900. 0s 0d
Balance c/f to next year	£ 89. 2s 3d	£76. 19s 8½d	£ 43. 8s 4d	£ 59. 13s 2d	£ 113. 18s 8d
Train Mileage Passenger	16,442	9,806	nk	nk	11,520
Goods	5,113	1,910	nk	nk	1,790

The debentures interest represents 4% on £3,000 in 1903, on £3,316 in 1906, on £3,300 in 1911, and on £2,300 in 1912 and 1913.
The dividend on ordinary shares represents 7½% on £9,000 in 1903, and on £12,000 subsequently.

SOURCES: 1903 – National Archives MT6 1338/6: 1906 – Essex Record Office T/Z 43/1, unidentified cutting of 9.3.1907: 1911 – Essex Record Office T/Z 43/2, unidentified cutting of April 1912: 1912 – ditto, cutting of 22.2.1913: 1913 – National Archives MT6 2265/2.

Chapter Three

PEACE AND WAR: KYNOCHS AND THE CLR 1901 – 1921

Although the years of peace 1902-1914 brought lower demands on the armaments industry than had been the case during the Boer War, it would seem that the Kynochtown works was still flourishing at the time of the *Essex Review* visit in 1907 (p.9). But after 1907 Kynochs generally fell upon leaner times, partly because the new Liberal government cancelled all their cordite contracts. This was purportedly because mercury had been found in the cordite, but party politics were suspected by many!

The works did not actually produce much goods traffic for the CLR and LT&SR pre-1914. Coal for the works came in by sea, as did acid, and the majority of the output went upriver to Woolwich Arsenal in Kynoch's own barges. In 1913 the LT&SR's traffic with the CLR still amounted to only £95 inwards (to CLR) and £648 outwards (from CLR). The inwards goods were 'empties and cordite paste', the outwards 'cordite and gunpowder'.

'Internal' CLR traffic included bricks from the brickworks to the main works, and perhaps coal from the pier to the brickworks.

In addition to Kynoch's own traffic, the CLR was carrying a very small amount of 'public' goods traffic. The Thames Stores Ltd (the Kynochtown shop / Post Office) received 'groceries of a very small carriage value' – although the shop was really part of Kynochs anyway. Coal and other goods wagons were brought in for local merchants at Corringham, and it appears that there may have been some traffic from local farmers as well, but hard evidence is lacking. Goods for the CLR were consigned by stations elsewhere to 'Thames Haven', and one imagines the CLR made a small extra charge for taking the wagons on from Thames Haven.

The limited goods traffic did not prevent the CLR from making a good profit. The figures for several years for which the annual accounts have been found are presented in the table here. The company paid a 7.5% dividend in every year 1901-1918. This made it one of the best-paying railway companies in the UK, although the point was not of any public interest given that CLR shares were not traded on the market in practice. It was somewhat odd for a company to pay exactly the same dividend for so many years in a row, and one suspects that some creative accounting was engaged in. Working costs were kept very low by the minimal number of staff – probably only the loco crews.

The 'goods train' figures must be taken with a pinch of salt as it is unlikely that anything resembling a 'train' ever ran, let alone a timetabled train; wagons were simply taken to and from Thames Haven as necessary, and the compilation of goods 'mileage' figures must have relied on loco crews' guesses at best.

The CLR had no running powers over the LT&SR into Thames Haven yard, however it would seem that at some periods CLR locos were allowed on to LT&SR metals there. The Midland Railway's * 1915 report on the Thames Haven branch noted (1) that 'traffic for the Corringham Light Railway is placed by us in sidings at Thames Haven Depot on the down side, from which Kynochs work it away. They deposit traffic for us in the same sidings'. This will be referring to the sidings either side of the cattle pens, which had lost their original purpose in the 1890s. The CLR loco probably *propelled* from Kynochtown as a rule. At other times, though, it seems to have been the practice for the CLR loco to leave wagons (again propelled) on CLR metals just short of the junction, and similarly for any wagons for the CLR to be left at that point by the LT&SR locos. The Midland report also noted that Midland locomen were in the practice of using the CLR line as a shunting neck for their own purposes, which they had no legal right to. One hopes they kept themselves well-informed as to when the CLR loco was propelling loaded ammunition wagons towards them!

THE PASSENGER SERVICE 1901-1914

As noted earlier, the CLR had issued a printed timetable of passenger services in June 1901. Unfortunately no copies of this are known to survive, and the CLR did not appear in *Bradshaw*, although it ought to have. The 1905 *Locomotive Magazine* article states that seven trains a day are run each way on weekdays, and four each way on Sundays.

The only other timetable information available for the pre-1914 period is what was given to the *Railway Magazine* in 1913:

From Kynochtown
Mons-Fris 6.10am, 12.35pm, 5.10pm, 6.15pm.
Sats 6.10am, 1.10pm, 2.5pm, 5.10pm, 6.15pm, 7.0pm.

From Corringham
Mons-Fris 5.40am, 6.40am, 8.48am, 1.15pm, 5.35pm, 6.35pm.
Sats 5.40am, 6.40am, 8.48am, 1.40pm, 2.40pm, 5.35pm, 6.35pm, 7.40pm.

No mention is made of Sundays but we must not assume from that that there were no Sunday trains at this date.

There must also have been empty workings from Kynochtown to form the 5.40am and 8.48am from Corringham.

The timings show that the majority of the workforce was starting at 6am or 7am and finishing at 5pm or 6pm. The 8.48am from Corringham (and the 2.5pm from Kynochtown on Saturdays) would be for the office staff. It is not evident what the lunchtime trains were for, or the 7.0pm/7.40pm Saturday extras. The service given here would also provide for any workers on 12 hour night shifts, but it is not clear how much night working there was 1902-14.

This timetable involves 38 passenger trains each way per week, an annual passenger mileage of 8,180, which does not correlate too well with the 1913 accounts figure of 11,520.

We cannot guess how much the timetable in other pre-1914 years resembled this 1913 timetable. The passenger mileage figures in the annual accounts vary considerably.

The 1913 annual accounts passenger revenue figure of £353 equates to only £7 per week, or about 100 people travelling each way daily on the basis of the 1s 3d weekly season price. The 1903 figure would represent 350-550 daily users.

Whilst the majority of passengers were Kynochs employees, the CLR was quite used to carrying the 'public' in the form of a very few LATHOL workers, and from 1916 a few Shell workers. The Midland report noted that the CLR passenger service 'is worked absolutely according to the requirements of the employees of the firm, and although there are very few other people who wish to use the trains, anyone may, by paying the fare demanded, travel'. However the line remained virtually unknown to people outside the immediate area.

Even with the more frequent service of these earlier years, the CLR was probably of minimal use to most people living in Kynochtown. Corringham itself had few attractions beyond those available at the Kynochtown shop and Institute, and if one were making for the wider world the best option was to cycle along the Thames Haven line to Stanford-le-Hope. What is not mentioned anywhere, though, is how Kynochtown people and their visitors got anywhere with luggage in the earliest years. Their cosmopolitan origins probably made them rather more prone to making long journeys than the

---

* For the benefit of 'non-railway' readers it should be explained that the Midland Railway had taken over the London Tilbury & Southend Railway in 1912. In 1923 the Midland Railway was itself absorbed into the London Midland & Scottish Railway (LMS).

Probably the earliest known photograph of a CLR train – summer 1901? The Kitson loco is in 'as bought' condition, with large block buffers (on which smaller blocks have been mounted), a single side-step, and cab with rear cut-outs. The view is at Corringham; it is about 6pm and the strong evening light has made conditions difficult for the photographer. If the train has just arrived, it is surprising that the workmen are still in the coach – but perhaps the excitement of being photographed made up for getting home five minutes later.

The great majority of CLR train photographs, at all periods, show the locos chimney towards Kynochtown. In fact the Kitson loco is that way round in all the five known views.

above
Our next view of the Kitson shows it after standard buffers had been fitted, but still with the cab cut-outs, probably c1903. It has just arrived at Corringham with the Kerr Stuart composite coach, from which at least thirty men have alighted, including a couple of 'bowler hats' from the First Class. Again it is 6-7pm. One of the traincrew is walking back down the line, probably to change the loop east end points. The full length of the passenger platform is seen at its original 150ft length.

This is also the best view of the loading bank section of the platform in its early years. The loop west end points are also well seen, in their original position as shown on the 1919 OS map. There is a sleeper (?) placed across the rails at centre, which is not present in any other view. Was this to stop wagons in the spur from running away? If so one suspects that the locomen must have got fed up with having to move it every time they ran round.

At left are the two 'Baden Villas' (named after Baden Powell).

Ivor Gotheridge collection

left
The Kitson loco and one of the Kerr Stuart coaches at Kynochtown, at a later date after the cab cut-outs had ben filled in. The high ballasting of the period is again evident. It is less clear what the men are up to!

average Essex villager of the day. Perhaps they had to use the CLR and get horsedrawn 'taxi' conveyance from Corringham to Stanford-le-Hope station?

Kynite was the principal passenger train loco up to 1915, and photographs show it variously with the Kerr Stuart composite coach only, the composite plus the LT&SR coach, or all three coaches. (It is to be assumed that trains were also sometimes formed of the two Kerr Stuart coaches only, but no photographs are known showing this). As all trains offered First Class accommodation, the composite had necessarily to be included.

The 1905 *Locomotive Magazine* article states that the Kitson loco was only used on Sundays or when *Kynite* was under repair. However the photographic record suggests that it was used rather more often than that (it is unlikely that any pre-1914 photographer visited on a Sunday). No photograph is known of the Kitson hauling more than one coach (the composite) and it may well have had trouble on the 1 in 55 up to Corringham with any heavier load.

It seems that goods wagons were sometimes used for carrying passengers. The most likely time for this would have been in the first few months, before the LT&SR coach was acquired. C.L.Webster, who was appointed as the Prudential rep for Stanford-le-Hope district in 1901 and made his rounds daily from then on, recalled in 1934 (2):

'I have a very vivid recollection of the first time I saw the tiny engine of the Corringham Light Railway, hauling a train consisting of one carriage – similar to those on Southend pier – and two or three coal trucks, packed with men. The men swarmed over the sides of the trucks when the engine failed to negotiate the rise into Corringham station – which, however, it managed to do after most of the passengers had alighted. Those who occupied the carriage were then able to alight with dignity on the platform'.

This was most likely the Kitson loco, seen in the first few months, before attempts to get it to haul more than one coach were abandoned? There are other references to goods wagons being used but they are more third-hand.

Derailments were also reported to be rather frequent (no doubt exaggerated by some!). The best first-hand report is in a letter by a former worker of the pre- and post-1914 period, Mrs A. Freeth, published in the summer 1956 issue of *Essex Countryside*:

'It was not uncommon for the carriages to come off the rails when rounding the bends, and it would then be all hands to the wheel brake [sic], which was in the carriage. We would then alight and walk the rest of the journey to the works'.

In the years up to 1914, a 'conductor' travelled on the trains to issue tickets (photos p.34). The actual issuing was probably mostly done at the stations before departure. In 1907 the CLR Secretary J.W. Ramsay caused puzzlement at the Board of Trade by enquiring 'what regulations of your Board apply as to the running of the railway apart from the special order under which it is inaugurated. In particular the information is required regarding attendants on trains'. When the Board sought clarification Ramsay caused further confusion by saying that he wished to know about 'the limit of men to be in charge of the scheduled trains'. The correspondence then fizzled out! The Board of Trade officers wondered if Ramsay had come across some reference to the action that had been taken previously against the Rother Valley Railway after allegations of danger to conductors moving between carriages en route.

WARTIME EXPANSION AT KYNOCHS 1914-1918

After the onset of war in 1914 the government had to forget its objections to Kynochs as cordite suppliers. In March 1915 (the war having failed to be over by Christmas) they asked Kynochs to produce an extra 120 tons of cordite a week, and works expansions at Arklow and Kynochtown were authorised in consequence. The most notable development here was the construction in 1915 of an entirely separate subsidiary factory, the Shell Haven Works, dedicated purely to cordite production (although the main works continued to make cordite as well). Details of this Shell Haven Works are somewhat scanty. It was situated close to Shellhaven Farm house and had its own power house,

Only a very poor copy has been found of this Edwardian postcard (entitled 'Ye Olde Kynoch Express'). Most likely *Kynite* has just arrived from Corringham with the composite coach only, or is about to take out such a train. At left we see the brake wheel on the conductor's balcony end of the Third Class coach.
Thurrock Museum

The approach to Corringham station as seen by the aproaching workman after tramping from 'old' Corringham or Stanford-le-Hope. The sun-lit roofs of the station buildings can just be made out under the tree at right.
Bill Hammond collection

Another 1900s view, with *Kynite* (unusually chimney towards Corringham) awaiting departure from Corringham with a lunchtime train, formed of the Kerr Stuart composite and the LT&SR four-wheeler.

but only one distant view is known (3). The separate site was chosen on the basis that it should be 'sufficiently far from our other works to allow of either being destroyed by an explosion without affecting the other' (4).

The main works received a number of additional buildings. It was surrounded by a barbed wire entanglement, with blockhouses manned by soldiers stationed nearby. The most notable change however was a massive increase in the number of workers, to 5,000 or more (5). The manufacturing units went on to permanent 24 hour operation on two 12 hour shifts. In the first months of the war the extra staff numbers required were achieved by local recruiting, but from 1915 on this had to be supplemented by bringing in young women and unconscripted men from elsewhere. Many of these were housed in wooden huts in two 'colonies' (6). The 'girls' colony', housing 600, was at Herd Farm near Corringham station (see 1919 OS map p.40). The residents travelled to and from work on the CLR. The men's colony housed 800 and was situated in Fleet Street, Kynochtown, on previously unused ground adjacent to the Institute. The separation was no doubt intended to enforce 'morality', as the women would disappear to their remote

above
Kynite captured at Corringham by Ken Nunn on Wednesday 16th June 1909, with the Kerr Stuart composite only, awaiting departure as the 1.15pm.
(LCGB/Ken Nunn Collection)

middle
Shortly afterwards the crew posed en route just outside Corringham. The loco is a few yards short of the Ballast Pit Siding points.
(LCGB/Ken Nunn collection)

bottom
Kynite on the 12.30pm from Kynochtown on 16th June 1909, passing a mysterious signal, said to be near the triangle. There are no references to signals in the 1901 inspection reports, and it is difficult to see why anything like this should have been erected. It appears to be worked by the lever on the post, so it cannot be showing the lie of the triangle points. The fishtail should not be taken to imply any 'distant' function. Nobody other than the loco crew could have worked this signal, and nobody other than them could have ever seen it!
(LCGB/Ken Nunn Collection)

opposite
A c1910-14 view, showing the Kitson loco after it had been fitted with double side-steps, and the Kerr Stuart composite coach after it had been completely enclosed (something which clearly only happened after 1909, given the Nunn photos). The First Class section seems to have been left unaltered. In this midsummer afternoon view, the train has stopped some yards short of the train in the front cover photo, between the footpath crossing and the Ballast Siding points. Fobbing church tower can be seen in the background. The houses to the left of the tower are on the west side of the High Road and the east side of White Lion Hill. The crew are driver Arthur Baker (on footplate) and Fred D'Aumont (on ground).

There was a 'Whistle' board on the approach to this crossing and the twice-daily whistling on the arrival of the morning and evening trains was part of the pattern of life for those living nearby in the 1920s-50s period.

settlement by train as soon as their shift was finished. Needless to say this was not entirely successful, as can be judged from the fact that two of four female employees interviewed in the 1970s actually got married to fellow workers during their time there! When the colonies opened, a good number of employees who had hitherto been travelling in daily from across South Essex also moved into them for the greater convenience.

The best account of wartime life at the works is by J.H. Freeman (7):

'All sorts of girls came to us – flower girls from London, actresses, Society women and so on. After a time the men were sent and came in batches; we had tin miners from Cornwall, First League professional footballers from the north, and so on. Their hours were very long – 12 hours a day, so that the work might be continuous, six days per week. The work, though, was generally very light, very clean and generally pleasant. There were good work buildings, with nice surroundings, flower gardens, splendid messrooms, with cooking arrangements and attendance'.

'All explosive workers were provided with special fireproof clothing, and in the case of men it consisted of boots and shoes, cap and cape; in the case of girls, shoes, frocks, cape and cloak. The changes took place in special changing rooms just before entering the danger area. The work was most interesting, with a flavour of risk, and the feeling too of doing something to finish the war. In addition to training girls for explosive work, girls too were trained for the inspection departments and for the laboratory'.

'In the usual way, an explosive factory is all lighted. During the war, conditions were very different owing to the fact that there was no outside lighting, and all buildings had to be heavily curtained. The workers had, therefore, to move about in the dark during the night shift, and move material from one building to another also in the dark. Even under these conditions, they behaved specially well. Many soldiers were stationed in the works for protection purposes – usually Scottish Borderers or West Kents, together with gunners. During the war I know of no attempt being made to enter the works by unauthorised persons, though several bullocks were shot because they would not halt when challenged at the barbed wire entanglements'.

'We were very fortunate during the war, insomuch that we had no explosions. We had, though, three distinct fires, a cordite stove being involved in each and burnt to the ground. In the first, the lives of two men were lost, one being in the stove itself. Shortly after the armistice [actually on 11th September 1918 - the victim was Ada Jane Wakeling of Southend] we had a very bad fire in the guncotton rubbing room. All got out except one girl who lost her life. Great attempts were made to save her, without success. We had too an ignition in the cordite press. A girl had her arm cut right off, and a bad fire followed, three press houses being involved and gutted.

Many dug-outs were constructed for the workers, specially for the girls. On an air raid notice being given, all work was stopped. The workers left the danger area. We received special telephone messages of impending air raids, usually when the craft left the other side. This gave us about half an hour, during which plant would be left in a safe condition, ready to be restarted, and during which workers left the explosive area. Most remained in the open to watch the excitement – watching the efforts of searchlight apparatus to pick up the opposing craft, and those in control of machines, on the other hand, making superhuman efforts to get out of the rays, and then to watch how closely our gunners were getting, as seen from the smoke trails. A few only, who were rather timid, found shelter in local houses, carriages on the railway, etc. The dug-outs were little used. There were of course many air raids both by Zeppelins and aeroplanes. The Zeppelin that was brought down by gun fire at the Thames estuary passed right over the works and dropped a sort of lighted parachute. Fortunately for all concerned, it just missed the cordite incorporating room. Usually the machines passed over us east to west or west to east. Many bombs were dropped, but little damage was done. One of the huts in the men's colony was hit and gutted. As it happened shortly after 6 o'clock, the place was empty: one shift had gone on duty, and the other had come off. There was of course risk from our own gunfire. Many dud shells dropped in the works, together with much shrapnel'.

Freeman's views on the working conditions were not shared by all! The conditions at the government-run Woolwich Arsenal were known to be decidedly better. The Kynochtown rose beds were real enough, but the buildings were poorly ventilated and rat-infested. Most of the work involved standing up for a 12-hour shift, and on occasions staff worked 24 or 36 hours on the go. Pay at first was 32s a week for men, 24s for women; but wages were increased in 1917/18 after inflation. Some men actually felt glad to be out when they were called up. The women seemed to recall their time here with greater pleasure – 'we were a happy crowd, singing as we worked'. In normal working the shift workers in the manufacturing units were divided up permanently into an 'A' shift and a 'B' shift, doing alternate weeks of days and nights. The day shift was 0600-1800 Monday to Saturday, the night shift 1800 Monday to 0600 Sunday.

The school log book records the air raids affecting Kynochtown:
13th June 1917, am – 'children dismissed 11.45'.
14th June 1917, pm.
31st October / 1st November 1917, overnight.
18th December 1917 – 'air raid 6.30pm, several bombs dropped on Kynochtown. School – two panes glass broken, some tiles off roof'.
17th / 18th February 1918, overnight.

These later panoramic views were taken in 1917/18, both from the same viewpoint. Most of the buildings correlate with those shown on the 1919 OS map.

above (full spread)
This view looks northwards. The main east-west roadway can be made out, also the main east-west rail siding. The vans on the left are on the siding curving away to the south. The power station is seen at right, near the pier. It had two 200hp and one 80hp engines, and provided electric power for the whole site. The section of tramway in the bottom right hand corner is not shown by the OS.

right
Looking east (there is an overlap with the previous view) the prospect is a little more bucolic. In the distance are two rakes of Midland and GWR vans, in the sidings at the far end of the works standard gauge network. The functions of the nearer buildings are not known.
Thurrock Museum

left
Looking east over the north end of the site (c1915?) towards Holehaven Creek, with the later Cordite Range running across the view. At several points in the works Kynochs made an effort with extensive lawns and flower beds. This Cordite Range garden also had a fountain. The beds look very new here (compare the 1917/18 view at p.45). At top left Westwick Farm on Canvey is seen.
Ivor Gotheridge collection

left
A wartime portrait of the office staff outside the main office block. There are more young men than one might have expected.
Thurrock Museum, F.Z. Claro collection

right
The works entrance in the war years. The YMCA hut was erected as a recreational facility for the men at the 'colony'. Trees have grown up since 1897 to soften the original bleak scene. At left is the ramp up to the station platform; the platform fencing between the ramp and the level crossing betrays the c1915 extension of the platform at the east end.

37

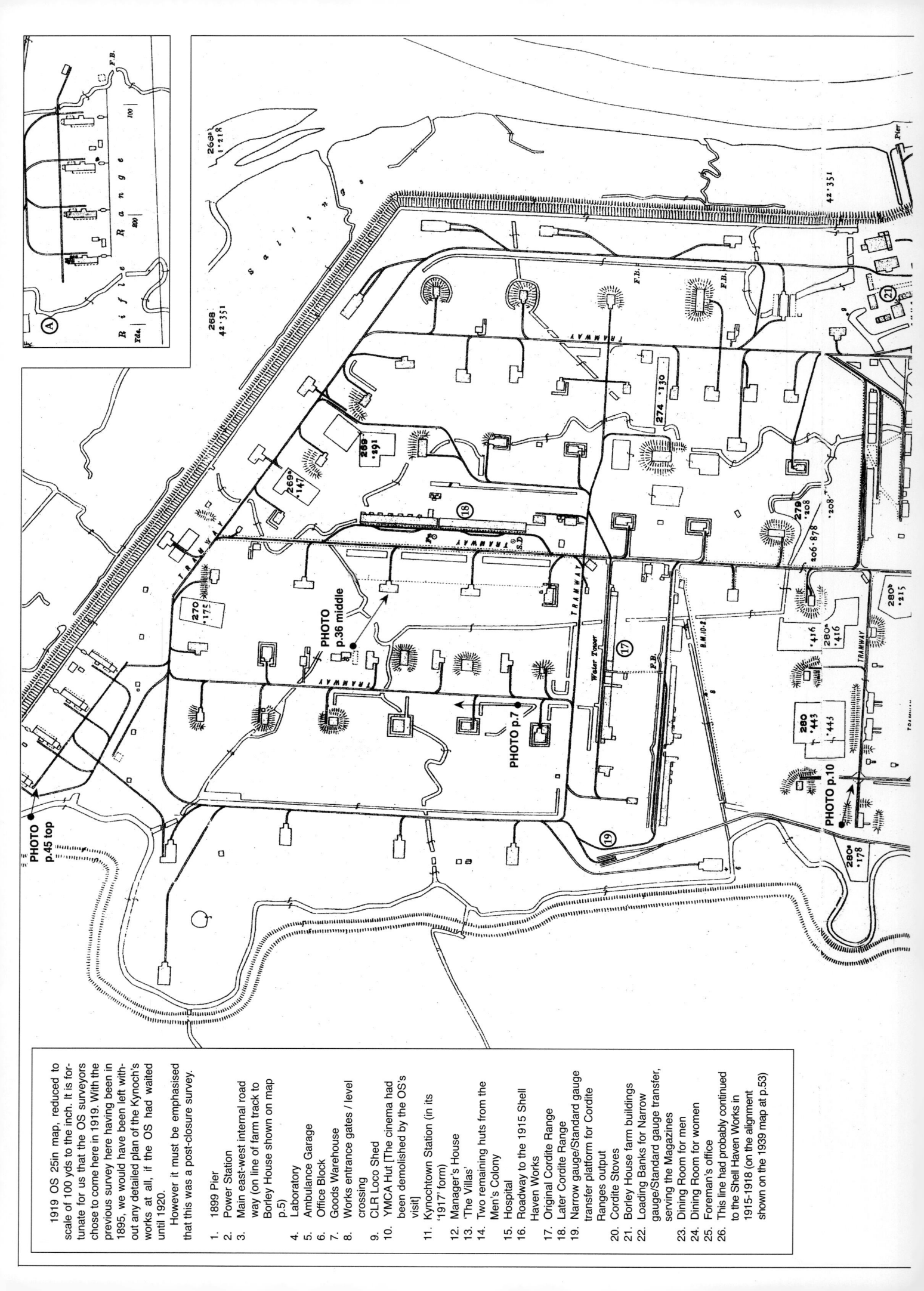

1919 OS 25in map, reduced to scale of 100 yds to the inch. It is fortunate for us that the OS surveyors chose to come here in 1919. With the previous survey here having been in 1895, we would have been left without any detailed plan of the Kynoch's works at all, if the OS had waited until 1920.

However it must be emphasised that this was a post-closure survey.

1. 1899 Pier
2. Power Station
3. Main east-west internal road way (on line of farm track to Borley House shown on map p.5)
4. Laboratory
5. Ambulance Garage
6. Office Block
7. Goods Warehouse
8. Works entrance gates / level crossing
9. CLR Loco Shed
10. YMCA Hut [The cinema had been demolished by the OS's visit]
11. Kynochtown Station (in its '1917' form)
12. Manager's House
13. 'The Villas'
14. Two remaining huts from the Men's Colony
15. Hospital
16. Roadway to the 1915 Shell Haven Works
17. Original Cordite Range
18. Later Cordite Range
19. Narrow gauge/Standard gauge transfer platform for Cordite Ranges output
20. Cordite Stoves
21. Borley House farm buildings
22. Loading Banks for Narrow gauge/Standard gauge transfer, serving the Magazines
23. Dining Room for men
24. Dining Room for women
25. Foreman's office
26. This line had probably continued to the Shell Haven Works in 1915-1918 (on the alignment shown on the 1939 map at p.53)

Explosives Works

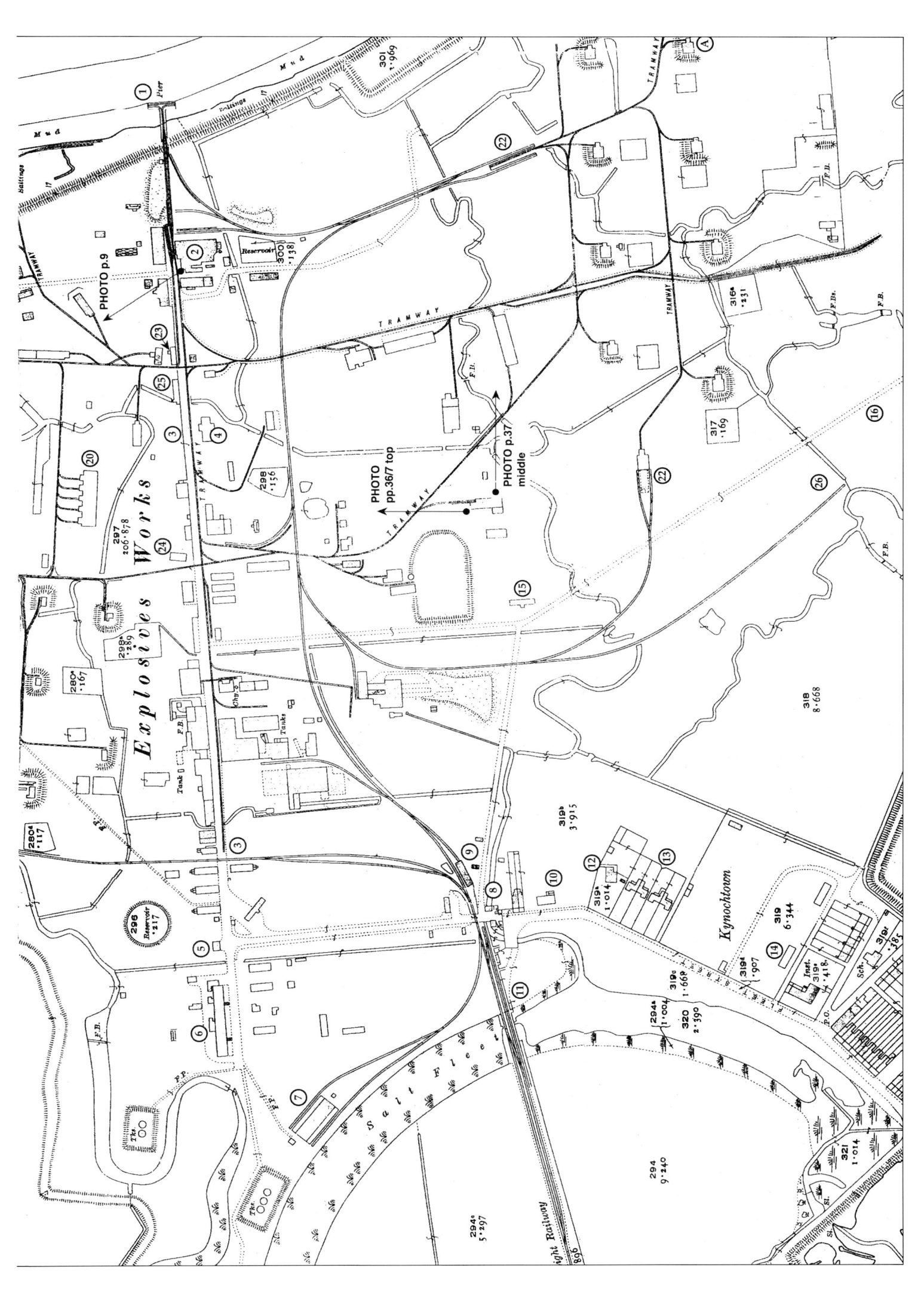

Kynochtown

Salt Fleet

PHOTO p.9
PHOTO pp.36/7 top
PHOTO p.37 middle

Corringham and Fobbing area, 1919 survey OS 25in map, reduced to scale of 100 yds to the inch.

The former Kynoch Estate Co's Brickworks is shown as disused – one wonders if it had still been active during the war? It seems likely in consequence that the CLR Brickfield Siding serving the loading bank alongside the main line had also fallen out of use by 1919. The next we see of it is in the 1920 photograph at p.49, where the track is wholly removed. The longer Ballast Pit Siding (plot 193 is presumably the pit?) may have still been in use in the 1920s, but the connection had been taken out prior to 1936, although the rails beyond were still in situ then.

Most (but not all) of the Herd Farm Colony buildings were still present when the OS surveyors visited. The entrance to the colony was in Herd Lane next to the school, although one suspects that the girls also made some shorter unofficial path direct to the station. This land has remained in the ownership of Corys / Vacuum /Mobil up to the present day. In 1950-3 the area formerly used for the Colony was quarried to obtain gravel for constructing the new refinery. Then in 1959-61 new buildings for the Mobil staff 'Pegasus Club' were erected in Herd Lane, and landscaped sports pitches laid out on the ballast pit and Colony area.

The Estate Co's two cottages in Herd Lane can be seen just south of the Colony entrance. They were removed c1960 along with the Herd Farm farmhouse.

The 51 new houses in Digby Road / Wingfield Road / Fobbing Road were still quite separate from the rest of Corringham village at this date. They occupied less than half of the field (No.158) bought by Kynochs as their 'Corringham Estate'.

For the benefit of non-Essex readers it might be explained that the 'Peculiar People' were a 19th century nonconformist sect, formed in the 1830s by John Banyard of Rochford. They never became numerous outside SE Essex. The chapel here was built in 1914, replacing a wooden hut at the bottom of White Lion Hill.

1. Wingfield Road (now Hill Terrace)	3. Digby Villas *alias* The Villas
2. Grove Terrace	4. Baden Villas

CLR/LTSR junction area, 1919 OS 25in map, reduced to scale of 100 yds to the inch.

1. CLR/LT&SR property boundary

2. Dock House level crossing

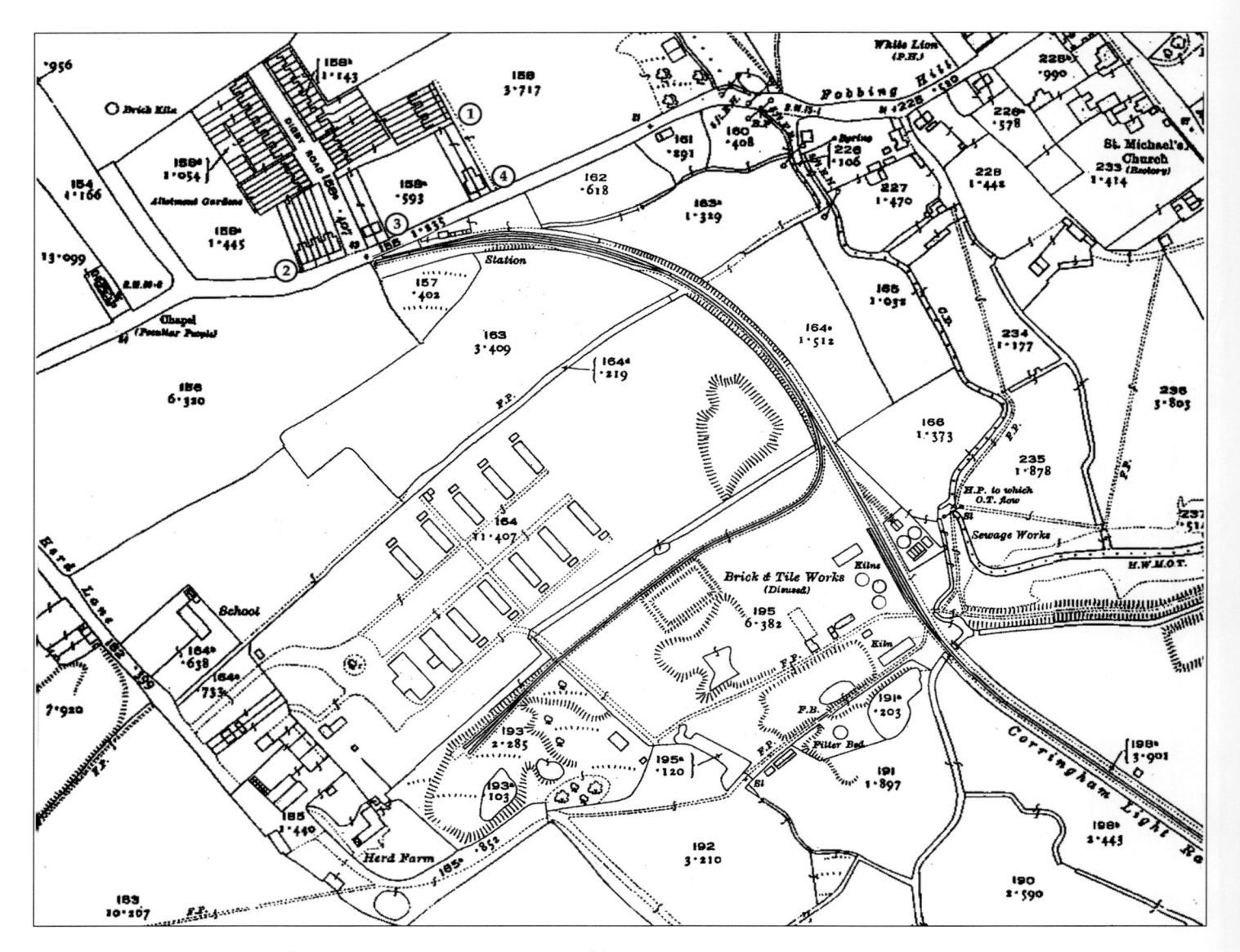

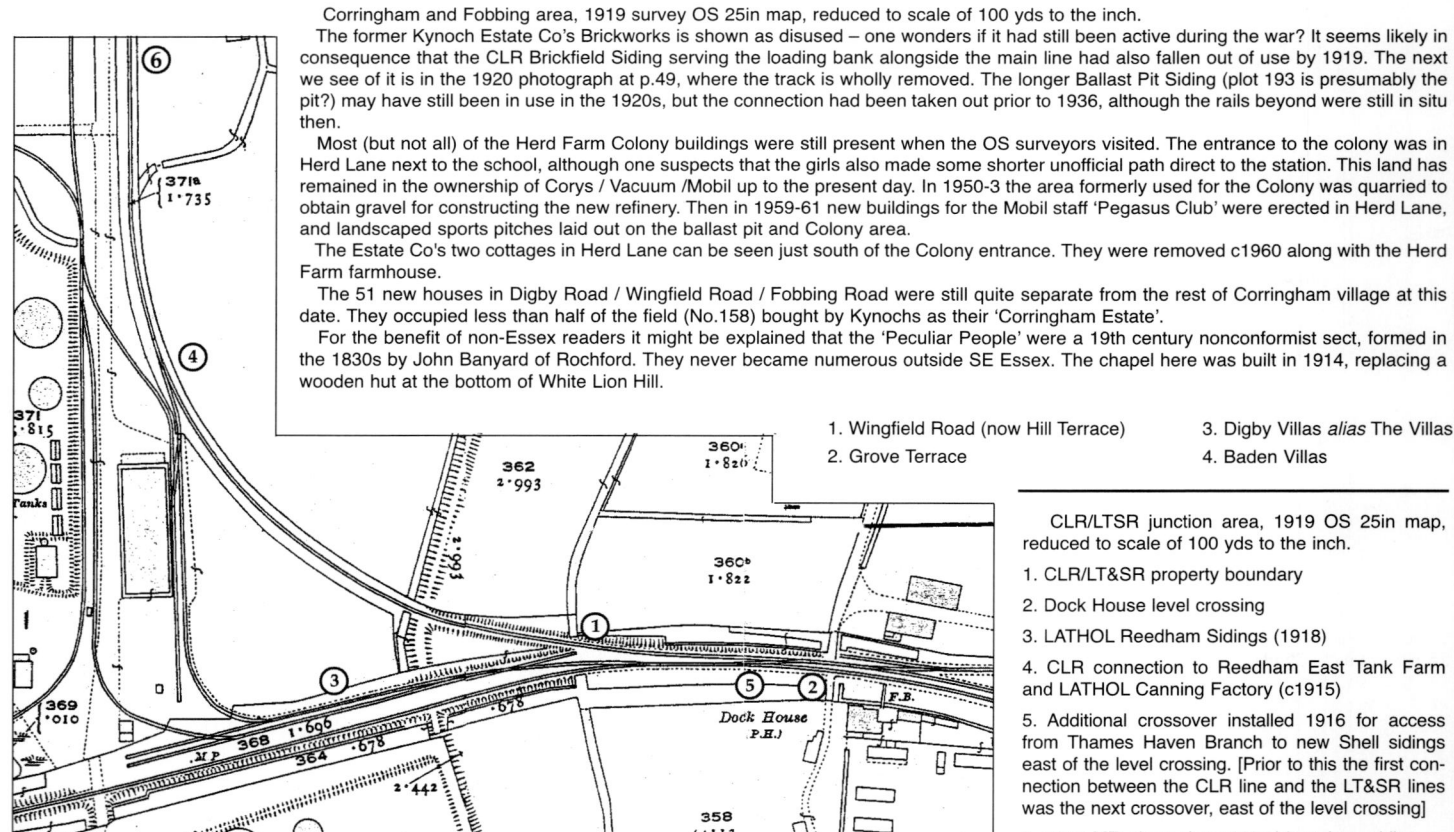

3. LATHOL Reedham Sidings (1918)

4. CLR connection to Reedham East Tank Farm and LATHOL Canning Factory (c1915)

5. Additional crossover installed 1916 for access from Thames Haven Branch to new Shell sidings east of the level crossing. [Prior to this the first connection between the CLR line and the LT&SR lines was the next crossover, east of the level crossing]

6. 1915 MR plans show 150yd long loop siding on west side just north of here (for military camp?), lifted by 1919 OS.

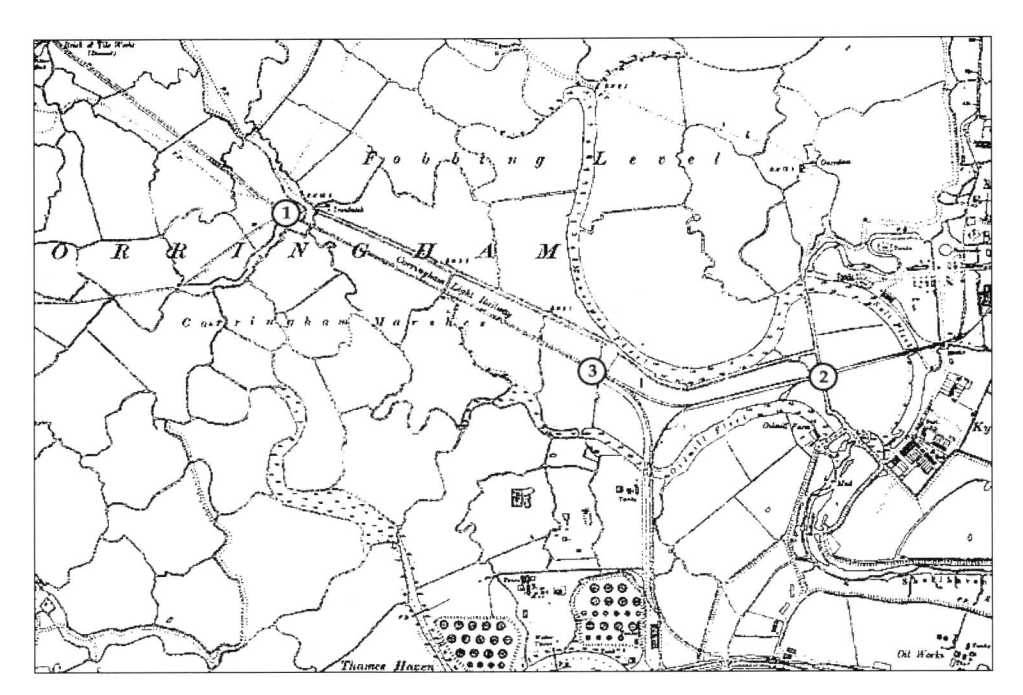

This 1919 survey Ordnance Survey 6in map (reduced to three inches to the mile) is included to show the intermediate sections of the CLR not included in the 25in extracts here. Comparison with the 1860s map at pp. 4/5 shows that there have been no changes to the basic landscape over the half-century; it has just had a lot of industry inflicted on it! Only matters related to the CLR and Kynochs are annotated here – for information on the various industrial sites at Thames Haven see *The Thames Haven Railway* pp. 36/7.

1. CLR / Manorway level crossing at Ironlatch
2. CLR / Manorway level crossing (Haven Hotel built adjacent 1924)
3. Proposed Manorway Siding site

The Herd Farm girls' colony, looking southwest along the central area. The September 1915 contract plans show a total of fourteen 73ft 6in by 19ft 6in two-storey dormitory blocks, eight in the northern row, and six in the southern row as seen here. (However by the time of the 1919 OS survey opposite there were only five left in each row). The blocks here were quite different in design to those in the mens' colony. Freeman's total of 600 residents would require 43 per block.

Former resident Catherine Brown later recalled (17):

'As the number of employees increased, it was necessary to find accommodation and so the colony came into being at Corringham. My sister joined me and I moved there. The colony was run by some very efficient ladies and was well organised. The charges were reasonable and we were supplied with individual lunches which we could get heated at the factory. Then on our return from work an appetising meal was ready which was very welcome. There was a large recreation room and social events were arranged. There were occasional dances to which we could invite a friend'.

Mrs W. Muir was the superintendent of the colony, and Miss Stritton the chief supervisor. They lived in the farmhouse (see p.18).

The residents formed a concert party, the Bluebirds, to raise money for the wounded troops recovering in local hospitals.

Thurrock Museum, F.Z. Claro collection

Another view of the Herd Farm colony, looking the other way along the central area from the main entrance roadway. The nearest building is the 90ft by 40ft Recreation Block, and the low building behind is the Laundry Block. The large Dining Block (demolished by the 1919 OS) is out of sight to the right.

Thurrock Museum, F.Z. Claro collection

The Kynoch's 'A' shift girls' football team, 1918. (Why is the ball marked 'GFC'?). Along with a 'B' shift team, they played in a South Essex league against teams from factories in Grays, Purfleet, and Southend. 'A' shift won the league in this year, beating Jurgens 1-0 in the final. They are wearing their work clothes over their football gear (but the berets were for the football). Some are sporting their triangular War Work badges.

The only team members identified are Edith Bone at back row centre, and goalkeeper Ivy Petherick in the darker shirt at right foreground. The man at centre is their trainer Charles Tighe; they practised twice a week after work. Standing at left is Jack Heatherton, Secretary of the local Corringham & Fobbing (men's) football club. 'A' shift played their home matches on a field at the rear of the Duke's Head in Corringham, 'B' shift at the Warren, Wharf Road, in Stanford-le-Hope.

Roy Woodall recalled that the Herd Farm colony 'regularly fielded more than eight football teams' – the others were presumably less serious teams who played against each other?

Thurrock Museum, F.Z. Claro collection

41

above
The men's colony, seen from the roof of the Institute. There appear to be 25(?) huts, which would require 32 men per hut to make up Freeman's total of 800 men here. The shift system meant that on weekdays there would never be more than half the men here at a time. In 1915 as in 1897 Kynochs were generous with the garden environment. One doubts if the occupants of The Villas entirely appreciated their 800 new close neighbours, though! Further down the street towards the works gates is the YMCA hut seen at p.37, with another building (the cinema in its original form?) to its right. There are a good number of rail vans in the works sidings in the distance.

below
A later view of the men's colony, taken in 1917/18. The gardens have been somewhat deformalised under the pressure of heavy male usage, and a 'porter's lodge' (?) hut has been provided at the entrance.
Thurrock Museum

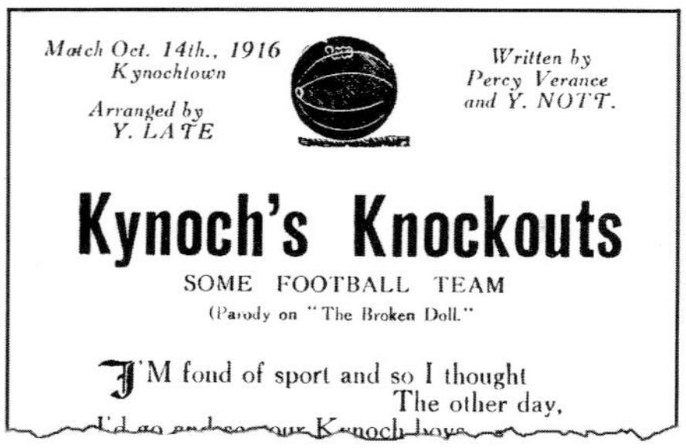

left (upper)
The Kynochs *men* did also engage in football! This card was produced to advertise a 1916 match with the locally-stationed troops of the Suffolk Regiment, and sold for 1d to raise money for Tilbury Hospital.

left (lower)
The local troops possessed thespian as well as footballing talents. This is part of the programme for a 1915 show at the Kynochtown Institute in aid of the YMCA facilities. The plot concerned the attempts of the German conspirators Von Sauer Kraut, Tirpitz Schmitz, and Von Blumer to cause devastation at 'Flynoch's'. It would seem that a spell here was better than the western front.
Thurrock Museum

below
The 'Hospital' was a wartime addition – previously any injured workers had to be taken to Stanford-le-Hope. It was located within the works, at the junction of the new roadway down to the Shell Haven Works, some 300 yards due east of the 'lion gates'. The building was still there in Cory's years but no longer used as such.
Thurrock Museum

In December 1967 the *Coryton News* reported the retirement of Roy Woodall, Planning Foreman of Maintenance Division. He had started as an apprentice electrician at Kynochs in 1916 and, apart from having to finish his apprenticeship with LATHOL in 1919-22 after Kynochs shut down, had worked here throughout his 51-year career for Kynochs, Corys, and Vacuum / Mobil. A fair number of men had worked through in this way.

Roy came from a family which had been in the explosives trade since the eighteenth century. 'As a boy, Roy was always playing with explosives, either black powder which was sold loose by ironmongers, or cordite sticks which he carried in his pockets. He used the cordite in place of fireworks as it gave off lovely sparks when lit'. His father was killed in a factory explosion in Kent. His grandfather was a manager at Kynochtown and arranged the apprenticeship. 'The electricians were responsible for supplying light and power to the factory, the village, and adjacent establishments, including the two colonies and the Kynoch Hotel on Canvey Island. They were also responsible for the telephone and emergency alarm-bell systems.................Roy was also made responsible for operating the cinema apparatus for the weekly film shows given in the 200-seat wooden structure outside the factory gates'.

'For the first six months Roy was in lodgings at Red Lion Hill, Horndon, and walked to Corringham every morning to catch the 5.20 light railway train to the factory. In bad weather he sometimes attempted to travel by the two-horse brake leaving Stanford Church at 5.30am, but was usually required to give up his seat to any senior who came along. After six months he moved to Corringham and was able to take an active part in the social life centred on the Institute. He became a member of the cricket and football teams, and was a keen billiards and snooker player. He also spent many happy hours fishing from the sea wall and walking one or other of the factory girls over the marshes by moonlight'.

top
'Inspection Department'. Bundles of cannon cordite await examination on the table. The girls here were no doubt better-educated than those in the manufacturing units, and produce a scene reminiscent of a prewar summer evening prep session in a girls' boarding school.
Thurrock Museum

middle
Interior of the 1901 Laboratory. The girls are wearing the same white uniform with broad red (?) waistband as used in the Inspection Department. It was clearly vital to have a man with a hat present as well!
Thurrock Museum

right
The 'Girls' Mess Room'. Few things were so vital as tea for defeating the Hun! The notices include 'Cycling in the Factory' and 'Military Passes'.
Thurrock Museum

43

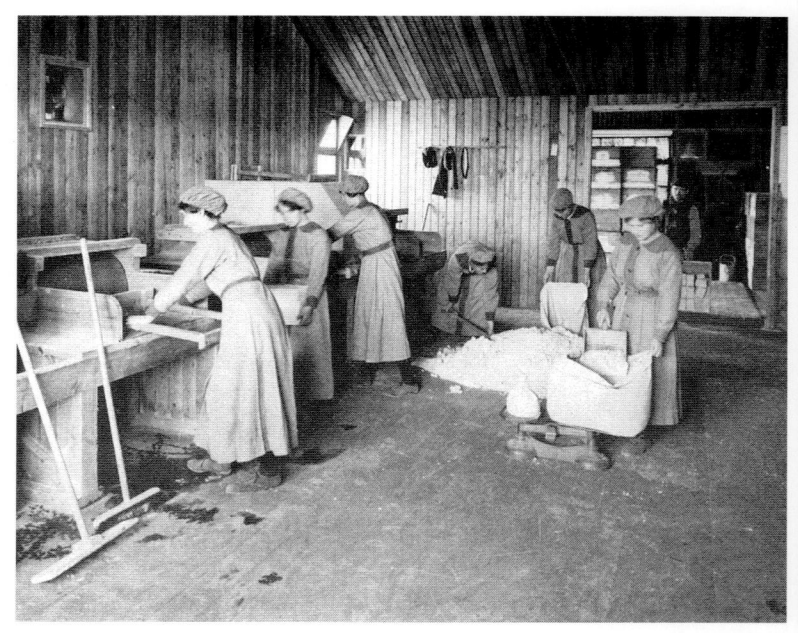

above (left)
The Rifle Press Shop. Foreman Lew Grover surveys operations. The women here have plain khaki uniforms, indicating that this shop is outside the Danger Area.

above (right)
'Rubbing gun cotton'. Note the special rubber shoes. Gun-cotton was used for other purposes as well as for cordite.

below
'Guncotton Girls'. They are posed outside the building seen in the background in the view at p.45 top. The girls in the front row are sitting on the tramway. The uniform for the guncotton drying sheds was white, with white rubber hats, and Wellington boots.
Thurrock Museum

opposite (top)
The two girls here are outside one of the guncotton drying sheds, and are loading sacks of guncotton on to an (invisible) narrow gauge truck. The sacks will then be covered over with the sheet. The location is identifiable on the 1919 OS map (p.38), at the far north end of the works, although the OS does not show the short stub siding. The wooden 'rails' used on the elevated sections of the tramway show up well here. They are laid on longitudinal boards here and at p.7, but on transverse boards at p.10. No record of the gauge has been found but clearly it was around 2ft.

One suspects that the operation of the narrow gauge system was carried out by a separate staff (rather than by workers from each building moving trucks around as they saw necessary). Otherwise it is difficult to see how a system which had no 'passing loops' en route could have been 'controlled' - without a defined person responsible for truck movements on each part of the network, truck-pushers would have continually been meeting others coming the other way on the single track!
Thurrock Museum

opposite (bottom)
The exterior of the later Cordite Incorporating Range (*cf* photo p.36 taken earlier). The gardens have become more splendid and almost give the impression of carefree prewar summers! The narrow gauge line passes along the whole length of the range, this side of the building acting as 'loading bays'. The sundial (dutifully recorded by the OS) attracts admirers.
Thurrock Museum

44

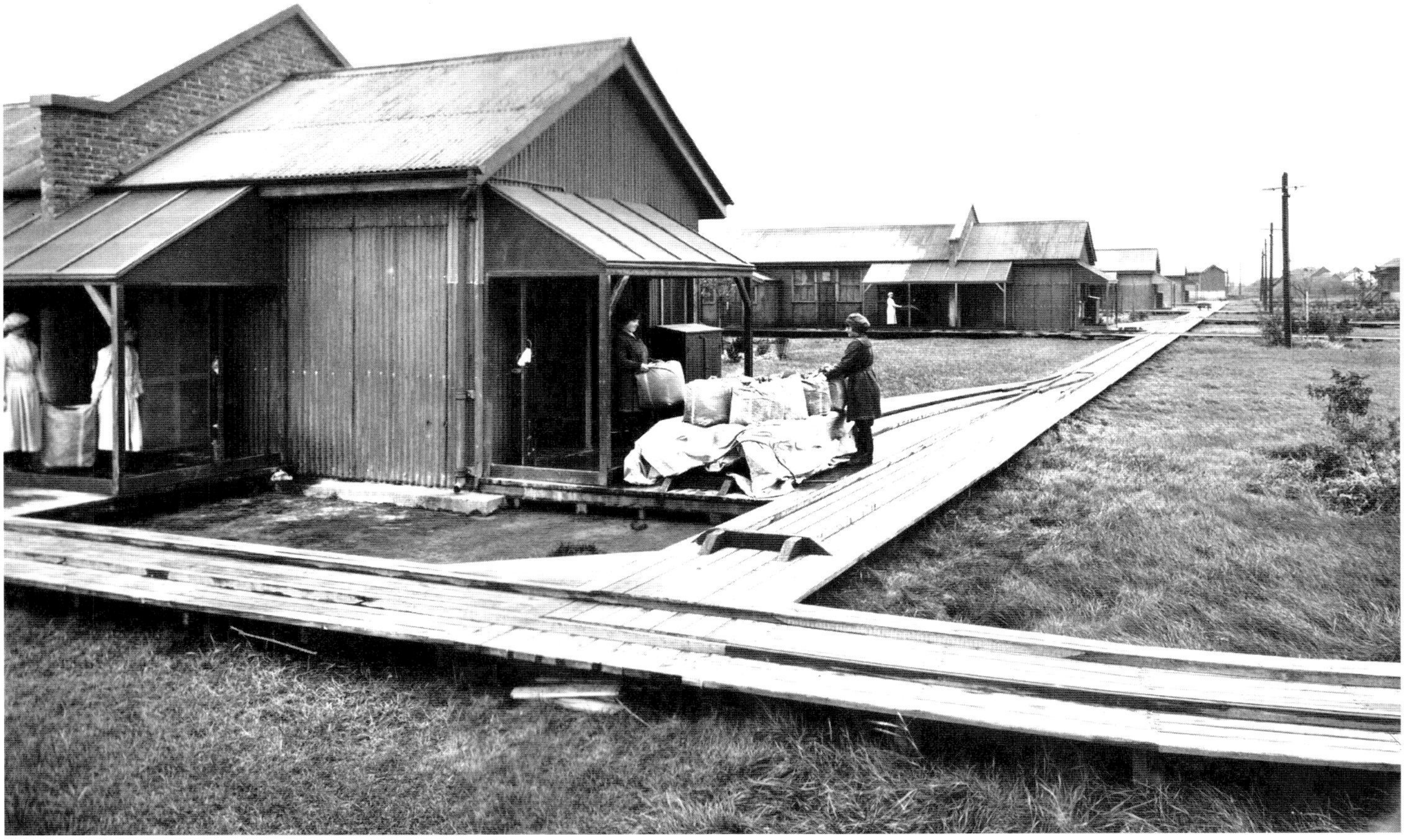

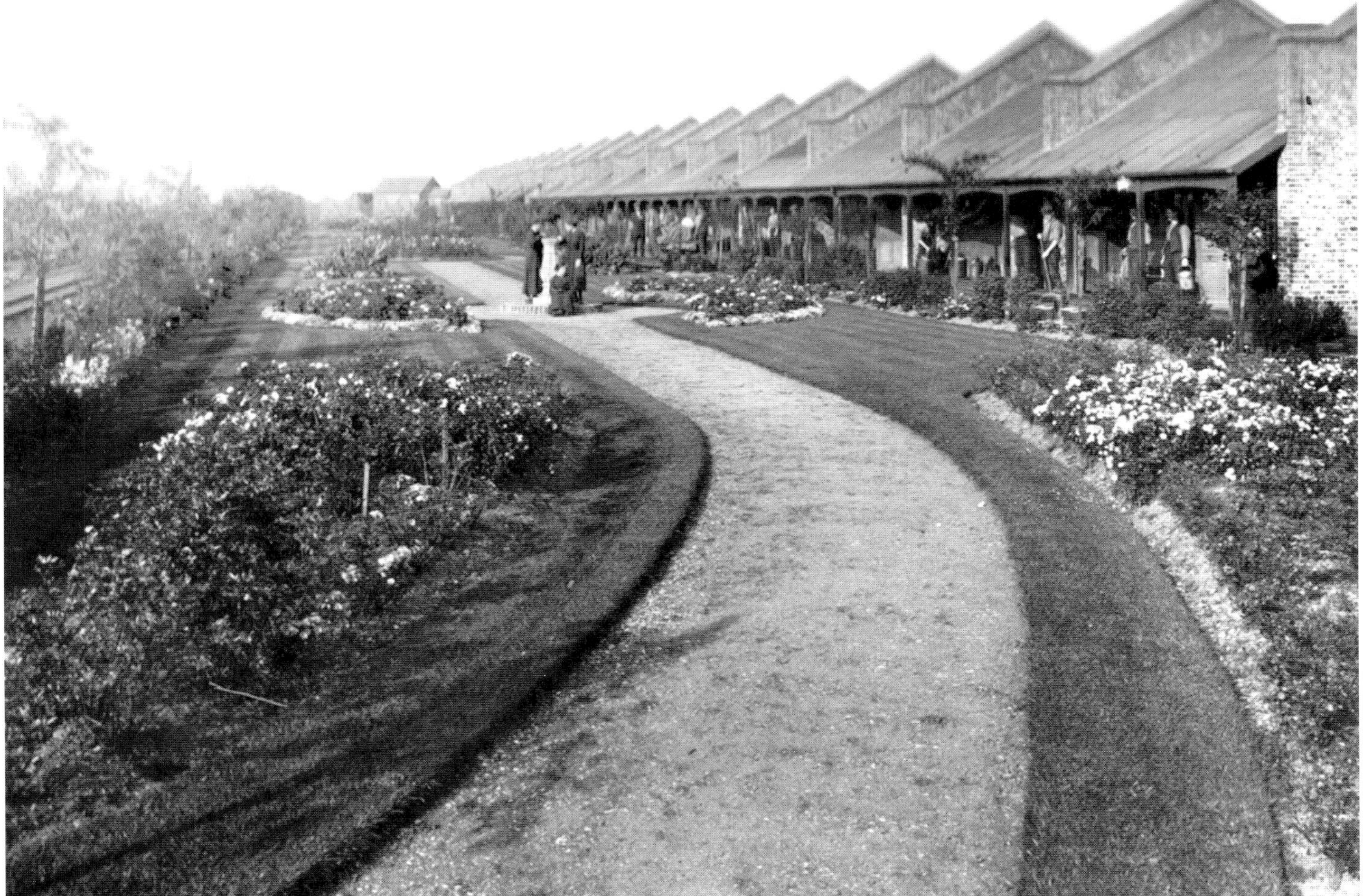

CLR GOODS TRAFFIC 1914-1918

The effects of the expanded output of the works on the CLR's goods traffic can be seen in the report prepared by the Midland Railway in December 1915 regarding the Thames Haven branch traffics and the need to adopt new working methods in the light of increased traffic (1). The £95 inwards / £648 outwards CLR traffic in the twelve months ending September 1914 had increased to £1,487 inwards / £4,445 outwards in the year ending September 1915. The increase in inwards traffic was mainly because coal for Kynochs was now coming in by rail. Kynochs were also bringing in 'timber and materials for new buildings'. The report noted also that 'materials for various contractors erecting new factories and works on adjacent lands leased by the London & Thames Haven Oil Wharves' were also now being brought in by the Midland for transfer to the CLR. This must be referring to the LATHOL canning factory, and the LATHOL 'Reedham East' tank farm which was constructed c1915. The wagons would only have been conveyed a few yards over the CLR. The connection between the CLR and the LATHOL Reedham East sidings, marked on the map at p.40, was probably provided c1915 for this traffic.

The Midland officers pondered on 'the desirability of our taking over at least so much of the Corringham Light Railway as is simply used by Kynochs for hauling their traffic to and from Thames Haven station', but this was not pursued.

There are no figures for the CLR goods traffic in 1916/17 and 1917/18, but it was most likely higher than in 1915.

The CLR traffic was still only a small fraction of the Midland's total Thames Haven branch traffic, which was £107,782 in 1914/15.

One of the horse brakes used to carry workers between Stanford-le-Hope and Corringham station in the war years. Many more had to walk!

THE PASSENGER SERVICE 1914-1918

Most of what we 'know' about the wartime passenger traffic is seemingly based on tales told to enthusiast visitors in the interwar years, who then wrote up their accounts long afterwards. Add to that much copying from one subsequent author to another, and a good deal of embroidery, and we do not end up with anything very solid. J.C. Mertens writing in the *Model Railway News* January 1931, based on a visit made c1927, spoke with decent restraint of wartime 'trains of several bogie coaches'. But by the time of D.M. Smith's March 1936 *Railway Magazine* article, this had been expanded to 'trains of 14 coaches, hauled by the two locos together'. By the 1947 *Trains Illustrated* article we get 'as many as fourteen vehicles, most of them open wagons, which required the services of both tank engines coupled together'.

What *is* known is that the CLR, in or about 1915, purchased a number of Midland bogie coaches, and further LT&SR four-wheelers, from the Midland Railway (see p.87). At the same time a larger 0-4-0 saddle tank locomotive was acquired from Kerr Stuart (p.77), and the Kitson loco and the original Kerr Stuart coaches probably went out of use, being inadequate for the new passenger numbers. (*Kynite* too would scarcely have been up to hauling trains of many bogie coaches). A further and more powerful 0-6-0 saddle tank locomotive was subsequently bought from Avonside in 1917 (p.77).

As to wartime passenger numbers, the much-copied figure of '10,000 passengers a day' seems to first appear in the 1936 *Railway Magazine* article. It is unfortunate that Freeman did not mention this subject. The '10,000' is presumably to be interpreted as 5,000 individuals a day, each making a return trip. It may not represent any more than someone taking the stated total number of workers and doubling it! (and there is certainly no reason to think that it comes from CLR ticket records). However it is possible to make a fair guess at the maximum CLR traffic levels by considering the number of workers able to get to work *without* using the CLR. These would be the 800 in the men's colony, 100 or so in Kynochtown, and however many cycled in direct from Stanford-le-Hope, or from Grays and Tilbury which were some nine miles distant via easy flat roads. Even if these cyclists were only a few hundred, we still have well over a thousand *not* using the CLR. Thus if the workforce did not actually exceed 5,000, only some 3,800 a day at most would have been using the CLR – i.e. '7,600' in passenger journeys terms. The figure of '10,000' would only have been reached if the total workforce ever exceeded 6,000 (8).

The sole surviving wartime photograph (opposite) shows a train of ten (?) coaches, which could have accommodated around 800 including some standing. This seems insufficient for a shift change, but we have no information on the CLR timetables at any time during the war.

To accommodate the longer trains, major platform and track alterations had to be carried out at both Corringham and Kynochtown

left
A 1917/18 view of the double-sided warehouse at the end of the siding that curved away north from the CLR line immediately west of Kynochtown level crossing. Built some time 1902-14, this was the only 'goods shed' on the standard gauge system. It lasted into the 1960s.
Thurrock Museum

opposite page
This is the only known view of a CLR passenger train in the war years. The date is probably summer 1917; the 1917 Avonside loco still has the shine of newness upon it, and the second platform extension, in brick, has not yet had a rear fence fitted. Further along is the previous timber extension of c1915, with fencing. At far right is one of the two extra platform access ramps put in at this period to handle the wartime passenger crowds. The 1901 station building is out of the picture. The train is formed of four Midland bogie coaches, two LT&SR four-wheelers, and four (?) more bogie (?) coaches at the rear which are very blurred even on the original. The first coach is a 40ft luggage composite and the second a seven-compartment Third. The man on the footplate is presumably an accomplice of the photographer.
Thurrock Museum

c1915 (see plans p.58). At Corringham the platform was extended eastwards from 150ft to about 340ft, and the run-round loop line extended similarly. At Kynochtown the existing 100ft-only platform and lack of any run-round facility meant that more drastic changes were needed. The platform was extended at both ends in timber c1915 to around 360ft, and then further in brick at the west end to about 440ft c1917. At one or other of these dates the platform line was extended much further westwards to new points only 80yds from the Haven Hotel level crossing. Crossovers were also provided at each end of the platform. These alterations should have been notified to the Board of Trade, but no inspection was ever made. One naturally questions why the platform at Kynochtown should have had the second extension making it so much longer than Corringham. Is it possible that the practice was introduced of *running trains up to the stops* at Corringham and passengers using the goods section of the platform as well? That would have provided a total length of some 400ft here. Note that whereas in earlier photographs the fencing between the passenger and goods sections runs across the full width of the platform, in the 1920 photo (p.49) the outer half has been removed.

The extended run-round loop at Corringham was of about 350ft clear length, and no train could have been run longer than this, unless (a) it had a locomotive at each end, or (b) it was *propelled* (hopefully empty!) in one direction. We simply have no hard evidence to decide whether either of these things happened regularly or at all, or whether trains were kept to a length that enabled running-round at Corringham.

There is also no evidence to support the claims that have been made (not traceable back beyond Gotheridge in 1983) that through trains were run between Fenchurch Street and Kynochtown (9).

The only references that have been found to additional trains being run by the Midland for Kynochs staff are from early 1917. In January an extra Sunday morning train, the 8.10am Stanford-le-Hope to Shoeburyness, was introduced for workers living in Southend off the Saturday night shift, specifically noted as being for 'Kynoch's workpeople' (10). This however did not satisfy the Southend workers who proceeded to get up a petition to the Minister of Munitions and the Minister of Labour complaining about the Midland's refusal to run through trains daily to Thames Haven for them. It was noted (11) that

'some hundreds of workers travelled each day from Southend to Kynochs, and the only means of conveyance was by a motor charabanc to Corringham and then by Light Railway.........the motor service continually broke down, and two or three hours were then spent in getting to the factory. Men and girls had to leave Southend about 4am and did not return home until 10pm. This inconvenience is reducing the efficiency of the workers……..'

The charabanc(s?) was presumably only used for getting to work at 6am on the day shift, as there were suitable trains at other times. The workers even sought the help of the renowned Southend Railway Travellers Association. They never got through trains to Thames Haven but it was reported that a 4.55 (?) am Southend to Stanford-le-Hope would be put on for them from 1st March 1917 to eliminate the charabanc. However it is not clear that this actually came off (12).

The war brought the CLR's only known fatal accident. At 10.55am on Sunday 30th April 1916, Private Joseph Statton of the Manchester Regiment was hit by a passenger train from Corringham whilst 'patrolling' the CLR line. Driver Thomas Johnstone walked back to find his mutilated body. An inquest was held at the Dock House Hotel the next day.

CLOSURE OF KYNOCH'S WORKS: 1919

Investigations by the Ministry of Munitions in 1917 revealed that ammunition from private companies was costing the government far more than that from its own factories. Furthermore, it became clear by late 1917 that the shortages of 1915 had now been turned around to such an extent that there was an overwhelming stockpile of munitions. Although there was of course no idea that this stage that the war would soon be over, it was realised that output needed to be cut back. At meetings between the Ministry of Munitions and the principal firms in January 1918, it was agreed that their output should be reduced to 60% of capacity, and that factories that did not produce direct from raw materials would be closed. There was no specific list, but Kynochtown would have fallen under this heading. In February the Ministry ordered cordite production nationally to be cut to half the existing levels. Almost overnight, the heroic ammunition workers found themselves become the unwanted. Notices were put up at Kynochtown stating that the works was to be closed 'by order of the Ministry of Munitions'. However when representatives of the workforce met Lord Moulton, the Chairman of the government Committee of High Explosives, on 26th March, he denied that the government had issued any such order. This was no doubt true in a strict sense, but they had ordered that *cordite production* should cease at Kynochtown and Arklow, which was pretty much a death knell! Clearly the government and Kynoch's management were both trying to make it look as though the other party was responsible.

The news that cordite production at Kynochtown was to be stopped at an early date, and that only 12% of the male staff, and none of the female staff, were likely to be redeployed at other works, led to a protest meeting at the cinema in Stanford-le-Hope on 15th May 1918 (13). This resulted in the resolution:

'From the tradespeople, workers (in the villages of Corringham, Kynochtown, Fobbing, and Stanford-le-Hope), and members of the following unions: Toolmakers, National Union of Labour, Heating & Operative Society, Electricians Union, Plumbers Society, Zinc Workers Society, and A.S.E., protesting against the closing down of the Kynochtown explosive factory. We ask, that the order may be cancelled, and in view of the fact that unnecessary hardship may be caused thereby, ask that the workshops may be used for other work of national importance'.

In the event the works was kept open at this stage. The government backtracked and merely reduced the Kynochtown quota for cordite from 120 tons a week to 81 tons in June 1918, and indeed it subsequently went up again to 136 tons a week in September when national stocks were falling. After the armistice ideas were floated of increased black powder production here to keep the works open, and even (according to one former worker interviewed in the 1970s) using the cordite presses to make macaroni! – but nothing came of this. Different departments at Kynochtown were then shut down at different dates from January 1919, cordite production ending in March. A few workers were kept on into 1920 for tidying-up operations (14).

As early as spring 1916 the four largest manufacturers (Kynochs, Nobel, Eley, and Curtis & Harvey) had been discussing the possibilities of merging. A report from a leading firm of accountants was received in May 1916, and the Kynoch's Board agreed to a merger in March 1917, with the intention of it being implemented by the end of the year. This however was delayed. A new company, Explosives Trades Ltd, was registered in November 1918 (and soon renamed Nobel Industries Ltd). Formal approval to the merger was given by Kynoch's shareholders at their February 1919 meeting. Arthur Chamberlain Junior (who had succeeded his father as Kynoch's Chairman in 1913), and Cocking, secured places on the Board, and became leading members of the new company's 'Birmingham Committee' set up to control Kynochs and other factories in the area. (Cocking however resigned all connections in 1920). It was quickly confirmed that the Arklow and Kynochtown works were surplus to requirements. However the main Kynoch's plant at Witton continued in full operation. In 1926/7 Nobel Industries Ltd merged with several other firms to form Imperial Chemical Industries Ltd.

After Kynochtown closed, much of the plant was sent to Witton for further use. The remaining plant and buildings were sold off at auction in October 1919, the *Grays & Tilbury Gazette* reporting on 1st November that 'by direction of Messrs Kynoch Ltd, Messrs Grimley & Son conducted a dismantling sale at Shell Haven Works, Kynochtown, commencing on Monday and ending on Thursday. The sale included portable buildings, plant, machinery, tramlines, etc, and buyers were attracted from a very wide area. Some of the larger huts fetched £190 and £200, and there was good competition for the lots generally' (15).

No record has been found as to how many Knyochtown staff were transferred to Witton; probably it was only a few of the higher-grade and technical staff. The extra wartime workers left the scene for good. Many of the longstanding workers living in Kynochtown stayed on in their houses (16). J.H. Freeman tried to find new jobs for them, which included an offer from Shell to take on any men from the village. Other houses in the village were let to anybody who wanted them.

The CLR's goods and passenger traffic must have collapsed in 1919. There is no suggestion that the passenger service was ever *given up* in the 1919-22 period – if it had been this would surely have been recounted to later visitors. (*Per contra*, there is no specific proof that it did run continuously throughout). Again, there is no information as to the timetable in these years. The additional Kerr Stuart loco of 1915 was transferred away, leaving the 1917 Avonside loco and *Kynite*.

In January 1919 the CLR shareholders were sent a circular letter stating that Kynoch Ltd was willing to buy their shares at 23s per £1 share (the 3s representing the equivalent of two years dividend at the previous rate). Only one shareholder (owner of 100 shares) rejected this offer, and all the necessary transfers of share certificates to Kynoch Ltd had been effected by July. The purpose of all this was presumably to enable Kynochs to offer the railway as well to any prospective purchaser of the site, without the nuisance of having to arrange a CLR shareholders' meeting. It also served to ensure that the major shareholders (including the Directors who made this decision) got a good price for their own holdings before the CLR's profitability slumped!

left
Another uncaptioned view from Morris Paley's albums, almost certainly showing demolition at Kynochtown, although the particular building is not identifiable.
Courtesy Marion Paley / Stuart Brand

right
Letter sent out to CLR shareholders in January 1919. The handwritten note at the top, by Arthur Chamberlain (Junior) the Kynoch's Chairman, reads 'Do not complete this [i.e. the transfer of shares to Kynoch Ltd] for any of the [CLR] Directors until Kynoch has transferred into their names the necessary Directors' qualification'. Cocking, Chamberlain, and Kerly wanted to get 23s each for their own shareholdings before the CLR went into decline! – but they had of course to continue in possession of at least 250 shares each in order to continue as Directors so that the administration of the company could continue. Hence the wheeze of a purely notional transfer to them of 250 shares each from the shares bought back by Kynoch Ltd, at the same time as their own actual shareholdings were sold.

---

1. National Archives RAIL 491/788/1 and 2.
2. *Grays & Tilbury Gazette* 10.2.1934.
3. Photo 7876 in the Kynoch's album at Thurrock Museum. There are no plans showing the Works, and all the buildings were gone by the 1919 OS map which, surprisingly, shows no trace of the site at all.
4. From National Archives MUN 7/152, which has the March-April 1915 correspondence between the War Office and Kynochs.
5. The only 'contemporary' evidence for wartime staff numbers is J.H. Freeman (see ref. 7 below). He was reported as saying that 'about 5,000 people were employed – about a thousand in non-danger areas, and the rest in the Danger Area, two thousand of each sex'. As a Kynoch's manager Freeman should have known at the time exactly how many were employed, however he was speaking many years later. Figures of '5,000' and '6,000' have been repeatedly quoted by late twentieth century authors, without any sign that they had seen original sources. The figures for the numbers of the colony residents also come from Freeman.
6. The drawings for the erection of the girls' colony buildings are dated 23.9.1915 and they were most likely erected very soon afterwards.
7. *Grays & Tilbury Gazette* 15.7.1933, report of talk given by Freeman to the Grays Thurrock Rotary Club. It is of course possible that the journalist writing the report introduced corruptions.
8. There is in fact an unexplained problem as to where all the 5,000 plus workforce could have been living. The known origins of those coming in via the CLR are:
600 from the Herd Farm 'colony'.
Say 300 living or lodging in houses in Corringham, notably Digby Road, and Fobbing.
A large three-figure number living or lodging in Stanford-le-Hope and walking, cycling, or using the horse-brakes to Corringham station.
A fairly small number coming in horse-brakes from elsewhere to Corringham station, known providers being Campbells from Pitsea (see p.92) and Mr Wiles the Basildon coal merchant.
'Several hundred' coming by train from the Southend area to Stanford-le-Hope (see below) and making their own way to Corringham station.
An unknown number coming in by train from the Tilbury direction, likewise. (There were however no trains arriving early enough for the 6am shift start).
This seems to leave us with the best part of 2,000 with no known place of residence!
9. There is no reference to such trains in the available Working Timetables for the war years, those of July 1916 and October 1917; nor in the Midland weekly notices for 1918, where they would have been mentioned had they been introduced since the October 1917 WTT. The December 1915 Midland report on the Thames Haven branch states clearly that there were no passenger trains on the branch at that date. The notices for the introduction of 'Pilot Guard' working on the branch in 1916 make no reference to passenger trains, and it is highly unlikely that this method of working would have been countenanced if there had been passenger trains. Two new connections were put in near Dock House crossing in 1916-18, uninterlocked; they would have had to be interlocked if any passenger trains were running. And all the points in Thames Haven yard were uninterlocked; this would have had to be dealt with if a passenger service had been commenced.
10. This train was not publicly advertised and is not in the October 1917 Midland public timetable book. It is in the October 1917 Working Timetable.
11. *Grays & Tilbury Gazette* 24.2.1917.
12. No such train appears in the October 1917 Public or Working Timetable books, which still show the 5.20am from Shoeburyness (arriving Stanford-le-Hope 6.7am) as the first up train.
13. *Grays & Tilbury Gazette* 18.5.1918.
14. Thurrock Museum has a notice of dismissal sent to Arthur Wright 'Principal Foreman in charge of all general labouring in connection with foundations for buildings, the construction of railways and tramways, the unloading of goods and machinery at our railway sidings and wharf, etc', stating that his services will be terminated on 23.12.1920.
15. If the auction was only of the plant at the *Shell Haven* Works, there must have been another auction later at the main works. In this context it might be noted that there is no trace of the Shell Haven Works on the 1919 OS map, whereas almost all the buildings and tramways at the main works are still shown.
16. The attendances at Kynochtown school in autumn 1920 were 60 plus, more than in the latter part of the war, proving that the village was still well populated in the 'gap years' 1919-22.
17. Essex Record Office T/Z 162/1.

These views are stated to be 1920, and as they came to be preserved together, and are taken in similar conditions, it can be assumed that they were taken on the same day.

This Corringham station view was taken about midday. The most notable feature is that all the trees have been cut back (probably the last time this was ever done). This was scarcely the sort of thing manpower would have been expended on in the war years – was it perhaps a work-creation exercise for the remaining staff in 1919? The platform is still weed-free throughout, reflecting the many boots that had so recently been treading it. The telegraph poles have appeared since the 1900s views. The station nameboard is not to be seen, so one assumes it had been moved further east when the platform extension was made c1915 (it was later moved back to the original position). The wagon has been left in a position where it would have to be moved by the loco every time a passenger train was run round. If there was some particular good reason for leaving wagons at this precise point, that may explain why the points were moved soon afterwards. The Peculiar People's chapel is seen in the distance to the left of Grove Terrace.

Jim Connor collection

This photograph must have been taken around 5pm. We are looking towards Corringham; the loco is on the running line at the Brickworks Siding. The sewage works fence can be seen beyond the LBSCR wagon (high bar wagon No.4333). The 1917 Avonside loco is still in very good external condition, with the lining-out clear.

Geoff Goslin collection

The LBSCR wagon has now been left alongside the Brickfield Siding loading bank. We can guess from this view that the siding itself had been lifted in the months between the 1919 OS survey and the taking of this photograph, but some sort of further traffic had then arisen subsequently, requiring this plank arrangement for loading.

John Scott-Morgan collection

49

Chapter Four

THE CORY'S YEARS 1921 – 1950

The works site was put up for sale in 1921, together with Kynochtown village and the Corringham properties. The only expression of interest came from Cory Bros, and the Kynoch's Board minutes of 19th July 1921 record that 'after negotiations lasting six months' the whole of Kynoch's Essex properties had been sold to them for £35,000. The purchase went through in August (1).

Cory Bros & Co Ltd were one of the largest businesses in South Wales. The firm had been built up in the 1850s-70s by the brothers John and Richard Cory, expanding on a shipowning and shipbroking business owned by their father Richard Cory. They created a worldwide network of coal depots and agencies, and also bought up a large number of South Wales coal mines. The Limited Company was formed in 1888. Their UK coal distribution network led to them owning over 5,000 railway wagons, claimed to be the UK's largest private wagon fleet. John Cory was also a principal figure in the promotion of the Barry Railway, and both were leading public figures in Cardiff. John died in 1910 and Richard in 1914, so by the time of the Essex purchase the company was headed by John's son Sir Clifford Cory, Liberal MP for the St Ives division of Cornwall 1906-24. In the early 1920s Cory's decided to move into the oil refining and distribution business, for which they obtained powers in 1922, and it was for this that they wanted the Essex site.

As part of the deal the whole of the shares in the Corringham Light Railway (which had escaped being taken into one of the new 'Big four' railway companies under the 1921 Act) were transferred in 1921 from Kynoch Ltd and the Kynoch's directors to Cory Bros and the Cory's directors, Sir Clifford Cory becoming the new CLR Chairman. A General Meeting of the CLR Company (in reality, of the directors only) was held on 19th September 1921 to elect the new Cory's CLR directors. The situation therefore remained that the CLR was still independent in law, but was a wholly-owned part of Cory's in reality. When the enthusiast J.C. Mertens visited c1927 he asked the driver whether the railway was owned by Cory's, and got the answer 'It is and it isn't' !

At the time of the sale to Cory's, the CLR was in debt to Kynoch Ltd to the sum of £5,426. 1s 6d, for 'rebates on traffic under an arrangement made during the war'. Kynoch Ltd had to formally agree a release of this debt so that the CLR company could be sold free of liability.

When Cory's took over the works site the great majority of it was empty apart from the many earth blast mounds, as almost all of the wooden buildings had been removed, as had the narrow gauge tramway system (apart from a short length near the pier – see map p.53). The whole of the former 'Danger Area' at the north end of the works was wasteland, and Cory's never did anything with it. However, many of the larger buildings did remain alongside the main east-west roadway, from the offices block to the power station and pier (2). The power station was brought back into operation, and the pier continued to be used for coal ships.

Some preliminary work was done on the site in 1922, but it was not until 18th January 1923 that Cory's issued a press statement confirming that they were to start work on an oil installation here, at a cost of £250,000. As can be seen on the 1939 OS (p.55), they built a small oil refinery and a tank farm at the far south-eastern corner of the site near Shellhaven Point. An American engineer A.D. Smith was in charge of construction. A second pier was provided at the refinery for use by oil tankers, and one of the existing rail sidings was extended nearly a mile to serve the refinery. Cory's therefore operated a 'split site', with a large area of still-undeveloped marsh between the refinery and the older ex-Kynochs buildings.

No detailed description of the refinery has been found. Roy Woodall's recollections refer to 'a coal-fired distiller, a tube reforming unit, and a cross cracking plant for the processing of grozny and batuum crude oils'. As was generally the case in the UK prior to the 1950s, there was no primary refining of crude oil. The cracking plant also proved unreliable. Some blending of oils was done in steam stills. Fuel oil and motor spirit came in already refined.

Kynochtown village was renamed 'Coryton' (pronounced COARY-ton) in 1923 (9), and all other traces of the word 'Kynoch' were eliminated similarly.

Continuity was provided by J.H. Freeman who was appointed as Kynoch's sole Manager here around the time of closure. He now became Works Manager for Cory's, and moved from his former house in Stanford-le-Hope to the Manager's house in Fleet Street, remaining there until he retired after the 1950 sale to Vacuum Oil. As part of his job he was also 'Secretary and Superintendent' of the CLR. Indeed he was both 'Mr Coryton' and 'Mr CLR' throughout the interwar years.

CLR GOODS TRAFFIC 1921-1950

There may have been a significant traffic in construction materials during the building of the refinery in 1923. After that the principal CLR traffic was oil tankers. There are no figures for the CLR traffic in the interwar years but the tonnage was no doubt higher than pre-1914. There were three general goods trains a

J.H. Freeman takes centre stage at the annual Coryton village fete in his own front garden, c1932. His wife Jessica and the Rev. Ernest Gardner, Rector of Fobbing (studying his hat) are seated to the right.

John Henry Freeman was born in 1889 and brought up in Birmingham where his father was a builder. He attended King Edward School, where he excelled in science and rugby, and then studied chemistry at the University of London. After joining Kynochs he transferred to Kynochtown in 1910. From 1919 he was the sole remaining Manager here, and would have been responsible for demolition and sale of assets. In 1921 he transferred to Cory's. His political activities were perhaps initiated by the limited work activity in 1919-22! He was elected to Corringham Parish Council in 1919, and soon onto Orsett RDC also. When the new Thurrock UDC was set up in 1936 he became its first Chairman. He was also an Essex County Councillor for some years. From 1936 he was a JP, and held many other public posts in Thurrock, including Civil Defence Officer in the war years. He was Manager of the Stanford and Corringham primary schools. In short he was by the 1930s one of the most influential men in south Essex.

He retired from the UDC during a spell of ill health in 1947, but continued as Cory's, and then Vacuum's, local Manager until 1952, when he retired at 63, moving to a house in Lampits Hill, Corringham. In 1952 also he was awarded the M.B.E.

He was married to Jessica Reeves in 1912; she died in 1935 and he remarried subsequently. They had one son, John, who was killed in August 1940 whilst serving as a radio officer in the merchant navy.

Freeman was regarded by the village as a kindly man – he saw it as his role to find a job for any boy leaving school. But he was of course very much *Mr* Freeman, and would not stand for any nonsense. He died on 19th October 1960 aged 71. *Courtesy Win England*

Cory's refinery and tanks, c1925, seen from the sea wall. The tanks were erected by the Palmer Shipbuilding Co of Jarrow.
Padgett collection, Southend Museums Service

above
The new Cory's pier on the Thames at Horseshoe Bay, c1925.
Padgett collection, Southend Museums Service

right
Cory's motor tanker drivers, loaders, and others pose beside Scammell petrol tanker lorry No.34. CLR loco driver Arthur Baker is third from right. A lot of fuel was already going out by road in the interwar years. The loading area seen here was presumably at the refinery but it cannot be identified on the 1939 OS. Motor spirit was also sent to a depot in Wandsworth by barge.

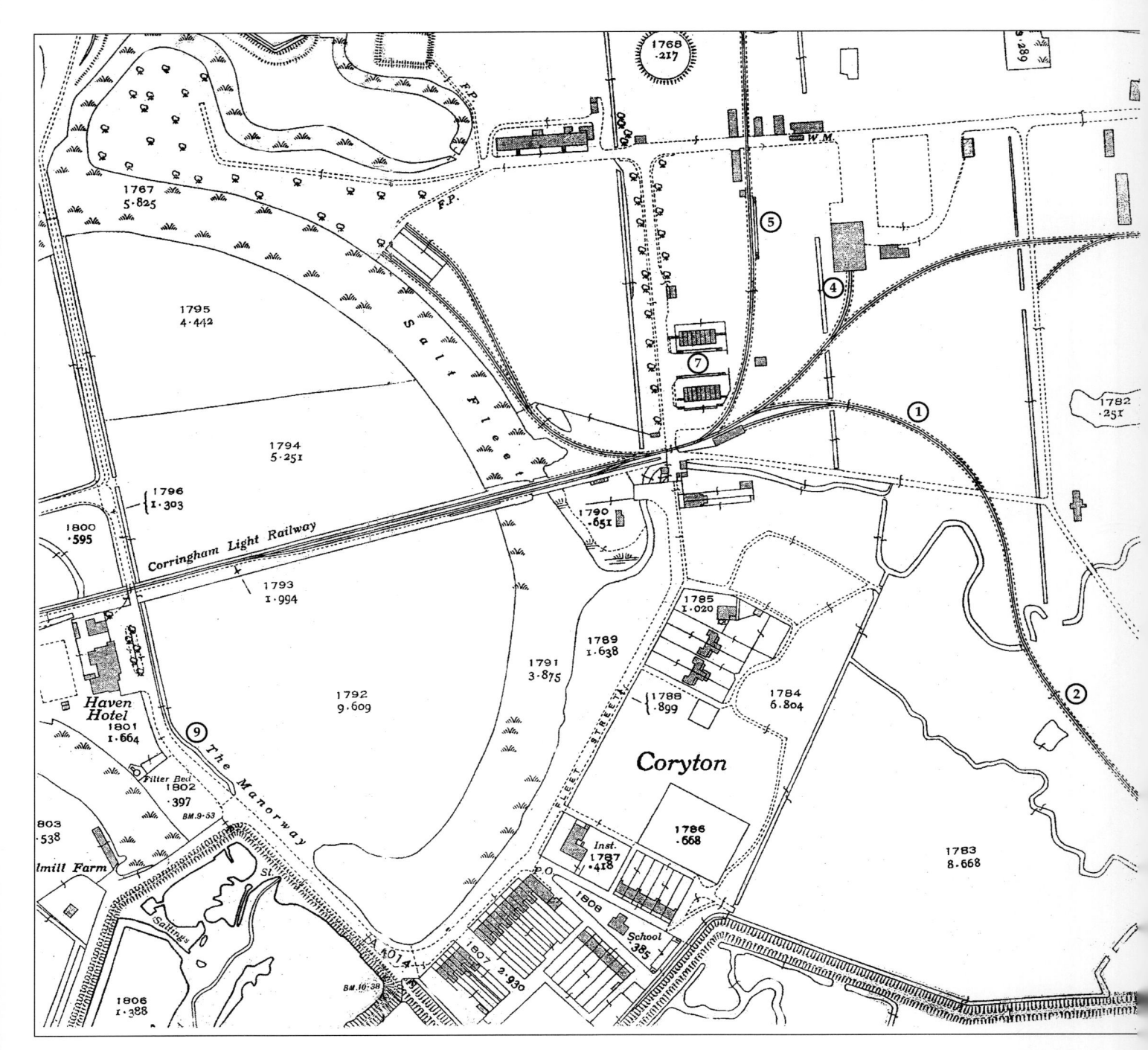

day on the Thames Haven branch at this period, which would have brought in and taken away the Cory's tankers.

After the Cory's takeover *Kynite* is only heard of as a stationary boiler (see p.76). It then rusted away on site until 1952. The 1917 Avonside was the only loco in use until 1933 when a second identical Avonside was bought as a spare loco, a function it continued to fulfil until the end of steam in the 1950s.

The CLR's limited non-Cory's goods traffic probably came to an end in the 1930s; the last known photograph showing a wagon at the loading bank at Corringham is c1935, and the end of the track here is quite overgrown in postwar views.

1939 - 1945: GOVERNMENT EDIBLE AND VEGETABLE OIL STORAGE

Information on the Cory's period is far less readily available than for the Kynoch's years. By the late 1930s the site was effectively serving as a distribution depot only (ship to rail/road/barge). 'In 1938 Coryton was merely a storage concern handling 1,000,000 tons of oil a year' (3). Whereas the 1914 - 18 conflict had brought the line to its peak, the 1939 - 45 war was to bring the lowest ebb on both the passenger and goods fronts. It is unlikely that any oil came in here in 1940-44 at least, as there was a general government-dictated diversion of oil imports to the west coast (see *The Thames Haven Railway* p.47). Instead most of the tanks were used for storing edible and vegetable oils for the Ministry of Food. One-off excitements were the unloading at the jetties of a cargo of Canadian apples in June 1941, and the bunkering of naval vessels in 1943 (to use up remaining fuel oil stocks??).

Coryton village was evacuated in 1940, along with the Shell and LATHOL housing, as it was feared to be at serious risk from air raids on the tank farms. In the event, though, only two houses in Coryton (the pair by the lion gates) were destroyed by bombing, and the Army took over the empty village houses for locally-based troops for the remainder of the war. The village was not re-occupied for several years after 1945, and only a few of the previous occupants moved back, so the 1950s Coryton was largely a different community.

After the war, the storage of palm oil, nut oils, molasses, etc continued, 'with the occasional visit of a factory ship discharging a cargo of whale oil from the Antarctic seas' (3). This went on until 1950 when the vegetable oil stocks were 'liquidated as soon as possible' after the sale to Vacuum.

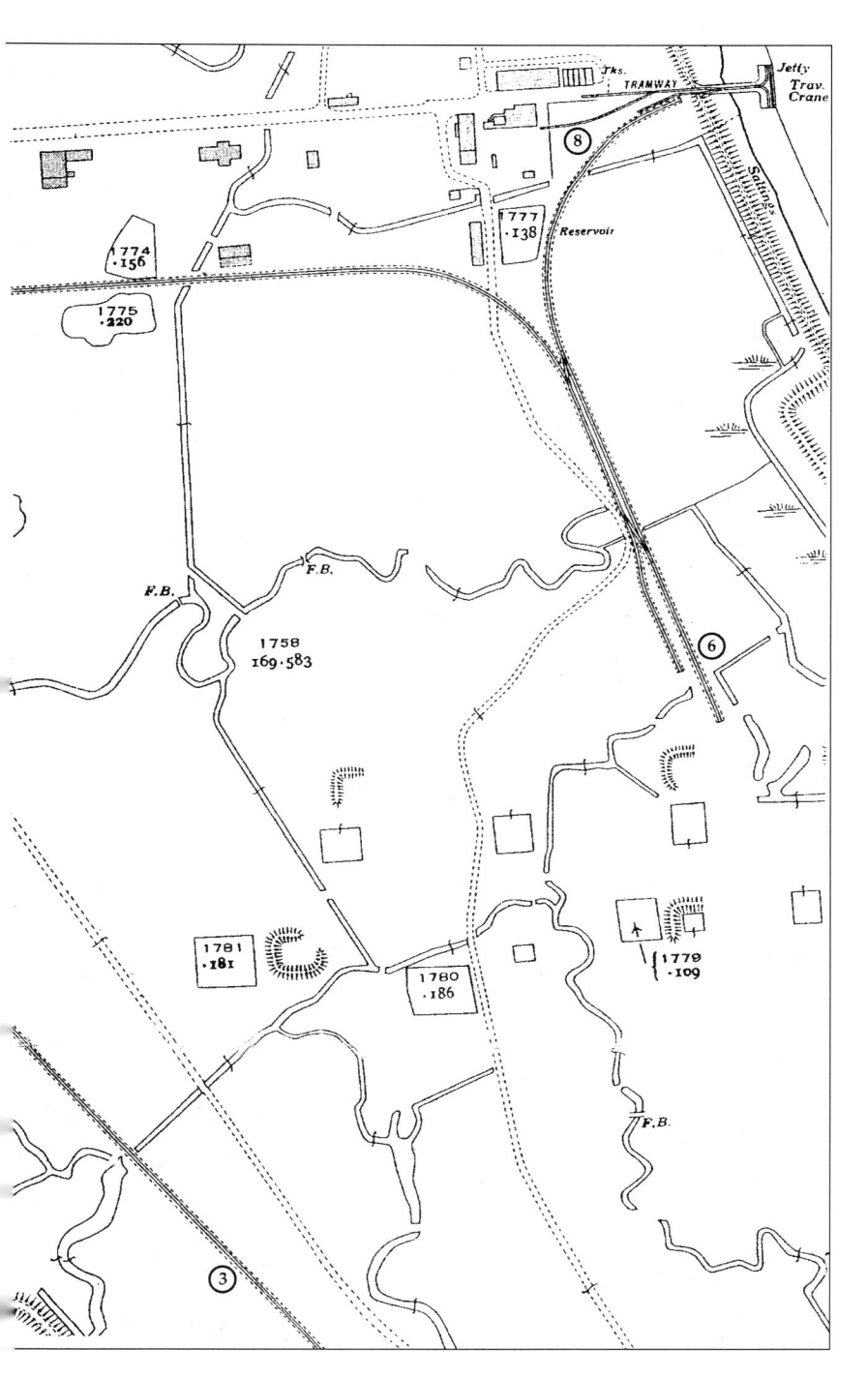

left 1939 survey OS 25in map, reduced to scale of 100yds to the inch.

This gives us our best view of the site in the Cory's period. Coryton village is quite unaltered since 1919. Amongst the surviving Kynoch's buildings within the works area are the offices block, the Laboratory, the Hospital, and the Power Station.

For changes in the Coryton station layout see the plan at p.58.

1. New line c1923 and new connection to loco shed in consequence
2. Section of existing line incorporated into new line to Refinery c1923
3. Line extended to Refinery c1923
4. Siding altered to run into (existing) shed 1920s/30s
5. Loading platform (?) added 1920s/30s
6. Loading platform removed and siding slightly extended 1920s/30s
7. New Cory's buildings 1920s/30s
8. Residual (and additional) sections of narrow gauge track
9. Road straightened c1924

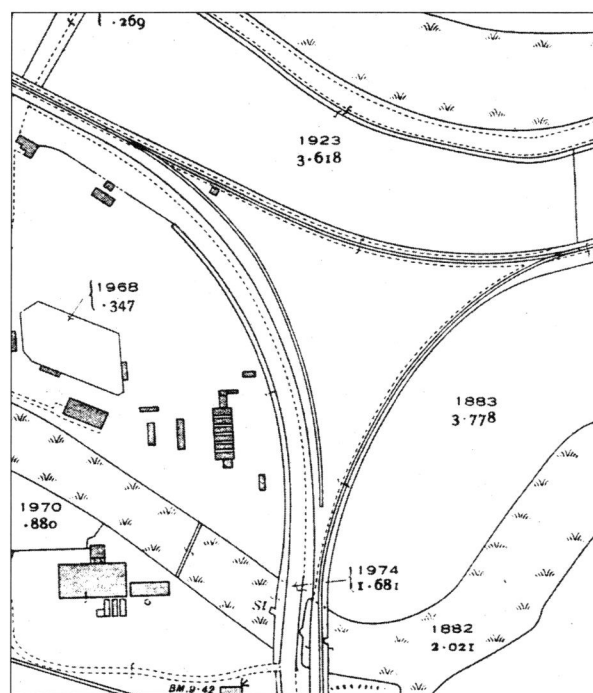

The 'triangle' as shown on the 1939 OS, with the southern junction points removed. The ex - Reedham Farm occupation crossing at top left is now the entrance to LATHOL's extensive 'Reedham' site operations. (It later became one of the entrances to the Shell 'West Site'). This occupation crossing became much busier from the 1920s, but there are no references known to any problems – presumably the trains went very slowly here.

The 1936 *Railway Magazine* article had included a map showing the south-west curve as 'track removed', but this produced a letter from 'Hestor' in the June 1936 issue stating that 'on examining this spur, I have found that it was still there, but overgrown entirely by grass'. So was most of the track left in place until the postwar years, and perhaps only lifted in 1952? It was certainly lifted by the 1960 OS.

1930s view of one of the Avonside locos at Coryton level crossing, either about to propel empty tanks to the refinery (where there was no run-round facility, per the 1939 OS), or bringing loaded tanks from the refinery. The loco would have had to run round the train in Coryton station loop in one or both directions. The requirement for barrier wagons would have complicated this, but the layout would have enabled it.

The wooden gates across the works roadway closed on the south side only. They had replaced the iron gates seen at p.33. Immediately either side of the crossing are the point levers for the siding connections.

53

The 1939 OS also provides the only known plan of the Cory's Refinery. It seems probable that the arrangements seen here do mostly date back to the construction of the Refinery in 1923. The principal structures are clustered around the end of the rail siding, and their small extent is evident.

Unfortunately the 1939 OS maps omit all oil tanks for 'security' reasons (which did little to prevent the Luftwaffe identifying the sites!). The fenced-off rectangular enclosures mark the 'tank farms'. Photographs show nine large tanks in parcels 1818/19 (off extract here) and 1820/21, and a group of small tanks in 1824; but the principal Cory's tank farm area was at the east end in parcels 1828/9 (plus some small tanks in 1840/1). Many of the tanks here were retained in use into the later Mobil period.

Note the new Cory's pier of c1923, with its own narrow gauge tramway, and the subsequent additional jetty to the east.

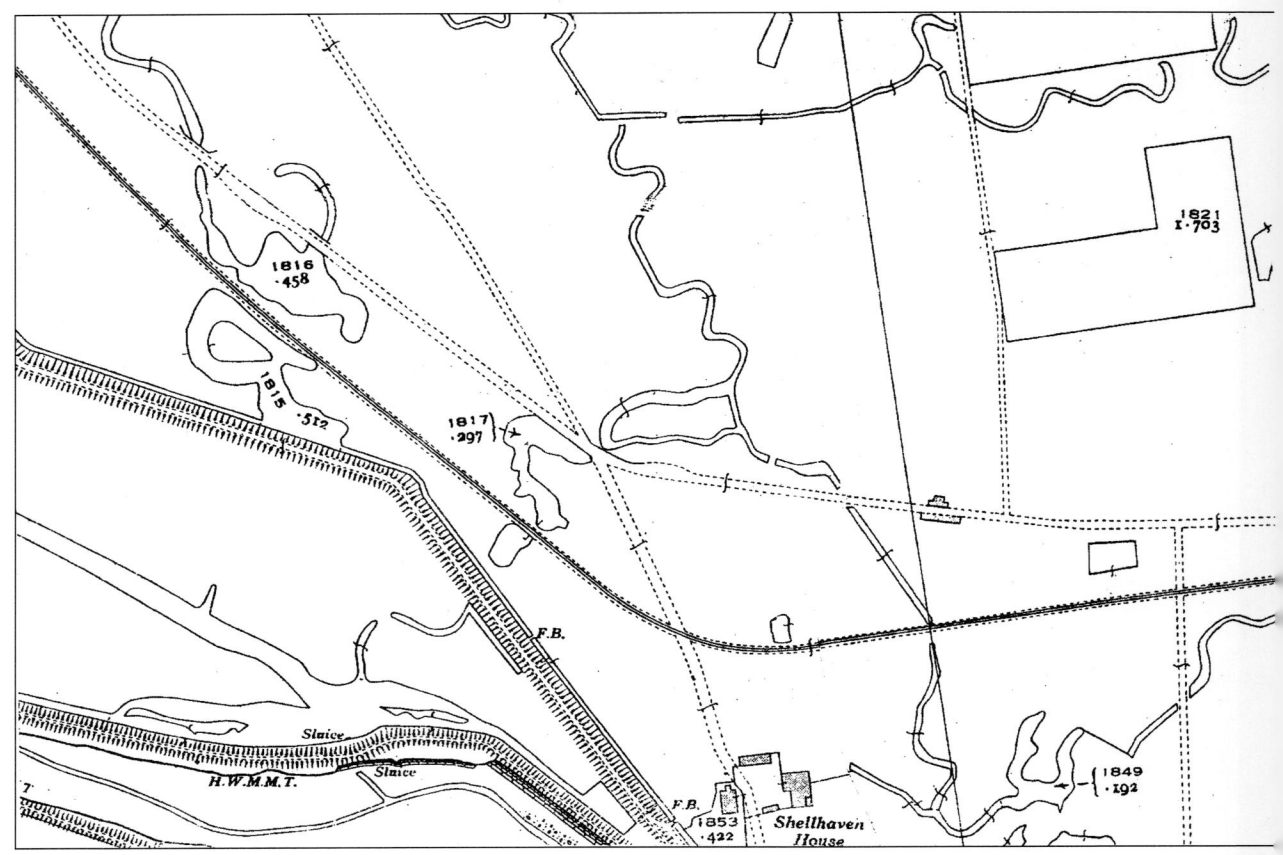

THE CLR PASSENGER SERVICE 1921-50

Nothing is known as to the service operated in the 1921-23 period. The Cory's works employed fewer than 200, so the CLR passenger trains would never again be as busy as in the Kynoch's years. In the early 1920s, Shell were running lorries to carry their own staff between Stanford-le-Hope and Thames Haven, and these made additional trips between Stanford and Corringham station to assist Cory's workers travelling on the CLR (4).

The principal nail in the coffin of the CLR passenger service was the transformation of the Manorway into a modern motor road around 1925, after which regular bus services were introduced (for details of which see p.92). The majority of workers changed over to the buses. By the time of J.C. Mertens' visit c1927 the CLR passenger service was already down to two trips a day, recalled by him as 'about 7.10am' from Corringham and 'about 5.25pm' from Coryton, with corresponding workings in the other direction in each case. The 1936 *Railway Magazine* article reported a similar service and it seems fairly safe to assume that this is all there ever was after the buses began. From the late '20s on the trains were used principally by those living in the immediate vicinity of Corringham station, which was often referred to as 'Digby Station'. The train became known as 'Cory's coffee-pot'.

Some time in the 1920s, when it became clear that there would be no more lengthy passenger trains, the whole of the timber sections of the station platform at Coryton were removed, leaving only the 80ft long brick section of c1917 at the west end. The timber station building was resited at ground level a few feet to the west of its original position. The brick platform at Corringham was not altered.

One bogie coach at least was still in service for several years after 1919 – Mertens referred to 'one bogie coach devoid of all paint' forming the train on his visit. Otherwise the Midland coaches acquired c1915 were left to rot after the war. Mertens noticed 'several old bogie coaches standing on a siding at Coryton, seemingly derelict'. The 1930s visitors made no mention of seeing these coaches; Gotheridge was told that they had been 'sold for scrap to a firm called Fyne'.

Even in the early 1920s the train sometimes consisted of only one LT&SR four-wheeler. A former Shell worker, R.Smallacobe of Grays, in his recollections recorded in 1990, spoke of his first day at work in September 1923 when, on cycling down the hill from Corringham,

'I saw the engine and one passenger wagon behind it, from Corringham, a four wheel coach, about forty or fifty men in it. After a few minutes I came across the gate across the road, whilst the engine and coach passed through. This was my first sight of the old Iron Latch'.

By 1930 there were only two LT&SR four-wheelers left in service (and seemingly no other coaches left on site). R.W. Kidner visiting in 1937 photographed the two coupled together and one assumes forming the train on that day, and photos here also show both coaches in use, but several other 1930s photographs show only one coach in use, and it would seem that the second coach was omitted more often than not.

The CLR ran occasional special trains as well as the timetabled service trains. Trains had been run for Sunday School children in earlier years, and these continued (5). At Easter, Christmas, and other high days, the Coryton Sunday School children went to Fobbing church instead, by special train. Village weddings, christenings, and funerals also had to be held at Fobbing, and a suitable request to Mr Freeman would produce a special train. Conversely, when there was a big event in the Institute at Coryton, special trains might be run for those coming from Corringham. This was still happening for dances in the postwar years, the train travel being included in the price of the ticket.

The first recorded special trip for railway enthusiasts was that organised on a Saturday in April 1935 (?) and recorded in *Trains Illustrated* in 1947 (6). This trip was privately organised and the party consisted of 'about fifty, including ladies and schoolboys'.

'The journey to Grays by the 1.55pm fast train from Broad Street – an unusual crowd for that little-known service – and the subsequent tour from Grays by two Eastern National coaches, do not concern this narrative; sufficient to say that having interested the Rector of Fobbing, the Rev. Gardner, we were met by him outside St Michael's church, and whilst awaiting the arrival of the 'special', were regaled with blood-curdling stories of lurid times such as the insurrection of Wat Tyler...........'.

'Undirected by signposts, we found Corringham station only by stumbling over it! The bold and wet-painted signboard 'Corringham' was impressive, and the station buildings, although ancient [sic], might suggest activity were it not for the weed-grown platform and the entire absence of lamps, officials and official notices; as for the rails, they rotted in rust and rickety joints.

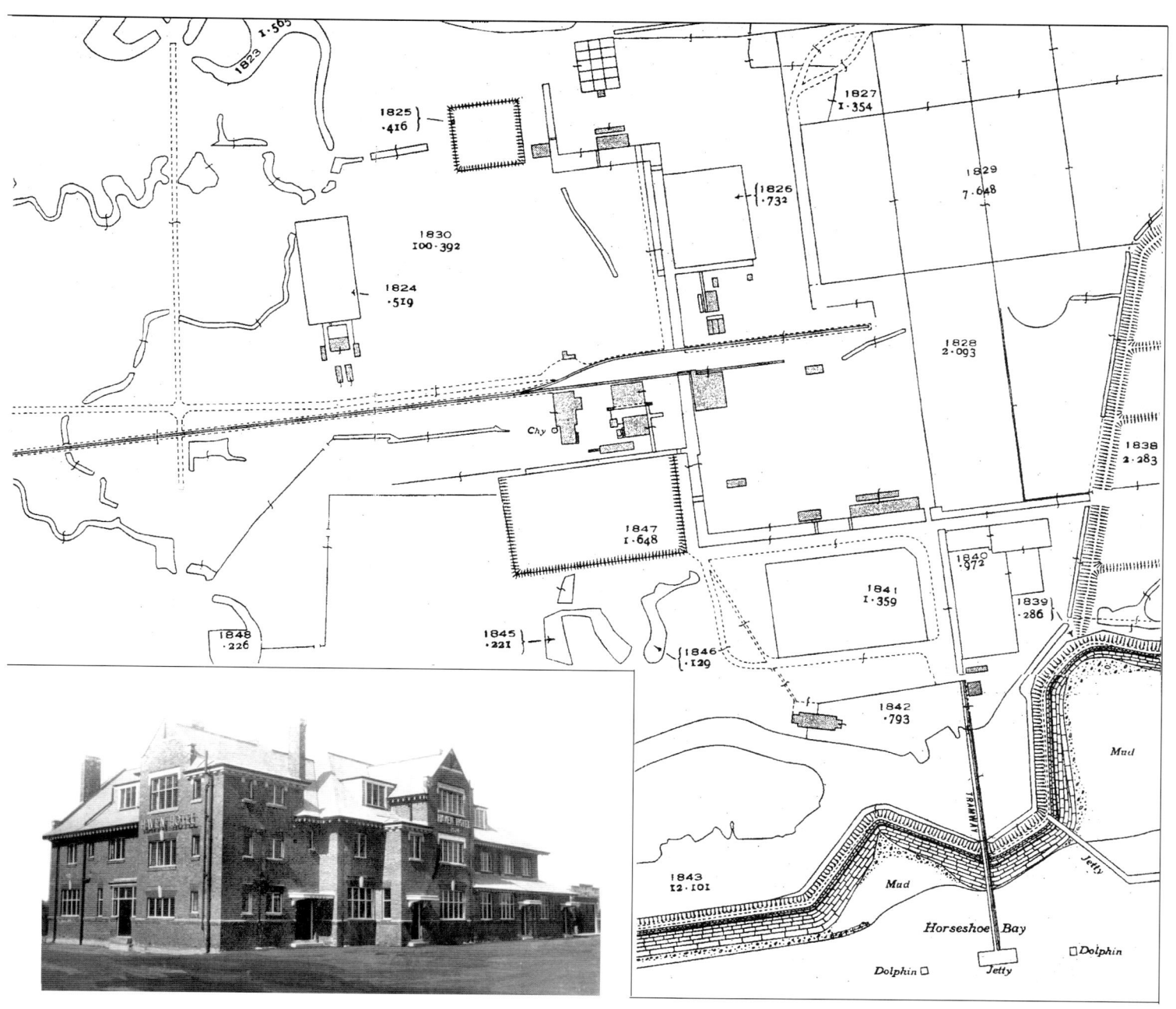

above

At the same time as the Manorway was improved, the 'Haven Hotel' was erected in 1924 adjacent to the CLR level crossing. This veritable palace was intended to be a more upmarket replacement for the Dock House pub at Thames Haven, although that did not stop the Dock House landlord Sid Wise being transferred here. It was provided with a bowling green. Some Coryton people used it as their 'local'. The Hotel rooms were intended for use by Thames Pilots, and by ships' captains staying here with their wives during the then-leisurely unloading process.

Unfortunately the demolition of Coryton village and the Shell houses took away the immediate customer base, and the increasingly fast unloading of tankers reduced the time their crews had to spend here. This brought closure and demolition around 1980.

Thurrock Museum

right

The majority of the 'new' Manorway road of c1925 was simply a modern tarmac surface on the existing alignment, however at Corringham a wholly new section of road had to be built, christened 'Thames Haven Road' (from grid reference 702802 to 711829). The previous access to the Manorway at Corringham had been via Church Road and Rookery Hill, but it would have been undesirable to have large lorries coming this way through the village centre. This c1926 view is taken looking east at the junction of Chase Road. Road markings had yet to make a general appearance in UK practice. It is about 5.30pm on this summer's day and large numbers of cycling workmen are making their way home. The climb up from the marshes at this point was the only place they needed to put in any effort! In typical interwar years fashion, bungalows are already springing up with direct access off the new main road.

Padgett collection, Southend Museums Service

Gone were the days of 1915-18……. Promptly at 4pm our 'special' drew in, a train of two ancient four-wheeled carriages of Victorian vintage, both specially painted up for us. The older of the two……formed the guard's van for the journey to Coryton, the guard sitting amongst the passengers and working the hand brake. After the engine had shunted to the forward end, we entrained under the eyes of the entire local population, who had turned out to see the fun; probably no 'special' had ever before been chartered on that line in all its 35 years of running. This was history in the making and the whistle of the little engine sounded loud enough to awaken the ghosts of the wild men of Mucking, whom we expected at any moment to see charging down the platform'.

'Speeded on its journey by the resounding cheers of the onlookers, and with a couple of schoolboys on the footplate acting as assistant drivers, the train rounded the sharp curve and began to traverse the marshland, crossed by dykes and ditches, and bounded by the seawall. Mr Johnstone was in control of the train, acting the 'Pooh-bah' role of Engine-driver, Fireman, Porter, Gate-opener, Ticket collector – in short, he might have said 'The Corringham Light Railway – that's me!'. Stops had to be made at level crossings to open and close the gates; and the journey of about 2¾ miles [sic] to the terminus occupied the best part of fifteen minutes'.

'After passing a lot of hideous and odiferous oil storage tanks, we joined the incoming goods line from Thames Haven, and not long after we again crossed the main road near the Haven Hotel, and drew up in Coryton station'.

'Coryton station consists of enough sidings, but very little station, and has no ticket office or any sort of shelter from the weather. The single line continues past the station to the locomotive shed and works of Messrs Cory Bros Ltd, the petrol distributors, after whom Coryton is named'.

'Here we were met by Mr J.H. Freeman, Superintendent of the Line, who, among other features of the rather grey village, pointed out a building [i.e. the Institute] which immediately impressed us on hearing that it was both licensed and consecrated, and functioned alternately or concurrently as the local inn and the parish church!'.

'We found the Haven Hotel with its well-kept gardens, neat lawns, bowling green, and H & C in all rooms, a most attractive haven in this isolated outpost of the Port of London Authority, and very good it was at brewing tea……………'.

Some doubt exists over the running of the passenger service in the war years 1939-45. The *Railway Magazine* in 1946, having received conflicting letters from readers, wrote to the CLR requesting elucidation. The reply (no doubt from Freeman) stated that the claim made by some that the line was closed entirely during the war was 'not the case', and that 'there never was an entire suspension of the passenger train services, as a few trains ran' (7). This was virtually a statement that the trains did not run most of the time! – confirming the information provided by others that the CLR had run a bus instead during the war years. With petrol scarce to come by the logic of this is not evident, unless there was also no goods traffic on many days, in which case it would indeed have been wasteful to prepare the locomotive just for the passenger workings.

The *RM* was also informed that the regular daily passenger service had resumed on Monday 8th October 1945. The CLR sent its 1946 timetable which was:

From Coryton 6.30am Mon-Sat, 12.10pm Sat, 5.10pm Mon-Fri.
From Corringham 7.15am Mon-Sat, 12.30pm Sat, 5.30pm Mon-Fri.

The timetable remained similar until closure in 1952, except that by 1949 the Saturday end-of-shift trains had been altered to 12.0 and 12.20pm, and the Friday afternoon trains to 5.0pm and 5.20pm. From 1948 the CLR service was at last included in *Bradshaw*.

Even in these last years, male and female passengers were still kept apart at different ends of the coach – there was no lighting in the winter months!

From 1947 on the line was visited by more enthusiasts, most of them coming to travel on the Saturday lunchtime trains. Several special advertised trips were organised – by the Stephenson Locomotive Society on 17th May 1947, the Birmingham Locomotive Club on 12th June 1948, the Southern Counties Touring Society on 25th June 1949, and the Railway Correspondence & Travel Society on 3rd June 1950 (photo p.80). The CLR staff clearly enjoyed these occasions too. The photographs taken on these dates represent more than half of the total record of the CLR! – a selection are given here on pp. 62-64.

A 1930s two-coach train captured at the most scenic point on the line, southwest of Fobbing church. This required a trespass across the marsh fields, and only this one (unknown) photographer ever seems to have ventured here to photograph trains. The back cover photo was taken on the same visit.

John Scott-Morgan collection

left
The 1917 Avonside at Corringham in 1926 with a train comprised of a Midland 40ft Luggage Composite of 1882/3 – probably the same coach as at p.47 - and one of the LT&SR four-wheelers. Goods wagons for Corringham may well have been propelled from Coryton as suggested here. This is an ex-NER four plank open wagon.

above
The 12.10pm service waits departure at Coryton on Saturday 22nd August 1936. This is the 1914 loco (the photographer noted it), which was kept in good condition up to 1939 - the driver, almost certainly identified as Tom Johnstone, is demonstrating how. The fireman looks like the young Ted Mynett – he had started on the line around 1925.

Thurrock Museum

ESCAPE FROM NATIONALISATION

In 1947 the CLR along with other minor lines was reviewed by government to see whether it should be acquired by the British Transport Commission under nationalisation. The conclusion was that it need not be, as it was 'now used only to convey the firm's workpeople between Corringham and Coryton'.

The report noted that in 1946 the CLR had gross receipts of £3,994 and working costs of £4,818, resulting in a net deficit of £824. These are the only profitability figures we have for the CLR after 1923. No dividend had been paid in any year after 1918 (8).

---

1. In fact Cory's did not buy the *whole* of the Essex properties, as the Canvey land was sold separately in 1922, as described at p.19.
2. As we have only the 1939 OS to rely on, it cannot be proven how many buildings still existed in 1921 but had been demolished by 1939. One suspects only a few.
3. Article in *Coryton Broadsheet*, January 1958.
4. Letters in *Shell Haven News*: September 1955 p.12 from F.J. (Jimmy) Woodman one of the lorry drivers involved, and August 1955 p.4 from H. Burton his then lad assistant.
5. George Woodcock stated (*Essex Countryside* July 1965) that 'in the 1930s the present writer by permission of Mr Freeman the Manager made a return trip over the line on one of the Avonsides for such an outing'.
6. As the party travelled from Broad Street the trip must have been prior to May 1935. One suspects that they actually travelled from Broad St because it was known that that service was about to be withdrawn, in which case it must have been April 1935, as their CLR train ran in daylight after 4pm. Note also the reference to '35 years of running'.
7. *Railway Magazine* Jan-Feb 1947 p.58.
8. Reported so for 1919-35, and assumed so for subsequent years given that the traffic was less. It would seem likely that the CLR made a profit again from the mid-1950s, but no accounts are known for the Vacuum/Mobil period to confirm this. The article in *Mobil News* October 1970 re the forthcoming winding up of the CLR company states that it 'always makes a profit'.
9. In later years, however, many people used to pronounce the name CORRY-TON instead. There was and is another Coryton near Cardiff named after the company.

When the timber sections of the Coryton station platform were removed in the 1920s, a new timber ramp had to be provided at the east end of the remaining brick section (left). In the foreground is the crossover of c1915, the geometry of which would not win any prizes! This crossover having been installed *prior* to the brick platform extension, it was rather peculiarly located in relation to this remaining section of platform. The 1939 OS erroneously omits this crossover.

The CORYTON nameboard appears to be new, c1923. In the background is the Haven Hotel.

John Scott-Morgan collection

Somewhat blurred, but a good view of the 1901 platform buildings as resited in the 1920s, at ground level and a few yards west of their original position. The photograph was taken in 1931. It is early afternoon and the one LT&SR coach which constituted the 'train' by this date has been left out of the way between the two crossovers until the afternoon passenger working. The 1915 eastern crossover (behind the photographer) was still in use at this date.

Geoff Goslin collection

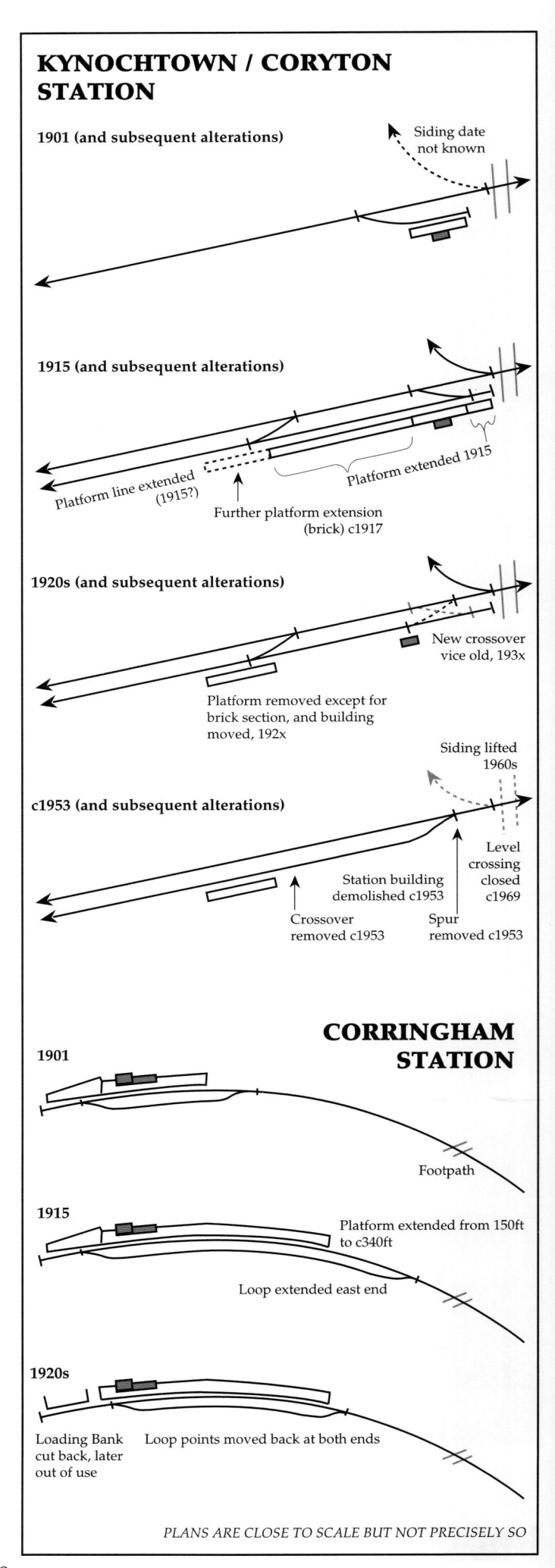

KYNOCHTOWN / CORYTON STATION

1901 (and subsequent alterations)

Siding date not known

1915 (and subsequent alterations)

Platform line extended (1915?)
Platform extended 1915
Further platform extension (brick) c1917

1920s (and subsequent alterations)

New crossover vice old, 193x
Platform removed except for brick section, and building moved, 192x

c1953 (and subsequent alterations)

Siding lifted 1960s
Station building demolished c1953
Level crossing closed c1969
Crossover removed c1953
Spur removed c1953

CORRINGHAM STATION

1901

Footpath

1915

Platform extended from 150ft to c340ft
Loop extended east end

1920s

Loading Bank cut back, later out of use
Loop points moved back at both ends

PLANS ARE CLOSE TO SCALE BUT NOT PRECISELY SO

In contrast, this September 1950 view shows the replacement eastern crossover installed some time in the 1930s (see plan p.58), the west end of which was adjacent to the old platform buildings. Here there is scarcely any curvature in the turnout at all! and the photograph highlights the generally primitive nature of the CLR's track up to the 1950s. The siding curving away to the north was clearly still in regular use at this date.
Brian Hilton, courtesy Charles Phillips

Corringham station, probably in the late 1930s. The station nameboard had been moved back to its original position. The platform has become completely grassgrown beyond the area trod by the passengers on one- or two-coach trains. However the line is still weed-free alongside the loading platform, and the vegetation is still being kept back from the run-round line.

below
A rare view (c1949) of the line at the point where it leaves the marshes and starts its 1 in 56 climb up to Corringham (the point at which the back cover and p.57 upper photos were also taken). Note the cycle tracks in the mud to the right of the track, where people from the Digby Road area cycled along the line to Ironlatch. The condition of the track on the curve lends credibility to the reports of derailments!
R.S. Carpenter collection, photographer unknown

These two views show the 1914 Avonside (recognisable by its shabby condition and missing chimney cap). The coach is also in a poor external state, so the photographs are probably c1946. Here the fireman is dealing with the gates at Ironlatch.

John Scott-Morgan collection

The same train awaiting departure from Corringham, a few minutes earlier.

John Scott-Morgan collection

A CLR CAB RIDE

This trip was made by Brian Hilton on Friday 15th September 1950, on the afternoon train from Corringham. The loco was the 1914 Avonside. (The 1672 works plate photograph at p.80 was taken at Corringham on this visit).

All photos - Brian Hilton (courtesy Charles Phillips)

right
Awaiting departure from Corringham.

below left
Looking west from Ironlatch crossing, after the fireman had shut the gates behind the train.

below right
Driver's eye view of Ironlatch looking east on 15th September 1950. It had become the custom here for the fireman to jump off well short of the crossing and run to the gates, in the hope of being able to shut them in the face of approaching cycling workmates!

below
Similar view of the Haven Hotel crossing. This crossing retained its single iron gates, which can be assumed original given their similarity to the original gates at Kynochtown seen at p.33. The points for the Coryton station loop are seen beyond the crossing.

right
The loco returns to shed. This view shows the 1923-1950/1 layout here, which was soon to be altered again.

61

STEPHENSON LOCOMOTIVE SOCIETY VISIT SATURDAY 17th MAY 1947

All photographs by H.C.Casserley

The party boarded the 11.06 from Tilbury to Stanford-le-Hope and made their way to Corringham to catch the scheduled 12.15pm (that was the time they were given) to Coryton. After an hour looking round the sights at Coryton, they were provided with a 1.30pm special working back to Corringham.

left
'High Noon' – members take up position at Corringham to photograph the arrival of the service train. Note the timbers between the platform wall and the track to prevent creeping (better seen in the inside front cover view).

above
The 12.0 from Coryton arrives behind the 1917 Avonside.

left
Driver Ted Mynett is clearly enjoying the occasion as he prepares to run round.

62

top
Note the sleeper across the rail at left – probably (by this date) because the track beyond was decaying.

above left
The party wait while the loco runs round. The normally-deserted station was no doubt always an attractive playground for the Digby Road children, but the arrival of so many strange men in a place not known for visitors must have given something extra to talk about.

above right
Ready for departure.

right
During the walkabout at Coryton, Ted Mynett chats with the visitors on the platform. This was how the history of the CLR was passed into print!

**BIRMINGHAM LOCOMOTIVE CLUB VISIT
SATURDAY 12th JUNE 1948**

Members pose on the 1917 Avonside after arriving at Coryton. Standing on the track to the right of the loco chimney, with dark tie, is Eric Tonks who was a leading figure in the Club's Industrial Locomotive section, which subsequently became the separate Industrial Railway Society.
See also the back cover photograph.
Roger Carpenter collection

SOUTHERN COUNTIES TOURING SOCIETY VISIT SATURDAY 25th JUNE 1949

The SCTS visit in 1949 seemed to result in a larger amount of film being expended than any other day in the CLR's life! It looks like early afternoon by the shadows here as the chaps await departure from Coryton, so they must have had an extra train arranged after the normal Saturday workings. The white headcode disc borne by the 1917 Avonside had no doubt been brought along by the party.

The party were conveyed from Stanford-le-Hope in Cory's Gilford bus EV 6952.
V.C. Jones, courtesy Alan Osborne

Exploring at Corringham. The vegetation seems to be closing in altogether here! Note the trolley in the foreground.
Ivor Gotheridge collection

Chapter Five

THE VACUUM/MOBIL YEARS 1950 – 1996

THE GENESIS OF THE NEW CORYTON REFINERY

The processes by which the new refinery came to be built in 1950-53 began in 1942 when the Cory Brothers & Co Ltd company was taken over by Powell Duffryn Ltd. This group was, like Cory's, heavily involved in coal mining in South Wales, coal shipping worldwide, and other fuel interests. The takeover brought no immediate visible change at Coryton (the Cory name continued to be used here until 1950).

Then in 1950 Powell Duffryn, seeking an investment outlet for the compensation money they had received under coal nationalisation in 1947, reached agreement with the US company Socony-Vacuum under which Powell Duffryn would take a 50% stake in their UK offshoot the Vacuum Oil Co Ltd, and put up 50% of the cost of the construction of a new refinery at Coryton to process Middle East crude. The Vacuum Oil Co took over the Coryton site in 1950 as part of this. At this time the oil industry at large was moving towards setting up crude oil refining operations in the UK and Europe (up to 1939 almost all crude refining had been done in the countries of origin, and Socony-Vacuum had no UK refinery prior to Coryton). Vacuum UK also had a financial incentive to set up a UK refinery, arising from the postwar 'dollar shortage', as all their oil hitherto had been imported from the USA and had to be paid for in dollars, whereas Middle East crude would be paid for in sterling.

For background to all this we must delve briefly into the complex history of John D. Rockefeller's Standard Oil Company and its successors.

The US Vacuum Oil Co was founded in 1866 and Rockefeller's Standard Oil acquired a 75% interest in it in 1879. Vacuum commenced UK activities in 1885 and set up a separate UK company, The Vacuum Oil Co Ltd, in 1901. In 1911, when the US government secured the break up of Standard Oil, seen as a dangerous monopoly, one of the many smaller successor US companies formed was the Standard Oil Company of New York (SOCONY). In 1931 SOCONY acquired the *whole* of the assets of the US Vacuum Oil Co, and changed its name to the Socony-Vacuum Corporation (from 1934, the Socony-Vacuum Oil Co Inc). The UK Vacuum Oil Co Ltd kept its name but its ownership changed in accordance with the US developments.

Up to 1950 Socony-Vacuum had only marketed lubricating oils in the UK and Europe, under the brand 'Mobiloil'. The Coryton refinery was to produce luboils but its prime role was to be the production of petrol to enable entry into the UK petrol retailing market. The first 'Mobil' petrol stations in the UK opened in 1952.

Powell Duffryn in the event withdrew from their share in Vacuum Oil after the refinery was completed, thereby passing from our story.

The US company was renamed again as the Socony Mobil Oil Co in 1955, and Mobil Oil Corporation in 1966. The UK company, similarly, became the Mobil Oil Co Ltd in December 1955. In consequence Coryton became a 'Mobil' refinery, and the Vacuum name disappeared.

Coryton village escaped being renamed again as 'Vacuum-town' or 'Mobiltown'!

BUILDING THE NEW REFINERY

As Vacuum UK had no previous experience of refinery construction, a team from the USA, known as the 'Texan Taskforce', was sent over to manage the construction project. The main contract was given to the Lummus Co of London in September 1950. Under them, John Laing & Son acted as principal civil engineering contractors, and Costain - John Brown Ltd as the principal mechanical engineering contractor (erection of structures). The new refinery was built on the same ENE-WSW / NNW-SSE 'grid' as the existing Cory's works, and most of the main Cory's tank farm at the eastern end of the site was retained in use. Several other 75ft tanks that were in the way of the new plan had a 'canal' dug around them and were floated to new positions pulled by men with ropes! The 1920s refinery

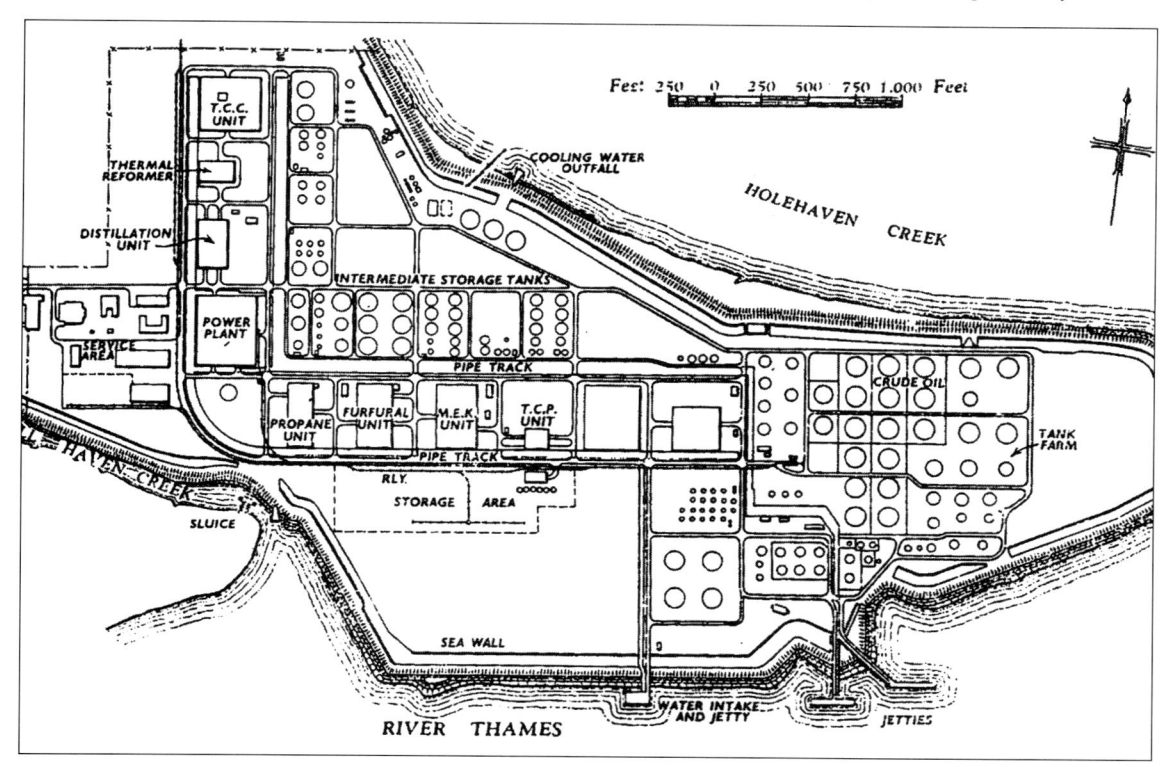

Plan of the new refinery as completed in 1953/4. All processing of crude oil began in the Distillation Unit. The Thermal Reformer Unit and Thermofor Catalytic Cracking Unit (T.C.C.) produced different grades of petrol and diesel. Along the south side of the refinery area, the Propane De-Asphalting Unit, Solvent Refining Furfural Unit, M.E.K. Dewaxing Unit, and Continuous Percolation Unit (T.C.P.), formed consecutive stages in the production of lubricating oils and waxes.

The two existing tanker jetties (*cf* 1939 OS) had been extended, and could now take 32,000 ton tankers at any state of the tide. The new water intake jetty to the west housed pumps to extract from the Thames all the cooling and processing water needed for the refinery.

Construction workers head home at the end of the day shift, probably in summer 1952 judging by the advanced state of many of the buildings. The temporary gates through which they are leaving are on the site of the new main entrance gate. The three chimneys at right belong to the power plant. The long queue in front of the power plant may be waiting for buses. Only one car and one bicycle are visible.

The aftermath of the 31st January 1953 North Sea flooding, showing the new refinery entrance road from the bottom end of Fleet Street. The contractors' hoarding reads 'New Refinery Under Construction For VACUUM OIL COMPANY LIMITED...Contractors THE LUMMUS COMPANY LIMITED', with the subcontractors listed below. Note the separate sign directing lorry drivers to the Bulk Terminal via Fleet Street. Coryton residents had to be evacuated after the flood but the waters did not rise high enough here to pose any threat to life. On the Sunday morning 1st February some 500 refinery staff came in after a loudspeaker appeal in Corringham and Stanford-le-Hope and helped put down thousands of sandbags before the next tide.

buildings were obsolete and were all removed.

The main part of the new refinery was on ground that had remained as undeveloped marsh hitherto, between Coryton village and the Cory's refinery. In consequence a large amount of fill had to be brought in and tipped on the marshes. 13,000 reinforced concrete piles then had to be driven to support the buildings. A new main road entrance was provided to the site, however the old entrance through the Kynoch's gates was retained as a secondary entrance, used mainly by road tankers to and from the new Bulk Terminal at the north end of the site. This continued until summer 1969 when a new road was opened direct from the Manorway north of the Haven Hotel crossing to a new No.2 Gate close to the Bulk Terminal, and the Kynoch's gates entrance was blocked off.

The first shipment of Middle East crude arrived from Kuwait in August 1952, starting the build up of crude stocks ready for the opening of the refinery.

The first unit to be commissioned was the Power House, on 1st January 1953. The Crude Distillation Unit followed on Saturday 31st January 1953. In a repetition of Kynoch's experiences in 1897, the east coast floods struck on the very first night after opening! However this only set back the commissioning by a few weeks. On 11th March a Charrington's road tanker took out the first load of processed fuel oil. Most of the other refinery units came into use later in 1953.

The formal opening ceremony was held on 27th May 1954, when HM the Queen Mother arrived from Tower Pier in the PLA's *St Katharine*, accompanied by the PLA Chairman Viscount Waverley. Before the ceremony the Queen Mother made a tour of Coryton village 'and visited one of the houses'.

The total cost was reported as £15 million. The refinery was designed to process 900,000 tons of crude per annum, producing
  300,000 tons of petrol
  160,000 tons of diesel
  100,000 tons of lubricating oils
  290,000 tons of heavy fuel.
These initial production figures would soon be greatly exceeded.

The initial workforce was 630.

All the crude oil came from the Middle East in the early years. The first North Sea crude arrived in 1976, and by the mid 1980s almost all the oil processed here was coming from the North Sea.

CHANGING TIMES ON THE CLR - MODERNISATION AND PASSENGER CLOSURE

The entire shareholding in the Corringham Light Railway company was transferred from Cory's (Powell Duffryn) to the Vacuum Oil Co Ltd on 1st September 1950, paralleling what had happened in 1921. A plaque was duly placed on the doorway of Mobil House in London announcing that this was the office of the Corringham Light Railway Company.

The new owners immediately announced a modernisation programme for the railway. The internal sidings were to be altered to serve the new refinery (done in 1951-3; see plan p.73). The steam locos would be replaced by diesels, and the track on the Thames Haven - Coryton section would be resleepered and reballasted. The *Railway Magazine* lamented in January 1951 that 'the railway is to lose those quaint characteristics which have attracted the railway enthusiast for many years'. The track improvement was supposed to have started in December 1950, but it is not evident that anything of substance was actually done at this time, and the new owners also allowed the line to become weed-infested in a way never seen before (p.70). It was a good number of years before the Thames Haven - Coryton section was eventually fully relaid with modern chaired track (photo p.75). Dieselisation was also delayed, the first diesel only arriving in 1955 and the steam locos continuing in use until 1956/7. In the event, then, the 'modernisation' to produce the 'new' CLR was a more gradual process than anticipated.

Nothing was announced about the future of the passenger service in 1950, but it would seem that the new management quickly came to see it as an anachronism. Indeed, it could have been taken off back in the late 1920s without significantly inconveniencing anybody! In due course it was decreed that Saturday 1st March 1952 would be the last day of operation. The local press were advised and John C. Gridley, Chairman of Vacuum Oil in the UK 1949-1968, came down from London with Mrs Gridley to make an event of it.

Corringham station buildings and platform were already being demolished when a *Railway Observer* correspondent visited on 12th April 1952.

The track on the Corringham line was also lifted within a few weeks of the end of the service: another *RO* reporter visiting on 12th June 1952 reported lifting complete 'except for a quarter of a mile at the Coryton end'. This residual section, from the triangle as far as the occupation crossing at the LATHOL site entrance (grid reference 73258265), is still in situ on the 1960 OS map.

above left

Our last glimpse of the workaday passenger service comes from a visit made by Frank Church on an unrecorded Saturday in summer 1951. Here is the 12.0 train waiting at Coryton, with the 1914 Avonside in charge. This may have been at the start of the 1917 loco's lengthy overhaul period (see p.77).
Frank Church

above right

The 12.0 arrives at Corringham and a few workers alight under the ever-expanding trees. The only known recorded usage figure for an ordinary day latterly is 11 on the 5.10pm from Coryton on 8th March 1951.
Frank Church

THE LAST DAY

The fact that the CLR passenger service was to end after Saturday 1st March 1952 did not become generally known in advance to the enthusiast fraternity, although there was a local press presence and several other local people turned out. These views were taken by Peter Wilde who had got the tip off at another recent visit and cycled here from Southgate to record the end. The 'last train', the 12.20pm from Corringham, had an abnormally large number of passengers, as this was the day of the annual Coryton children's party, and the children of staff living in Corringham always went by train. With Ted Mynett on this last train was fireman/shunter Clarrie Ockendon.

left
The 1917 loco in its recently-applied Vacuum scarlet livery, just west of Coryton level crossing on Saturday 15th March 1952. The Pegasus trademark used by Socony-Vacuum-Mobil was pronounced Pe-GAS-us by its US inventors!
Frank Church

middle
The 1917 loco with the tracklifting train on the Corringham line near Iron Latch some time in summer 1952. Fobbing church appears in the background.
Frank Church

A VISIT IN MAY 1954

Fewer enthusiasts came after the end of the passenger service, however Ken Butcher and Brian Pask made a visit on Saturday 8th May 1954. Although neither had a top-quality camera, these shots of the ordinary daily goods activities in the pre-bulk train period are a valuable record.

bottom
At Corringham the station buildings and platform had been wholly demolished.
Ken Butcher

opposite top left
Coryton station platform - the east end ramp, made up of old sleepers, had already collapsed. The crossover at the east end of the platform had been taken out shortly after the passenger service ended.
Ken Butcher

opposite middle left
Shunting activity west of the level crossing. The spur at the end of the platform line had also been lifted by this date.
Brian Pask

opposite bottom
In due course our visitors found this ensemble - the nearest thing to a goods 'train' in any CLR photo - ready for propelling from Coryton to Thames Haven, whereupon they successfully sought a footplate ride. The 1917 Avonside sports its recently-acquired spark arrestor, and number '2'. The two open wagons loaded with cylindrical tanks are LNER-built six-plank unfitted 12 ton open wagons with wood frames. The van is a Diagram 43 vacuum-fitted LNER ventilated fruit van (which were regularly used for more general purposes).
Ken Butcher

68

above
 More shunting, here seen by the loco shed. *Brian Pask*

below
 The undercarriage of one of the LT&SR coaches was found abandoned alongside the Salt Fleet on the siding that curved away northwards west of the level crossing. It was presumably this coach's body that ended up with a local farmer for some years. *Ken Butcher*

69

THE CORRINGHAM LINE AFTER LIFTING

below

For many years the line from Corringham station to Ironlatch had been used as an unofficial cycle- and footpath by those living in the Digby Road area, to avoid the more circuitous route via Church Road (see also photo p.59). This continued for a good while after the railway was lifted, hence the path being still clear in this 1960s view on the approach to Corringham station. But the number of cyclists later fell off, and then the station site was sold off blocking direct access from Fobbing Road. In 2007 the only walkable section of the trackbed at the Corringham end is for some 100 yards southwards from the footpath crossing at grid reference 715838 (used for unofficial back access to the Pegasus Club sports pitches).

left

This notice was erected by the CLR at Ironlatch after tracklifting, to prevent the trackbed becoming a legal right of way. Photographed in 1957.

Hugh Davies

left

Ironlatch level crossing in March 1957, looking east. As usual in such cases the rails across the road were left in situ.

Hugh Davies

below

Just east of Ironlatch, looking east along the still fenced trackbed, with the Manorway at left.

THE WEEDY LATE 1950s

Coryton station in the late 1950s weed growth period. Looking slightly out of place in the background is the 270ft steel tower of the Catalytic Cracking Unit, built in 1952/3. Note the 24-wire telegraph pole route to Coryton (nothing to do with the CLR).

Lens of Sutton Association

THE END OF THE CLR COMPANY (1971)

There was no need for the continued existence of the CLR as a separate company, now that the sole purpose of the remaining section was to convey Mobil's own freight traffic. In 1967 Mobil asked their Parliamentary Agents to apply for a Light Railway Transfer Order empowering the transfer of ownership of the railway to the Mobil Oil Co Ltd. This was obtained in September 1969. However the actual conveyance of the assets was not effected until some time in winter 1970/71. *Mobil News* in October 1970 carried a two-page feature with the tongue-in-cheek headline 'Mobil make takeover bid for the CLR', explaining that the end of the CLR was nigh, although 'no-one connected with it will be losing his job'. It continued 'Once the assets are transferred in accordance with the Order, the Secretariat will begin to negotiate with the Parliamentary Agents for the drafting and execution of a second order to be known as the Corringham Light Railway (Winding Up) Order'.

This second Order (S.I. 1971 No. 1494) was made on 6th September 1971 and wound up the CLR company with effect from 20th September 1971. It noted that 'the company have, owing to the sale of their undertaking, ceased to be in a position to carry out the objects for which they were incorporated'.

The company had seen 72 years of (somewhat notional) life - far more than most light railways created under the 1896 Act. It might be noted that up to 1970 the 'CLR' name had still been in regular use amongst Coryton staff.

THE END OF CORYTON VILLAGE (1970)

In the early years of Vacuum / Mobil ownership, it was assumed by all that Coryton village would have a permanent future. Indeed, in 1952 Vacuum built 16 new semi-detached houses in a new road on the site of the 1915-19 men's colony, named Freeman Avenue in commemoration of J.H. Freeman who retired at this date. A third pair of 'Villas' was also built around this time, and a further two houses in Freeman Avenue soon followed.

In 1965 the Church Avenue bungalows were declared unfit and the occupants were moved elsewhere. But as late as 1967 the houses in Fleet Street were all given a major refurbishment by Mobil. It therefore came as something of a shock when the company announced in 1969 that the whole village would have to be removed for an enlargement of the refinery. Within six months everybody had gone, most to council housing in Corringham and Stanford-le-Hope, others to Basildon. The village was then demolished in summer 1970. A new £220m Fluid Catalytic Cracker complex was built on the site in 1978-82, replacing the 1953 TCC unit. The Queen Mother made a second visit to Coryton on 4th November 1982 for the formal opening.

Subsequent growth of the refinery has seen some expansion northwards, nevertheless most of the northern end of the Kynochs site still remains empty.

MOBIL RAIL OPERATIONS 1953 - 1996

All rail distribution of oil products was from the start handled at the Bulk Terminal at the north end of the refinery. In its original form the rail component of the Terminal consisted of just two short sidings (track plan p.72) with no structures. Road tankers were loaded at adjacent covered loading bays. By 1958 the Terminal was handling 75 million gallons a year, the majority of which went by rail. Road delivery was used for shorter-distance deliveries across a wide area of south-east England.

From 1958 there were normally two or three diesel locos in use here: details are given in Chapter 6.

In 1964 the Bulk Terminal rail facilities were improved for increased throughput. The new equipment enabled top and bottom loading of all grades of fuel, with a rail tanker loading rate of 300 gallons a minute.

There had been no changes to the track layout in the Coryton station area when the refinery was built, but as traffic increased it became evident that there was insufficient siding capacity for tank wagons, and around 1964 a new yard with seven through sidings was opened close by the Terminal (to the east of Coryton level crossing). This entailed the demolition of the existing loco shed, and a replacement shed was built within the new yard.

In the early 1960s there was a rapid change to 'block train' operation. (In some cases the Mobil wagons were combined with Shell wagons at Thames Haven Yard to form a block train). Block trains from Coryton ran mostly to the West Midlands and East Anglia, either to inland distribution depots (notably Charringtons at Norwich, Cambridge, and Bedworth Hawkesbury Lane) or to large industrial customers' private sidings. A new ten-year contract between Mobil and BR was signed in 1963.

In the early Mobil years the CLR still handled a modest amount of general inwards rail traffic for the refinery (as indicated by the provision of a rail siding to the refinery stores building). However as happened everywhere this general traffic fell away in the 1960s leaving only the block train workings.

April 1967 saw the commissioning of an LPG Terminal comprising two sidings on the south side of the new yard. This was provided specifically for a new Block Train operation conveying butane and heavy fuel oil to Henry Wiggin & Co Ltd at Hereford, who had hitherto been receiving butane from

continued at page 74

Coryton village during demolition in 1970. The Institute, and two pairs of the Freeman Avenue houses, cling on. (*Mobil News* May 1970 had reported the start of demolition and noted that Freeman Avenue would be left till last). In the background are the 1953 Catalytic Cracking Unit and the three chimneys of the power plant; but the nearer refinery structures all represent 1960s expansion.

above left
A 1964 view showing one of the Bulk Terminal staff coupling the hose for bottom-loading one of the 8,000 gallon four-wheel Mobil tankers then recently brought into service.
Mobil

above right
The 'No. 1' half of the rebuilt Andrew Barclay loco is seen here working separately in 1970 at the east end of the Bulk Terminal. The northernmost siding, on which it is shunting, had been added c1964.
Mobil

left
A 1970 aerial view, looking north over the Bulk Terminal area. The then-new 19-bay road tanker facility is at top left; the rail terminal (in its '1964' form) at middle left; the new 7-road yard and new loco shed at centre; and the 1967 LPG Terminal (with all eleven of the butane tankers present) at bottom right. Coryton level crossing is just off picture at bottom left.
Mobil

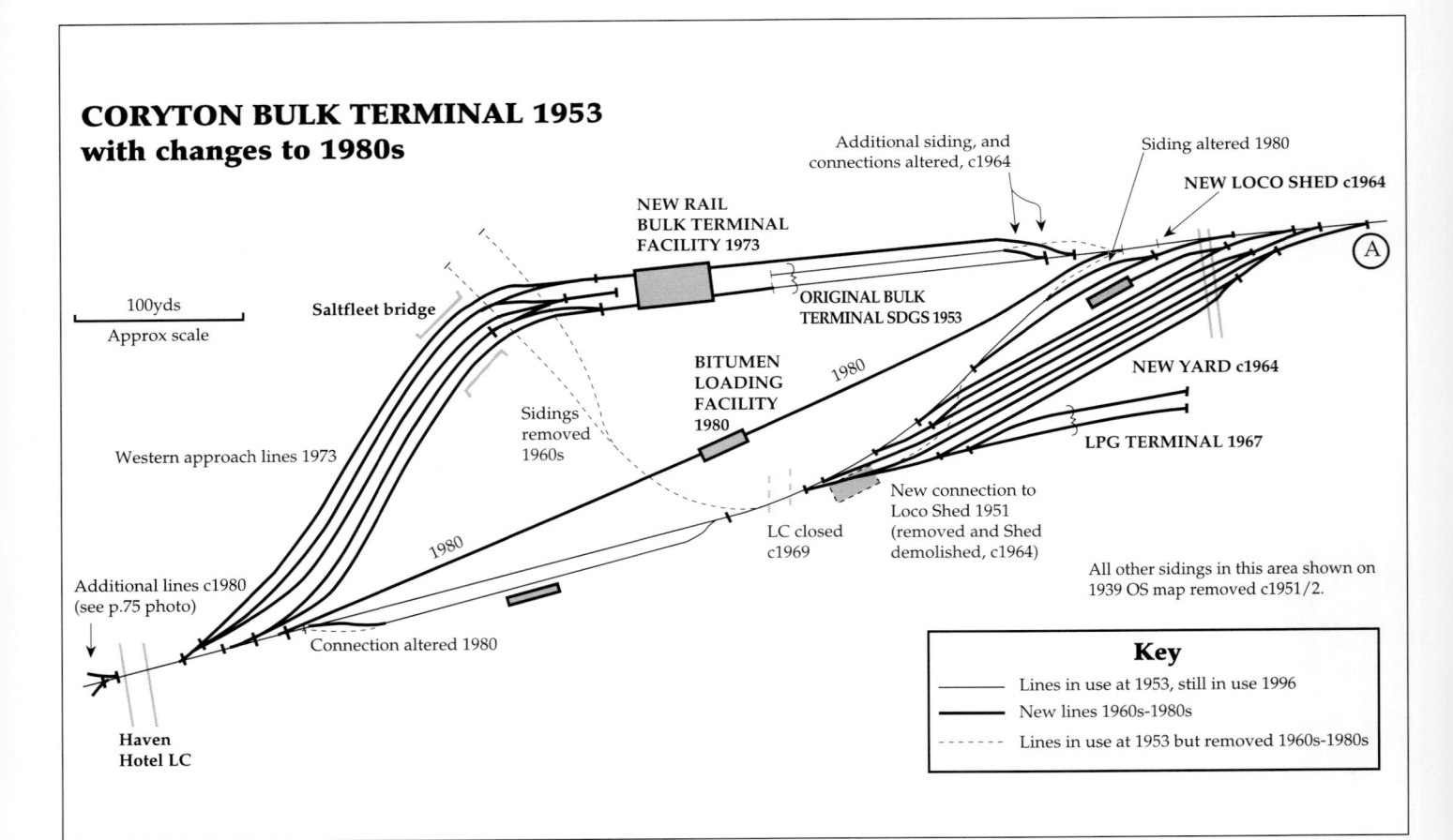

CORYTON BULK TERMINAL 1953
with changes to 1980s

Additional siding, and connections altered, c1964
Siding altered 1980
NEW LOCO SHED c1964
NEW RAIL BULK TERMINAL FACILITY 1973
Saltfleet bridge
ORIGINAL BULK TERMINAL SDGS 1953
100yds Approx scale
BITUMEN LOADING FACILITY 1980
NEW YARD c1964
Sidings removed 1960s
1980
LPG TERMINAL 1967
Western approach lines 1973
New connection to Loco Shed 1951 (removed and Shed demolished, c1964)
LC closed c1969
All other sidings in this area shown on 1939 OS map removed c1951/2.
Additional lines c1980 (see p.75 photo)
Connection altered 1980
Haven Hotel LC

Key
—— Lines in use at 1953, still in use 1996
━━ New lines 1960s-1980s
- - - Lines in use at 1953 but removed 1960s-1980s

72

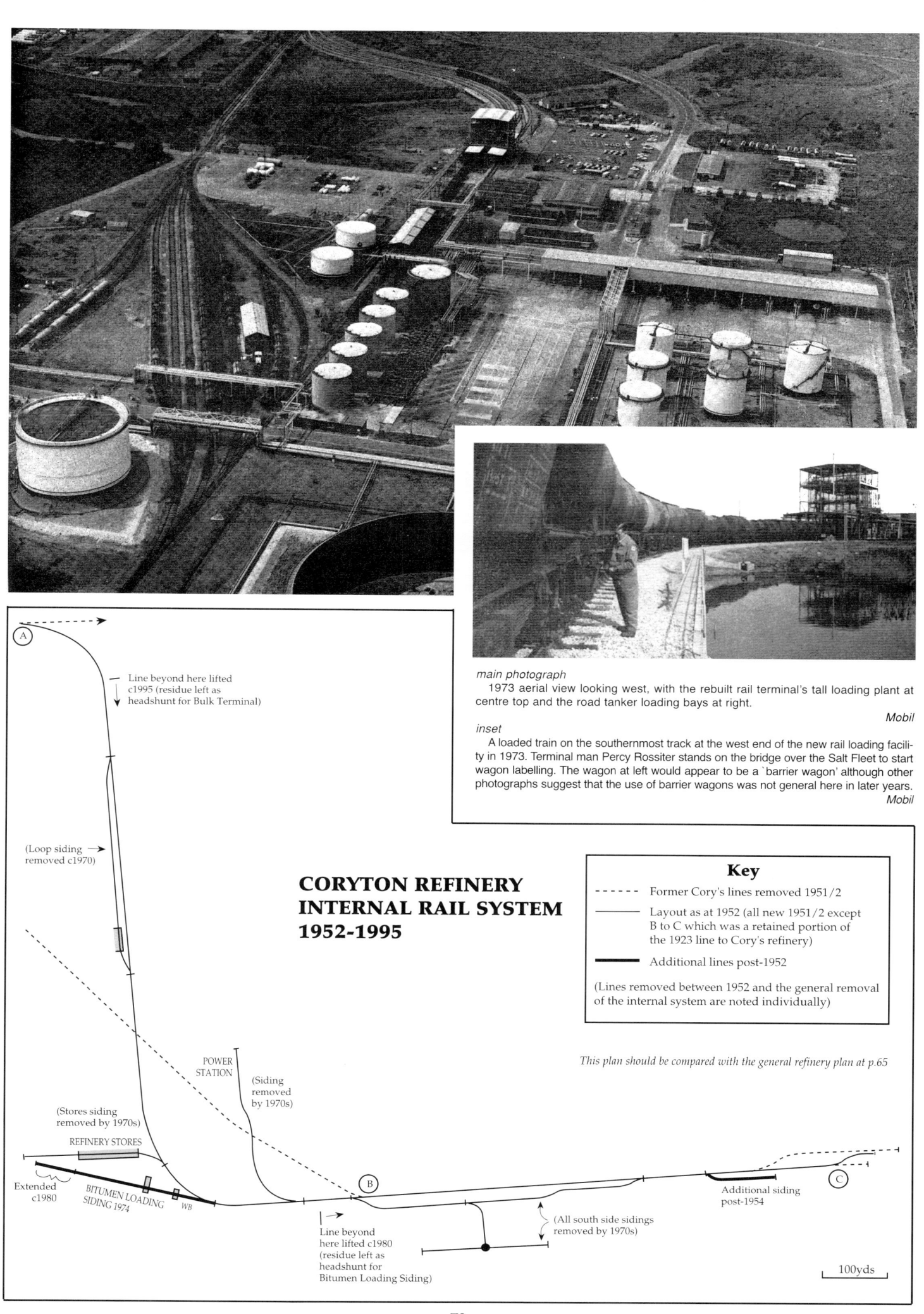

main photograph
1973 aerial view looking west, with the rebuilt rail terminal's tall loading plant at centre top and the road tanker loading bays at right.
Mobil

inset
A loaded train on the southernmost track at the west end of the new rail loading facility in 1973. Terminal man Percy Rossiter stands on the bridge over the Salt Fleet to start wagon labelling. The wagon at left would appear to be a `barrier wagon' although other photographs suggest that the use of barrier wagons was not general here in later years.
Mobil

CORYTON REFINERY INTERNAL RAIL SYSTEM 1952-1995

Key
- - - - - Former Cory's lines removed 1951/2
———— Layout as at 1952 (all new 1951/2 except B to C which was a retained portion of the 1923 line to Cory's refinery)
——— Additional lines post-1952

(Lines removed between 1952 and the general removal of the internal system are noted individually)

This plan should be compared with the general refinery plan at p.65

Line beyond here lifted c1995 (residue left as headshunt for Bulk Terminal)

(Loop siding removed c1970)

(Stores siding removed by 1970s)

REFINERY STORES

Extended c1980

BITUMEN LOADING SIDING 1974

WB

POWER STATION

(Siding removed by 1970s)

Line beyond here lifted c1980 (residue left as headshunt for Bitumen Loading Siding)

(All south side sidings removed by 1970s)

Additional siding post-1954

100yds

73

Aerial view of the refinery in 1974. The village has been completely cleared but the roads still stand out and no work has started yet on the new Catalytic Cracker complex. The new rail yard and the Bulk Terminal in its 1973 enlarged form are clear. Note the white bridge over the Salt Fleet for the Bulk Terminal approach lines. The second refinery entrance road of 1969, which was linked to the new Manorway roundabout in 1970/1, is at lower left.

Coryton by road tankers. Eleven new 'gas cars' were built for this butane traffic (photo p.72), and six new fuel oil cars. This train made one or two round trips per week.

In 1969/70 a new 19-bay road tanker loading complex was built to replace the 1953 road tanker bays. This was needed for overall increased demand, not because of any transfer of traffic from rail to road.

A new aviation fuel block train movement began in June 1970 to Salfords for Gatwick Airport. A ten-car train left Coryton at 9.41 am every weekday and was combined with Shell wagons at Thames Haven. Mobil had previously been serving Gatwick by road since 1964.

In 1971-3 over £1 million was spent on a considerable enlargement of the Bulk Terminal rail facilities. The new loading plant was served by the existing tracks from the east, and by five new tracks from the west, crossing the Salt Fleet on a wide bridge. An operator in the above-track control room worked the loading lances and the powered winch system for moving wagons under the loader. The loading rate was 1,800 gallons a minute - six times the rate of the 1964 equipment. This enabled a train of twenty 45-ton wagons to be loaded in 3 hours 15 minutes, or a train of ten of the new 100-ton bogie tankers in 2 hours 45 minutes. Men were still needed at trackside to open and close the tankers' hatches. The new system was designed to deal with 65 block trains a week.

By 1973 the Bulk Terminal was handling 800 million gallons a year (road plus rail). There were 92 Terminal staff including 30 road tanker drivers.

A Bitumen Plant opened at the refinery in January 1974. This product had at this date to be loaded close to the production point, so a road/rail Bitumen Blending and Loading Area was constructed, south of the refinery stores building. The new rail siding for this is shown in the photo at p.75 top. The first rail traffic from here was a block train movement to a terminal at Frome operated by Anglo-American Asphalt (Bitumen) Ltd, serving the coated stone plants at the nearby Foster Yeoman, Western Roadstone, and Hobbs quarries.

A new bitumen contract commencing in 1980 required a 25-car block train to Kilnhurst which could not readily be accommodated at the existing siding. Accordingly a Bitumen Loading Facility was constructed on a new siding adjacent to the Bulk Terminal (see plan p.72), and brought into use in July 1980. A mile long heated six inch pipe linked the bitumen plant to the new loading facility. This was to be the *last* expansion of rail facilities at Coryton.

As happened everywhere in the UK, oil traffic by rail started falling off in the 1980s as road transport became more competitive for longer journeys, thanks to new motorways and heavier lorries. This particularly applied in the case of the general distribution of petrol to garages, where rail transport meant a further transfer at the inland depot. Pipelines were also becoming a rival to rail for the major bulk flows. In the 1960s Mobil already had use of the UKOP (United Kingdom Oil Pipeline) which took oil from Thames-side to Mobil's own inland depots at Buncefield (Hemel Hempstead) and Kingsbury (West Midlands). A branch pipeline ran from Buncefield to Heathrow Airport which Mobil served from 1965. This was extended to Gatwick in 1983, replacing the rail flow. Then in 1985 a pipeline - served distribution terminal was opened at Wymondham to serve most of East Anglia.

After Shell opened their new 'Shellhaven Sidings' terminal in 1983, Thames Haven Yard was left with Mobil traffic only. An

above
The Bitumen Blending & Loading Area when new in 1974, looking east from the end of the siding. The overhead blending/loading equipment had three loading points below, two of which were road-only, and the third (on the south side) road or rail. Rail wagons were moved to/from the loading point by means of an endless cable driven by an electric winch, seen in the channel at right. *Mobil*

below
The Haven Hotel level crossing c1970, showing the manual barriers that had replaced the metal gates in the 1960s. *Mobil*

From the Haven Hotel level crossing looking east to Coryton station in the late 1970s, with the five lines to the Bulk Terminal curving away to the left. Half barriers had been installed in 1971 but the installation was discovered to be non-compliant for a public road, and on 12.11.1973 full lifting barriers were commissioned in lieu. These had traffic light signals for both road traffic and (right) trains.
Ivor Gotheridge collection

Looking west from the Haven Hotel level crossing on 2nd April 1988, showing the additional lines laid by Mobil on either side of the original running line at an unknown date c1980. The north side line has since been lifted.
Ken Butcher

A c1980 view at Thames Haven west of Dock House crossing, with a rake of tankers on the CLR Loop Siding, which was installed at an unknown date c1970. The Shell Reedham Sidings are straight ahead and the Thames Haven Branch running line curves away to the left. A view facing the other way can be seen at *The Thames Haven Railway* p.73 middle.
Chris Turner

The remaining section of Coryton station platform in 1991, now again weed- and shrub-free. It had been repaired by Mobil in 1986. The nameboard was bright red with the name in white painted letters.
P.D. May

agreement was made between BR and Mobil in 1986 under which Mobil paid £10,000 a year to 'lease' the Yard. Mobil locos, which had for some time previously been running beyond the CLR/BR boundary into the Yard, now also carried out the shunting there. Loaded trains from Coryton now ran into sidings 11-17, whence they were taken away by a BR loco. Empties were brought in by the BR loco into sidings 1-4, whence they were taken away by the Mobil loco. This change required the laying in of an additional crossover immediately east of Dock House level crossing, as there had hitherto been no direct connection between the CLR and sidings 1-4. (In 1959 during the discussions on a possible signal at the CLR/BR boundary, Mobil had asked the BR Traffic Manager for his thoughts on 'the longer term proposal of enabling our locos to haul wagons into your reception sidings instead of having to propel as now'. This might be taken as meaning that Mobil locos in 1959 were already propelling trains through into Thames Haven Yard, but is more likely to mean that they were still only propelling as far as the BR boundary).

When Shell abandoned rail distribution from Shell Haven refinery in 1993, the Mobil Coryton traffic was left as the only remaining traffic on the Thames Haven branch.

As the use of rail for purposes other than bulk trains fell off, the 1951-3 lines within the refinery itself were gradually cut back until there was only a short length left acting as a head-shunt for the Bulk Terminal.

The Kilnhurst bitumen contract ended in 1997, and this was the end of railborne bitumen distribution from Coryton.

Chapter Six

LOCOMOTIVES AND COACHING STOCK

CLR STEAM LOCOMOTIVES

KITSON T109 of 1884, *Cordite*

Acquired by the CLR late 1900, scrapped date not known.

0-4-0 Well Tank. 3ft wheels, 6ft wheelbase, weight in working order 10 tons 2 cwts.

A detailed article by V.J. Bradley on this locomotive (and the many erroneous 'facts' on it given in previous accounts) appeared in *The Industrial Locomotive* No.99 (2001) pp. 284-304. See also corrective letters in Nos. 112 and 113. Some further points on minor matters are added here.

This was one of three locos built as a batch by Kitson for the West Lancashire Railway in 1884. They were Kitson's T109/T110/T111 and the WLR's Nos 9, 10, and 11. The loco which ended up on the CLR was T109 / No.9. Along with T111/No.11 it had been sent back by the WLR to Kitson in 1885, owing to the WLR's financial problems. Both were in due course overhauled by Kitson and replated '1893'. T109 was sold by Kitson to the contractor J. Linton & Co, then working at Newport (S.Wales), and T111 to the Liverpool Overhead Railway. (The 1905 *Locomotive Magazine* article in saying that the CLR loco was 'built 1893' must surely have been relying on reports of the works plate. There are actually no photographs showing a works plate on the CLR loco, but it is known that T111 on the Liverpool Overhead Railway only had a works plate on the left hand side, and all the photographs of the CLR loco happen to be of the right hand side).

The *Locomotive Magazine* article stated also that the loco had been 'built for the Barry Dock Co'. In fact no such company existed - the docks at Barry were owned by the Barry Railway Company. There may nevertheless be some real fire behind this erroneous smoke. Linton & Geen (as they had become) offered their Kitson loco for sale in spring 1899 after giving up their Tredegar Dock contract in Newport, and it is *possible* that when it was bought by the CLR after that (or after an intermediate owner in 1899/1900), it came to Kynochtown by sea *from* Barry. A loco of this type might well have been refused travel by rail on its own wheels. There are actually no specific contemporary references to the purchase of the loco by the CLR, but it was on the CLR by late 1900. The statement made by the CLR to Von Donop in February 1901 (p.25), that this was not the engine actually intended for working the line, suggests that it may originally have been regarded purely as a stop gap until the arrival of the loco ordered from Kerr Stuart. In the event it was retained, and the photographic evidence suggests that it was in regular use up to c1914.

When the loco arrived on the CLR, it had large block buffers (confirming previous use by contractors) and cab cut-outs (an original feature of the three 1884 locos). The block buffers were soon replaced by standard sprung buffers, and later the cab cut-outs were plated over. Later still replacement double side-steps were fitted. These developments are illustrated in the photographs at pages 32 and 35.

The loco is in unlined livery in all known photographs. This may well have been red (like *Kynite*) but there is no contemporary record. It was named *Cordite*, as attested by the contemporary report quoted at p.29, however this name must have been somewhat inconspicuously painted as there is no sign of it in the one correctly-angled photograph (p.32 top). The *Locomotive Magazine* article mentions no name. In railway historical writing the earliest reference traced to the name is in Eric S. Tonks' 1950 book *Light and Miniature Railway Locomotives of Great Britain*. From there it was copied into the BLCILIS / IRS Pocket Books. In his 1957 *Branch Line News* article Gotheridge added the supposed alternative/subsequent names *The Major* and *Cordite Major*, which are not very likely, indeed the latter makes no sense.

There is no evidence of the loco being in use, or even present on site, after c1915 (although it probably did remain on site for several years). It certainly could not have handled the much heavier passenger trains after 1915, and goods traffic also increased then. It may have become superfluous as soon as the new Kerr Stuart loco arrived in 1915. There is no evidence but one assumes it was scrapped on site. The 'c1935' scrapping date given in IRS records may just reflect the 1936 published statements that it no longer existed; an earlier scrapping date is perhaps more likely.

KERR STUART 692 of 1901, *Kynite*

Acquired new by CLR 1901, out of use c1923, scrapped 1952.

0-4-2T, Kerr Stuart 'Waterloo' class. 2ft 9in driving wheels, 1ft 9½in trailing wheels, wheelbase 3ft 9in driving 9ft 9in total, weight empty 12 tons 11 cwts, in working order 16 tons.

Kerr Stuart records show this loco despatched to Kynoch Ltd Thames Haven on 21st March 1901, named *Kynite* (proving that the name was applied before despatch). The date is backed up by Von Donop's comments which show that the loco was not yet present on 11th February 1901 but had arrived by 4th June.

The 1905 *Locomotive Magazine* article notes the livery as 'brick red with black bands to form panels and fine yellow and vermilion lines inside. The name *Kynite* is painted on the side tanks in large gold letters shaded with light blue and black'. The lining out is not very evident in photographs. The brick red colour remained into the loco's derelict days.

As noted earlier, 'Kynite', after which this loco was named, was an explosive patented by Kynochs in the 1890s.

Comparison of the available photographs shows no significant changes in the loco's condition during its working life.

As with the Kitson there are no post-1914 photographs of this loco at work, however it seems highly likely that it remained in regular use until the first Avonside arrived in 1917, and perhaps until 1919. Several different withdrawal dates have appeared in print, all unsourced. The story given to Gotheridge that it was 'last steamed in 1922/3 to supply steam for lagging Cory's Cracking Plant' has an air of credibility. When first put out to grass it must have been in a fairly obscure corner of the works, as the earlier enthusiast visitors did not notice it. The 1920s Coryton village children were however very familiar with it as a play attraction! The first known photograph is of 1936. The postwar enthusiasts were all taken to inspect it. It was moved more than once in the last years. IRS records give a scrapped-on-site date of March 1952. The 1961 *Railway World* article adds 'by T.W. Ward'. [Thos W. Ward Ltd had a large depot at Grays].

KERR STUART 1283 of 1915

Acquired new by CLR 1915, transferred away 1919.

0-4-0 Saddle Tank, Kerr Stuart 'Huxley' class (but this 'class' was highly un-standardised). 2ft 9in driving wheels, 11in by 16in cylinders, weight in working order 14 tons 15 cwt 2 qrs.

Kerr Stuart records show this loco delivered to Kynoch Ltd Thames Haven on 28th April 1915, 'ex stock' and painted in War Office grey. The order had come from Kynoch's Witton head office. The CLR would have found a sudden need for a more powerful loco at this time. It must have done the harder work until the first Avonside arrived in 1917.

Per IRS records this loco was transferred to Eley Bros Edmonton in 1919 (i.e. when the Kynochtown works closed). It then went to Witton c1921 and remained there, apart from a period on loan to ICI Gowerton works c1947-51, until sold for scrap in 1954.

There are no known photographs of this loco on the CLR, perhaps not surprising given that it was only there for a few years in wartime. The fact that this loco was on the CLR when new also seems to have gone unmentioned in railway writing prior to the postwar years.

There is a small possibility that this loco too was named *Cordite*, as stated by Woodcock.

AVONSIDE 1771 of 1917

Acquired new by CLR 1917, scrapped 1957.

0-6-0 Saddle Tank, Avonside B3 class. 3ft 3in wheels, 9ft 8½in wheelbase.

Ordered by Kynoch Ltd 29.1.1917, price £1,930. This loco would have been needed because of the increasingly heavy wartime passenger and goods traffic.

Described in the 1936 *Railway Magazine* article as 'red, lined out with black and gold' (this was presumably based on the author's visit c1935). The lining shows well in the earlier photographs (pages 47 and 49), in the photo at p.56 it is only clear on the cab sides. Geoff Balfour visiting in May 1948 noted that this loco was 'badly in need of a coat of paint, a job which was to be executed in the near future'. [A comment difficult to reconcile with the good appearance of the loco in the 1947 photographs]. He noted that the colour scheme was 'a reddish brown, with black panels fringed with white on cab sides, saddle-tank, bunker, etc. Buffer beams appeared to have been the same colour, with black borders separated by a white line. The backs of the buffer beams were painted the same way. The flared top of the chimney was of copper'. [The lining is not evident on most published 1940s photographs, but can be seen on the better original prints].

The *Railway Observer* reported in December 1951 that in November the loco was being overhauled and that the existing 'lined brown' livery would be replaced by 'Vacuum Oil scarlet'. This new Vacuum livery is seen in the 1952-4 photos at pages 67-69. It incorporated lining out plus the company's Pegasus motif on the cab sides. The precise colour used is strictly unproven as none of the subsequent visitors made any note of it.

The loco had no number or name until the numbering as 2 c1953 (between summer 1952 and May 1954 photographs). Previously it had been distinguished from the other Avonside by being referred to as 'the 1917 loco'.

The only significant modification evident is that the rear portion of the cut-outs in the cab sides was plated over soon after acquisition (compare photo at p.47 with that at p.49). A spark arrestor was fitted c1953 (photo p.69).

This was the most-photographed of the CLR locos as it was in daily service throughout except when under repair or overhaul.

The exact withdrawal date is not recorded but was some time in 1955-7. The first diesel arrived in 1955 but this loco was most likely retained as standby after that. Per IRS records it was scrapped on site by Ray of Southend in August 1957.

AVONSIDE 1672 of 1914

Acquired by CLR c1933, scrapped 1957.

0-6-0 Saddle Tank, Avonside B3 class, identical to the 1917 loco.

New 1914 to the War Department, Shoeburyness Military Railway, No.7. (The order by them of 10.1.1914 was for a 2-4-2ST but they agreed to accept this loco in lieu). Sold by WD 1930 to William Jones Ltd, dealers, Greenwich; sold by Jones to the CLR c1933. It was with Cory's by October 1933 when they sent a spares order for it to Avonside.

Acquired by the CLR to serve as spare loco, and was so used throughout, remaining at the back of the shed except when the 1917 loco was out of service. Accordingly there are fewer photographs of this loco.

The 1936 *Railway Magazine* article states it was 'green'. Kidner in *Standard Gauge Light Railways* says 'blue'. These are possibly different descriptions of the same colour - both probably only saw it in the semi-dark in the shed. There are colour photographs taken in 1936/8 (reproduced in *Bedside Backtrack* 1993), which suggest a royal blue. Green paint often turned blue over the years.

This loco was kept in good external condition up to 1939, but after the war it was in a neglected state externally. There is no evidence that it was ever repainted in Vacuum livery (however the last known photographs are from 1951).

The loco had no name or number until c1953 when it *may* have had the number 1 applied (this is *assumed* from the fact that the other loco was numbered 2 - there are no photographs showing this loco numbered). Previously it had been referred to as 'the 1914 loco'.

The exact withdrawal date is not recorded. The *Railway World* 1961 article states that 'towards the end 1672 was unserviceable with a condemned firebox'. There was presumably no need for this loco after the first Ruston arrived in 1955. Per IRS records it was scrapped on site by Ray of Southend in August 1957 along with the 1917 loco.

An impression has always prevailed that the steam locos were legally the property of the CLR rather than Kynochs / Corys. The best evidence for this is that the CLR's annual reports include figures for the number of locos, coaches, and wagons owned, which should not have been done if they were legally the property of Kynochs. Compare also the 1904 statement (p.29) that the CLR company needed to raise further capital for the acquisition of rolling stock.

According to Woodcock, major repairs to the CLR steam locos were carried out at Dagenham Dock by Samuel Williams & Sons. This has an air of credibility but no other reference is known.

78

opposite top

Kynite somewhere within the works - the exact location is not identifiable from the OS. This photograph must date from 1903-5, as it was used in the June 1905 *Locomotive Magazine* article, yet the loco has fallen into a poor external condition so it can hardly be 1901/2. Other views of *Kynite* in its working days can be found at pages 33 and 34.

Ivor Gotheridge collection

THE FADING OF *KYNITE*

opposite bottom

When first put out to grass in the 1920s, *Kynite* was left on the remaining part of the works siding that had run north to the cordite loading platform (this siding having no special use otherwise after 1923). Here she is still largely intact in 1936. The front cover of the cylinder has migrated to the footplate above, and the steam chest lid of this cylinder has also been removed.

Thurrock Museum

top right

In May 1947 she was still resting on this siding, now minus chimney, worksplate, etc. The name had been chalked on by the visiting SLS members! The 1948 view on the back cover is also at this location.

H.C. Casserley

middle

Kynite's last years were more mobile. By 1949 she had been moved to this unidentified location elsewhere within the works sidings, together with the derelict LT&SR coach, a Cory Brothers & Co open wagon, and tanker No. 1585. This view was taken on the June 1949 SCTS visit.

John L. Smith

right

Then by summer 1951 she and the disused coach had been moved again to the stops of the platform line as seen here. This last move was no doubt provoked by the start of redevelopment work in the old works area.

Frank Church

79

left
Kerr Stuart 1283 at ICI (ex Kynochs) Witton Works in the postwar period. The fact that this loco was numbered '2' at Witton may be the source of the notion that it had been so numbered on the CLR.
Industrial Locomotive Society, Frank Jones collection

middle left
Works plate of the 1917 Avonside. This was always kept polished, up to the end. Note that the lettering is thicker than that on the 1914 plate.

middle right
Works plate of the 1914 Avonside.
Brian Hilton

below
On the June 1950 RCTS visit, the locomen were persuaded to get the 1914 loco out from the back of the shed to enable the two locos to be photographed together. They were all but indistinguishable (in black and white photographs) originally, but at this date the 1914 loco had its proper chimney and dome valve cover missing. (Both had been restored by September 1950 - see photographs p.61). The hose connection on the uncovered dome suggests that this loco may have been steamed on shed (at low pressure) when otherwise out of use, to wash out 1771's boiler.
Frank Jones

80

above
The 1917 Avonside, photographed in 1949. This loco carries a rerailing jack in most photographs (and 1672 does in all photographs).
Lens of Sutton Association

below
The 1914 Avonside at Coryton in 1936, again showing the good external condition maintained for this loco up to 1939. Note the oil bottle at the front of the footplate.
Thurrock Museum

VACUUM / MOBIL DIESEL LOCOMOTIVES

The diesel locos appear to have been the property of Vacuum / Mobil even in the years prior to the winding up of the CLR company.

RUSTON HORNSBY 386871 of 1955

New 1955 to Vacuum Oil Co. Sold 1962.

4-wheel diesel mechanical, Class 48DS. 48hp, 7½ tons. Engine no. 384782.

Delivered 4.3.1955. No number or name.
Sold 1962 to George Cohen & Sons. At Cargo Fleet to 1966, Cransley Works (Northants) 1966-8, Kingsbury from 1968. Scrapped at Kingsbury May 1981.

RUSTON HORNSBY 418791 of 1958

New 1958 to Mobil. Sold 1973.

0-4-0 diesel mechanical, Class 165DS. 165hp, 28 tons. Engine no. 421712.

Delivered 14.4.1958. IRS records give name 'Coryton' but this may be a statement of location, as on the Bagnall photograph here, rather than a name as such.
Sold 24.3.1973 to unknown buyer. Subsequent fate not known.

W. G. BAGNALL 3160 of 1959

New 1959 to Mobil. Sold 1979.

0-6-0 diesel mechanical. 305hp, 38 tons. Dorman 6QAT engine.

Built by Bagnall for stock but quickly sold to Mobil. 3160 and 3161 were to the same design as 3122 and 3123 of 1957. For details see article by Allan C. Baker in *Industrial Railway Record* No.115, December 1988. They were the last standard gauge diesel mechanical locos built by Bagnall. Delivered 18.10.1959. No number or name.
Sold c.December 1979 to Resco (Railways) Ltd, Woolwich Industrial Estate. After rebuilding as Resco L112, resold December 1980 to Tunnel Portland Cement Ltd, Pitstone Works, Ivinghoe, Bucks (later Castle Cement), their No.1. Transferred c.April 1992 to Ketton Works. To Staffordshire Locomotives 26.9.2005. Then to T.J. Thompson & Son Ltd, Stockton, where scrapped February 2007.

ANDREW BARCLAY 506 of 1965

New 1965 to Mobil, still at Coryton 2006.

0-8-0 diesel hydraulic. Two Rolls Royce engines of 252hp each. 70 tons.

Delivered November 1965. This larger loco was acquired because of the increasing length of bulk trains, which the existing locos were having to work as two trips to Thames Haven. The Barclay was intended to haul 1,500 ton trains.
Rebuilt 1967 (per Mobil) / 1969 (per IRS records) by Andrew Barclay as two 0-4-0 locos, as the curves at Coryton had proved unsuitable for the long wheelbase. The two locos could be operated together back-to-back, or separately. When coupled they could be driven from either cab.
After this rebuilding the locos were numbered 1 and 2.
Returned to Andrew Barclay again July 1981 - May 1982 for a £142,000 refit. This included additional ballast to improve the weight distribution, both halves now having a balanced weight of 40 tons; additional safety rails; modifications to meet the current code of practice for diesel locos operating in hazardous areas; deadman's control; and improved cab insulation. The numbers 506/1 and 506/2 were now carried.

THOMAS HILL 291v of 1980

New 1980 to Mobil, still at Coryton 2006.

0-6-0 diesel hydraulic. Rolls Royce engine. 70 tons.

Entered service 1.12.1980. Designed to haul 1,300 ton trains. No number or name.
Sent to R.M.S. Locotec Ltd Dewsbury for overhaul 1995, not returning until 11.2.1998.

THOMAS HILL 239v of 1972

Acquired by Mobil 1981, sold 1984.

0-4-0 diesel hydraulic.

New 1972 to Shell (Shell Haven), their No.24. Sold to Mobil c.July 1981. Probably acquired as a temporary measure whilst the Barclay was away for overhaul. No number or name when at Coryton. No photographs have been found of this loco at Coryton.
Sold to Gulf Oil Refining Ltd, Waterston, arrived there w/e 3.2.1984. Still there at 1996, their No. 245.

right
Rear view of the Bagnall, taken for a piece on the retirement of Driver Garland in 1963.
Mobil

below
Bagnall 3160 at Ketton in 1993.
Cliff Shepherd

left
Ruston Hornsby 386871 is seen here at Thames Haven on 9th January 1956.
Frank Church

above
This 'incident' reported in the May 1958 *Coryton Broadsheet* provides us with our best view of the then-new 1958 Ruston Hornsby 0-4-0 loco. The presence of the roadway alongside the line suggests that the location is somewhere on the new 1951/2 line within the refinery area. Driver G. Garland was bringing in two vans and a tanker when they derailed, seemingly on facing points. The refinery produced two mobile cranes to rectify things.
Mobil

left
In the last weeks of its service at Coryton, Bagnall 3160 stands in the yard on 26th September 1979.
Robin Waywell

CLR driver Albert Everard poses in 1968 to demonstrate the then newly-introduced VHF radio equipment. This had been acquired for driver-shunter communication in the terminal area after the increasing length of trains had rendered the previous informal methods impracticable.
Mobil

Andrew Barclay No.506 seen here on delivery in November 1965, at the east end of the Bulk Terminal loading area. Note the capstan head and rope.
Mobil

83

left
Thomas Hill 291v stands at the east end of the Bulk Terminal when only five months old in May 1981.
Robin Waywell

bottom left
The No.1 half of the Barclay, also in May 1981, shortly before it left for refit.
Robin Waywell

below
The Andrew Barclay pair photographed on return from refit in 1982.
Mobil

bottom
A decidedly less pristine-looking 291v c1983. The roller shutters for access to the engine compartment seem to have fallen out of favour.
Ivor Gotheridge collection

BP LOCOMOTIVES AT CORYTON

(Summary only)

THOMAS HILL 294v of 1981, *Hamble-le-Rice*

0-6-0 diesel hydraulic. New 1981 to BP, to Coryton 1997/8 ex BP Hamble Oil Terminal. Still at Coryton 2006.

THOMAS HILL 295v of 1981, *Kentish Maid*

0-6-0 diesel hydraulic. New 1981 to BP, to Coryton 1999 ex BP Isle of Grain Bitumen Terminal. Still at Coryton 2006.

HUNSLET 6950 of 1967

0-6-0 diesel hydraulic. To Coryton 1999 ex BP Isle of Grain Bitumen Terminal. Sold to Elsecar Steam Railway 2006.

HIRED DIESEL LOCOMOTIVES USED AT CORYTON

D2224

Hired from BR 1964 whilst one of the Mobil locos was away for overhaul. (Only known from a photograph, in which only the upper part of the third digit of the number is visible; however D2224 was at Stratford at this time whereas D2284 and D2294 were on other Regions).

H 011 (formerly D3538/08 423)

Hired from R.M.S. Locotec Ltd Dewsbury from September 1995 to June 1998, whilst TH 291v was away.

THE LOCOMOTIVE SHEDS

The 60ft long steam loco shed was built at an unknown date in the early 1900s (one imagines that *Cordite* and *Kynite* had to put up with some shack initially). It was a fairly substantial structure by Light Railway standards. Strictly speaking it was not on CLR property. In 1923, when the lengthy new siding down to the refinery was put in, the connection to the loco shed had to be altered to come off the new line (compare 1919 and 1939 OS). However in the changes of 1950/1 it went back to its original position.

above
1st July 1951, with the new track layout, and much evidence of rebuilding activity beyond. (Compare the 1950 photograph at p.61 showing the old layout). The sign at right must be one of the most remarkable ever erected on a UK 'Railroad' - but it should be remembered that the new refinery was being constructed by a US-led team! At far right is the internal roadway to Cory's refinery.

D. Trevor Rowe

left
The south side of the shed, taken on 3rd March 1957.

Hugh Davies

below
Also dating from 1957, this view shows the east end of the shed. The 1955 Ruston Hornsby loco was its only occupant at this date. The shed was demolished soon after the opening of the new shed c1965.

below
This poor quality 1954 photograph is included as it is the only known view showing the shed doors.

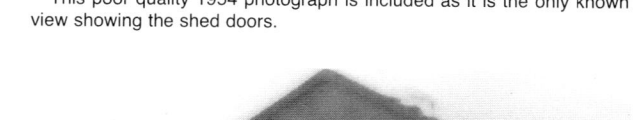

CLR LOCOMOTIVE STAFF

Apart from one reference to a 'Foreman' in the early years, the loco drivers and firemen/shunters seem to have been the only staff allocated to the books of the CLR company.

The following locomen are known of, either from press reports or personal recollections.

Tom (Thomas Charles) Johnstone   Driver 190x-c1939
Listed as Stationary Engine Driver in 1901 census. In the 1930s he lived at 78 Fleet St by the lion gates. He died soon after he retired).

Arthur (Edward) Baker   Driver 190x-1930s?   (Photos pp. 35 and 51. He lived at No. 10 Fleet St in the 1930s).

Fred(erick Edward) D'Aumont   Fireman   (Photo p.35. He lived at No. 17 Fleet St).

Ted (Edward Charles) Mynett   Fireman later Driver, cl925-1952   (Photos *passim*. He was born in 1900, the son of Charles Mynett a longstanding Kynochs/Corys employee. Lived latterly at No.2 Grove Terrace opposite Corringham station. He transferred to the Mobil maintenance division after the passenger service ended, but died in March 1961).

William Newman	Fireman 1940s
Clarrie Ockendon	Fireman c1940-195x
G. Garland	Driver c1949-1963
Albert Everard	Driver, c1960s (Photo p.83)
Alan Segasby	Driver, c1960s
Stan Edwards	Shunter, c1960s
George Martin	Shunter, c1960s
Paul Clark	Shunter, c1960s

Later rail staff were Mobil employees.

left
A closer view of one of the two primitive water cranes which appear in the background in other photographs. No reference is known to the loco water supply, which presumably came from the supply system already set up for the works in 1897.

below
The rebuilt Andrew Barclay pair, now numbered 506/1 and 506/2, outside the 1960s loco shed, c1983. The additional safety rails along the sides fitted during the 1981/2 refit are conspicuous.
Ivor Gotheridge collection

CLR COACHING STOCK

It is unlikely that it will ever be possible to provide full definite information on this subject; the following is the best available.

The Kerr Stuart coaches (1900)

Two lightly-constructed bogie coaches with 'toastrack' seating were obtained from Kerr Stuart in late 1900 for the start of passenger services, *cf* the January 1901 press report at p.26. (There is no known reference in Kynochs / CLR records to the acquisition of these coaches, or to Kerr Stuart being the supplier; the 1905 *Locomotive Magazine* article would appear to be the only source). One was a Third, with fully open sides; the other a First/Third Composite, with an enclosed First Class section and open Third Class section. Some time after 1909 the Third Class section of the Composite was enclosed (photo p.35). The Third remained open-sided, but Driver Ted Mynett recalled, from travelling in it as a child, that it had been fitted latterly with 'green curtains' to keep the weather out.

It seems unlikely that these coaches were used after 1915, but there is no specific evidence, and they may well have remained on site for some years after regular use ceased. There is no known reference to their disposal but they must have gone by the late '20s or they would have been reported on by visitors. It was in any case often found by other Light Railways with stock of this type that it was not long-lasting in service.

The first LT&SR four-wheeler (1901)

The two Kerr Stuart coaches were clearly found to be insufficient for peak passenger numbers at an early date, and a four-wheel Third was acquired from the LT&SR. This was definitely present by early 1902 (front cover photo). Despite this further acquisition the CLR continued to claim only *two* coaches in stock for many years after this.

It is not known what this coach's LT&SR identity was - indeed it has always been considered that *no* LT&SR coaches were ever withdrawn prior to 1912 (other than those damaged irreparably in the Pitsea accident). One wonders if it came on some loan arrangement? Nor is it known whether this coach was one of the two that survived into later years.

This coach had radiused corners to the vertical beading (i.e. curved framing at the head of the boarding) on the ends, as clearly shown in the photo at p.28. The coach that survived derelict in the postwar years also had this feature (photos p.79), which makes it more likely but does not of course prove that this was the '1901' coach. Radiused corners were not a normal feature of early LT&SR coaches, and it is not known how this/these coach/es acquired them. However they were a standard feature of GER coaches (on which the LT&SR coaches were modelled) from 1867 to 1881, and in some cases to 1884. The CLR coach that remained in use in the postwar years did not have this feature.

Three (?) further LT&SR four-wheelers (1915)

The earliest specific comment on the identity of the additional coaches acquired by the CLR in 1915 appears to be that in R.W. Kidner's *Carriage Stock of Minor Standard Gauge Railways* (1978). (Previous authors had only made general remarks about '12' or '14' coaches in total). Kidner had obtained, from a source now unknown, the information that three further LT&SR four-wheel Thirds were acquired, these being

LT&SR 2 (Midland 2445)
LT&SR 7 (Midland 2449)
LT&SR 9 (Midland 2451).

These were all from the initial 1876 batch of LT&SR coaches. They were rendered surplus to requirements in 1914 when the Midland brought further new bogie sets into use on the LT&S Section. Another source records that 2445 was withdrawn in March 1915, and 2449/51 in June 1915. The logic of all this makes one suspect that Kidner's information was correct.

By 1930 only two LT&SR coaches remained in use (and there were no others left on site). It is not known *which* two were the survivors - the coaches as observed in later years bore no evidence of their former identity, other than the '1876' date plate. In postwar years one of the two was derelict out of use.

One of the bodies was sold to a local farmer c1953 (*cf* photo p.69).

According to R.W. Rush, the coach still in use in the postwar years was LT&SR No. 11, but no source is known for this.

Eight (?) Midland bogie coaches (c1915)

The exact number acquired is uncertain. There are four at the head of the train in the photograph at p.47, and another three or four in the rear. The identifiable coaches are 1882/3 stock, but the numbers are not recorded. There was at least one Luggage Composite and at least one seven-compartment Third. It is perhaps surprising that the Midland did not offer more LT&SR four-wheelers rather than this bogie stock, although it was only six years younger.

By the end of the war the CLR was claiming 12 coaches in stock, which *may* equal four LT&SR 4-wheelers plus 8 Midland bogie coaches, but that is speculative. Gotheridge obtained from somewhere the story that a GWR coach had been acquired, but one would require further evidence for that.

At least one of the Midland bogie coaches was still in use in 1926/7 (photo p.56 and reported by J.C. Mertens from his visit). The others were observed derelict by Mertens. All seem to have been scrapped by 1930.

One CLR coach was bought from Cory's for 10s by their employee Luther Lord in the 1920s and used as a garage in his back garden in Fleet St.

LIVERY

It would seem from the evidence available that red (not necessarily of a consistent shade!) was always used for any coaches repainted by the CLR. D.M. Smith in his 1936 *Railway Magazine* article described the LT&SR coach seen by him as 'brick red', and all postwar accounts refer to the two surviving coaches as red. However the majority of the coaches acquired c1915 were probably never repainted, *cf* Mertens' reference to seeing 'a bogie coach devoid of all paint' c1927).

The Kerr Stuart coaches up against the stops of the platform line at Kynochtown, with a dumb-buffered wagon. This photograph was probably taken on the same day as that at p.28 top. For other views of these coaches see pages 32-35.

The coach that was still in use, photographed at Coryton on 15th May 1948. Geoff Balfour, also visiting in May 1948, reported that it had 'very recently been repainted. The coachwork was all-over bright red, with the footsteps, rails, and nearside lamp bracket at the ends painted black. Underframe black, wheels red with black bosses and tyres'. [In contrast he described the derelict coach as being 'a faded LMS red'].

The poor external condition of this coach prior to this 1948 repaint can be seen in the photos at p.60.

The most detailed examination of this coach was made by G.M.J. Chesmore in 1949 and reported in *Model Railway News* March 1950. He noted that the only significant external change was that some of the door drop-lights had been replaced by new ones with straight tops and square corners. He measured the length at 26ft 1in which tallies with the 26ft shown in the relevant LT&SR diagram. Internally there was only one full-height partition left, on one side of the centre compartment. [The derelict coach also appears to have had only one partition]. There was no trace at all of the lighting arrangements (which had probably been taken out when the CLR acquired it). The livery was noted by Chesmore as 'Post Office Red'. Traces of old maroon paint were found inside the coach.

Roger Carpenter collection

left
The opposite end of this coach, at Coryton c1950. *Roger Carpenter collection*

bottom left
Interior view of the coach, showing the brake handle fitted by the CLR, which only operated on the wheels at this end of the coach. Note the removal of the end seat. *Roger Carpenter collection*

below
The 1876 plate on this coach.
H.C. Casserley

CLR GOODS STOCK

This is a subject of still greater obscurity. The CLR annual returns claim ownership of '2' to '10' wagons at different dates, but we know from comments above that these figures cannot be trusted. The few photographs showing goods wagons on the CLR are mostly of 'visiting' wagons from the main line companies. Possibly all the CLR's wagons were 'internal user'.

Some Cory's open wagons were brought in in the interwar years but these would not have been CLR-owned. Similarly the oil tanker wagons would have been owned or leased by Corys / Vacuum / Mobil.

POSTSCRIPT: 1996 – 2008

In 1996 Mobil's fuel business in Europe was passed over to a joint operation with BP, in which BP owned 70%. BP then merged with Amoco as BP Amoco in 1998, and Mobil with Exxon as ExxonMobil in 1999. These changes left BP Amoco owning all the UK petrol stations, and in Europe the 'Mobil' name reverted to being a lubricant brand only, as it had been up to 1952.

BP/ BP Amoco also ran the Coryton refinery from 1996, and subsequently became sole owners of it.

The former Shell East Site (i.e. the area between Shellhaven Creek and Thames Haven sidings) was acquired in 1996 for future expansion of Coryton refinery.

By 1996, rail traffic from Coryton was down to about a dozen trains a week. The change of ownership did not much affect the number of trains, but did bring some changes of destination. Further changes came in 1998 when Shell ceased rail distribution from their other UK refinery at Stanlow, forcing customers who relied on rail to switch to other suppliers. Some turned to BP, and a number of 45-ton BP four-wheel tank cars were refurbished in 1998 for this traffic.

Following further decline in rail use in recent years, there is in 2008 only one service left, to Llandarcy. This runs 2-3 times a week and is attached at Ripple Lane to a Fords train, as far as East Usk. However it is expected that this Llandarcy working will itself cease at the end of 2008 when the plant at Llandarcy closes.

In June 2006 BP announced that it intended to sell Coryton refinery (leaving it without any UK refinery). The sale to the Swiss company Petroplus Holdings AG was made with effect from 1st June 2007, for £714m. The UK operating company is Petroplus Refining and Marketing Ltd. They had three other refineries in Europe, with a total capacity of 295,000 barrels per day - Teesside, Neuchatel in Switzerland, and Antwerp. Coryton with a capacity of 172,000 barrels per day was therefore a significant addition. Under the sale agreement Coryton will continue to supply BP retail outlets in the UK.

At the time of sale Coryton's production capacity was *ten times* its 1952 output, and consisted of 36% petrol, 27% diesel, 11% kerosene and jet fuels, 17% fuel oil, 4% lubes, 3% bitumen, and 2% LPG. The crude oil storage capacity was 4 million barrels, and there were 540 BP staff and 500 contractors' staff working on site.

Ownership of the remaining section of ex-CLR line was transferred to BP and then to Petroplus.

right
Twilight of the CLR - the same view as at p.75 top, now in autumn 2007. The rake of tankers are on the line to the 1980 Bitumen Loading Facility. The tracks on the western approach to the Bulk Terminal have been reduced from five to two.
Author

bottom left
There are few relics today of Kynochs or Kynochtown, however these houses in Wharf Road, Fobbing, made up of sections of the 1915 colony huts, can still be seen. They are said to have been bought in 1919 by Rev. Gardner. Given the large number of these huts sold off then, one suspects that an exhaustive search might reveal more still in existence!

bottom right
This seemingly-forgotten sign in Corringham still directs travellers down Rookery Hill to the old Manorway route to the industrial communites that have long since been removed.
Author

APPENDIX 1: CORRINGHAM LIGHT RAILWAY TICKETS

As noted in Chapter Two, the Light Railway Order had authorised maximum fares of 3d per mile 1st Class, 2d per mile 2nd Class, and 1d per mile 3rd Class. The distance from Corringham to Kynochtown was just over two miles.

It is not possible to reach any entirely definite conclusion as to all the fares charged at every period, as some of the evidence is confusing. The following account is the best that can be achieved.

Throughout the life of the CLR passenger service there were only two types of ticket available - singles, and weekly seasons. In the earlier years First and Third Class accommodation was provided (there was never any Second Class, not surprisingly given that Second Class was on the way out nationally by the time the CLR opened). The date of withdrawal of First Class is not known for certain, probably c1915 or whenever the Kerr Stuart composite coach ceased to be used. (However, at least one of the Midland bogie coaches purchased c1915 was a composite, so class distinction *could* have been maintained after then if desired). J.C.Mertens' 1931 letter confirms that there was 'now no First Class'.

The original fares would appear to have been
3rd Single	1d
3rd Weekly	1s 0d
1st Single	not known
1st Weekly	1s 6d

(The *Grays & Tilbury Gazette* report of the opening in 1901 states that the workmen were charged 6d per week, but this seems an extraordinarily low sum; perhaps the reporter was told that the fare was 1d and had assumed this to be a *return* fare? The survival of one low-numbered 3rd Single ticket with the 1d price, and of a Third Weekly with the 1s price overstamped 1s 6d, proves that these 1d and 1s fares had existed at some point at least in the first three years).

Some time in 1902-4 there was an increase to
3rd Single	$1^{1/2}$d
3rd Weekly	1s 6d
1st Single	3d
1st Weekly	2s 6d

(These fares are quoted in the 1905 *Locomotive Magazine* article). No new Weekly tickets were printed; the old stock continued in use with the new fare overstamped, as shown by the overstamped 1s ticket illustrated here, issued in 1907. New stocks of Single tickets were printed, although it is possible that the old stocks were used up by overprinting prior to that.

The Third Weekly price was as before the same as twelve singles, so no actual saving was achieved by purchasing a Weekly. The First Weekly was the same as ten singles - were some senior staff working a five-day week?

Subsequently however the Third Weekly was reduced to 1s 3d, equivalent to ten singles. A new stock of Third Weeklies was then printed with the 1s 3d price.

Finally there was a big increase in the Third Class prices (First having been withdrawn) to $2^{1/2}$d Single, 2s 6d Weekly. This may have been in 1917 when rail fares nationally were increased heavily because of wartime inflation. However there is no specific evidence; it may not have been until the 1920s. These fares remained until closure in 1952, but some time before the increase a very large number of Single tickets had been printed with the $1^{1/2}$d fare, and these continued in use until 1952 without being overprinted. Several enthusiast visitors from the 1930s on commented on the fact that the tickets said $1^{1/2}$d but the fare charged was $2^{1/2}$d. Similarly the number of 1s 3d Weekly tickets printed was such that these too were still being issued, unamended, in 1952. As no tickets were ever printed after 1923, the name 'Coryton' never appeared on CLR tickets. [The big printing of $1^{1/2}$d Single / 1s 3d Weekly tickets can hardly have been done in the dead years 1919-22, and the most likely date would be in the middle of the war when an ongoing large demand for tickets would have been anticipated].

All CLR Single tickets were thin paper tear-off tickets, with a stapled stub at left. The $1^{1/2}$d Third singles at least were in pads of 100. (Part-used pads with tickets 35888-35900 and 35901-35937 are preserved at the Essex Record Office, Acc. 10523). The backs were plain.

All CLR Weekly tickets were Edmondsons, again with plain backs. Both 1st and 3rd Class are known in four colours - blue, green, lilac and pink. It appears that a different colour was used each week in rotation to assist in ticket checking. Each colour had a separate number series.

Prior to 1914 tickets were issued or checked by the 'Conductor' on the train - the Kerr Stuart coaches were designed for this mode of operation. This would have been impossible after c1915. It is not known what was done during the war years. If up to 8,000 passengers a day were on weekly tickets, it is difficult to see how the ticket issuing could actually have been effected, so it may be that some type of longer-period passes were used then? By the 1920s, with passenger numbers down to 20-30 per train, tickets were being issued by the driver before departure.

Ted Mynett issuing tickets, probably in 1952. The ticket stock and takings were kept in his pocket, the money 'in an old blue handkerchief tied in a knot'. That some surviving tickets are on the grubby side is not surprising when one considers that they were issued and checked by a steam loco driver!

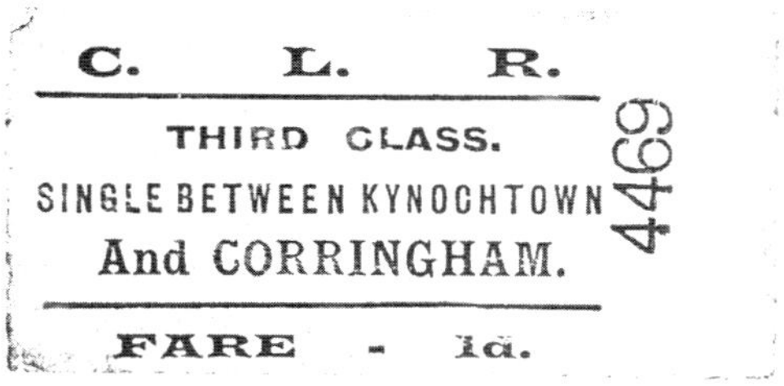

The sole surviving 1d Third Single ticket, assumed to be from stock printed in 1900/1. The non-serif serial number demonstrates that it was from a different printer to the surviving 3d First Single tickets (as one would hope, if the latter fare was a post-1901 increase). Colour white, 63mm by 31mm.

Ivor Gotheridge collection

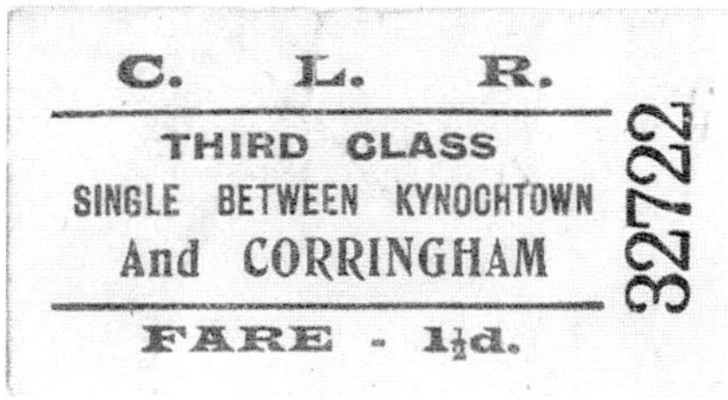

1½d Third Single of the later type, colour white, 55mm by 31mm. The number range of the (many) surviving Kynochtown to Corringham tickets is from 20113, issued to J.C. Mertens c1927, to 35939 sent by J.H. Freeman to the Vacuum UK Chairman John C. Gridley on 3rd March 1952 for preservation as the 'last ticket'. This suggests an issue rate of only 1-2 per day, which is possible given that most users bought Weeklies. However there may be a fallacy in this explanation!

Brian Pask collection

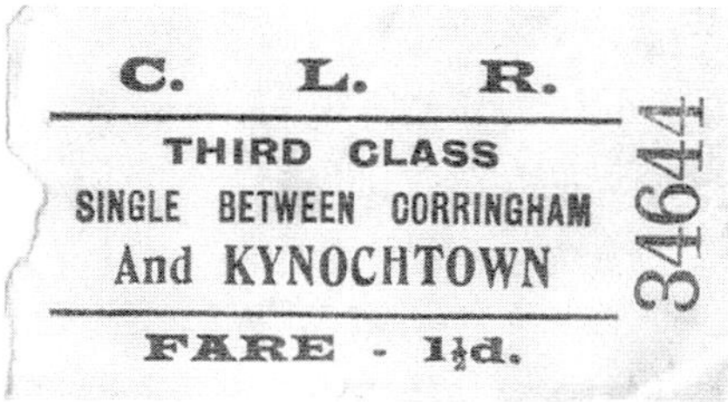

A corresponding Corringham to Kynochtown ticket. Fewer of these survive (it seems that the drivers were wont to collect tickets on arrival at Coryton - but perhaps they didn't dare attempt this at Corringham in the afternoon when the workers were all rushing off home?). The 'last ticket' in this direction was 39995, which does give a reasonable equality of numbers in each direction over the years. *Brian Pask collection*

left
Only three First Single tickets are known, all with the 3d fare. This Corringham to Kynochtown ticket is 63mm by 31mm, like the early Third Single specimen. Colour white.

Godfrey Croughton collection

right
Kynochtown to Corringham 3d First Single, 63mm by 31mm, colour very pale lilac, almost white.

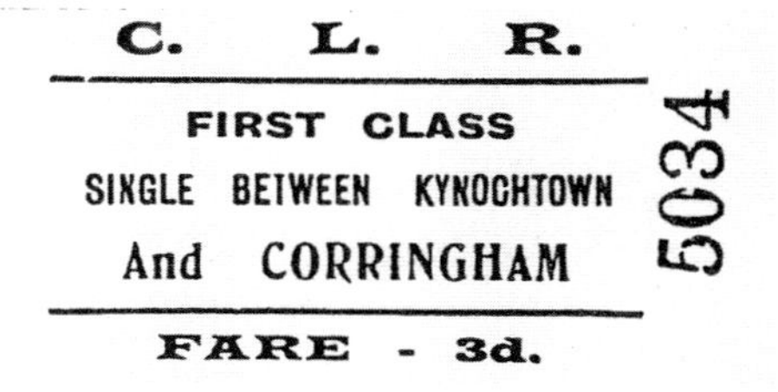

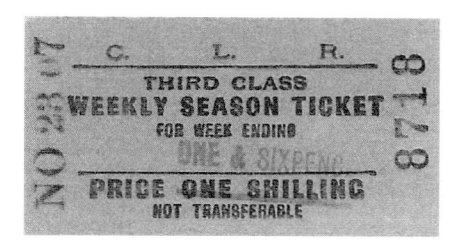

The only known Third Weekly ticket from the original 1900/1 printing, with the 1s price, is this blue ticket No. 8718. It has been overstamped 'One & Sixpence' and date-stamped NO 23 07. (23rd November 1907 was a Saturday, so the CLR's week must have been Sunday to Saturday). The date stamp has been wrongly positioned because of the fare overstamp. This ticket is, as one would expect, clearly by the same printer as the surviving First Weekly tickets (and is *different* in design from the later 1s 3d Third weeklies). Brian Pask has suggested Williamson as the most likely printer of these 1900/1 Edmondsons.

Godfrey Croughton collection

Green First Weekly No. 0982. The highest numbered known First Weekly ticket is 1546. All the surviving First Weekly tickets are from the same (original 1900/1) printing, and all are in fact unissued. It is to be imagined that they were after c1903 overstamped before issuing with the revised fare of 2s 6d, in the same way as the contemporary Third illustrated here.

Godfrey Croughton collection

Later style pink Third Weekly No. 21793. By the time these 1s 3d tickets were printed a new system of letter-stamping (here a K) had been introduced to identify the week of issue - hence the lack of any 'for week ending' wording. The A-Z stamping plus the four colours meant that the same combination only recurred once every two years. The known numbers of these tickets are 21660 to 37888 (although all the examples above 25500 are unissued, probably because they were sold to enthusiast collectors). The Glasgow Numerical Printing Co is considered the most likely printer of these tickets.

Godfrey Croughton collection

Lilac Third Weekly No. 23775. This ticket is unique in having a lower case letter-stamp. However the fact that it is horizontally-stamped may not signify much.

Godfrey Croughton collection

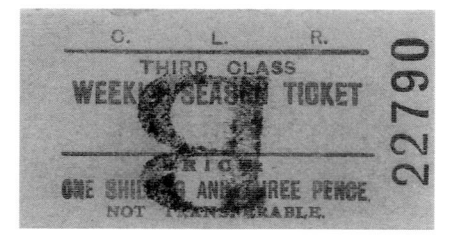

Pink Third Weekly No. 22790 with upside-down 'B' letter stamp.

Ken Butcher collection

Unissued Lilac Third Weekly No. 37381.

Godfrey Croughton collection

This is the only known CLR non-passenger ticket. It is a tear-off ticket like the Singles, 58mm by 31mm, colour pale peach. The 15mm wide stub is still attached. The 4d fare is decidedly on the high side. It is difficult to see many people wanting to send a parcel on the CLR!

Godfrey Croughton collection

APPENDIX 2: CORYTON / SHELL HAVEN BUS SERVICES

As with so many minor railways, the CLR's passenger traffic was heavily reduced once bus services began in the 1920s, with withdrawal of the passenger service becoming inevitable in due course. This account will also serve as background to the decline in the usage of the Tilbury - Thames Haven workmen's service (for which see *The Thames Haven Railway* p.52).

There were two principal bus routes, those from/via Pitsea and those from/via Stanford-le-Hope. Both ran (of necessity) via Corringham and thereby took away most of the railway's purely local traffic as well as those people who had previously 'enjoyed' slow connecting journeys. Both were introduced immediately after the Manorway was improved to a high-quality motor road c1925.

The PITSEA service was operated by J.W. Campbell & Sons of Pitsea and had its origins in 1915 when Campbell's started a horse brake from Pitsea station to Corringham station for Kynoch's workers living in Pitsea and Vange to travel to work via the CLR. In November 1916 Campbell's acquired a Whiting-Denby 30hp lorry converted for passenger use, and ran this instead (to Corringham station? or through via the Manorway?). This served not just the Kynoch's workers but also those working at LATHOL and at the Shell refinery. It is not clear what level or type of service was provided in the early 1920s, however Campbells had acquired their first proper buses by the time the Manorway was improved, and the service then became fully established as their bus route 4, Pitsea to Shell Haven. This ran twice a day for workers on the daytime shift. The route was via Lampits Hill (not via Fobbing). Cory's workers would have had to alight/board at the Haven Hotel. The times remained unaltered through the 1930s and '40s, and are shown in the 1942 timetable here.

Campbells never provided any advertised service for Shell and LATHOL three-shift workers in the 1930s and '40s. However the opening of the new Shell refinery in 1950/1 and the new Vacuum (Mobil) refinery in 1952/3, both of which operated on three shifts seven days a week, changing over at 6am, 2pm and 10pm, brought a big increase in the number of men on these shifts. From 1951 buses were run for the Shell three-shift men at 5.17am, 1.17pm, and 9.17pm from Pitsea / 6.10am, 2.10pm, and 10.10pm from Shell Haven, all daily. From 1953 additional buses were run to/from Coryton, Vacuum Oil new refinery gates, for their day shift workers (7.15am from Pitsea / 4.35 or 5.35pm from Coryton); but Vacuum three-shift men seemingly had to use the Shell Haven buses and walk to/from the Haven Hotel until 1955.

Eastern National were keen to establish themselves in Basildon once work on the New Town began. In 1955 they introduced a new route 242 from Whitmore Way in the first completed section of the New Town to Coryton: as shown in the timetable here, this provided for Vacuum day shift and three-shift men. By this date two of the three Campbell brothers were approaching retirement age, and negotiations were entered into for an EN takeover of the routes, which took effect from 19th February 1956. The 4 was renumbered 236. The youngest brother Albert retained some of the vehicles for excursion and tours work, which he continued until 1971.

In the years that followed, the 236 journeys were reduced in favour of the 242, and the 236 was withdrawn in June 1963. At the same time car ownership amongst the comparatively well-paid refinery workers was increasing rapidly, leading to the 242 also being withdrawn in June 1965. The 2C provided a residual service from Pitsea until 1973 (see below).

The Pitsea services were never of real use to those *living* in Coryton / Shell Haven, who would have had little urge to travel in that direction in any case (prior to the opening of the Basildon New Town shopping centre).

The STANFORD-LE-HOPE service was commenced in 1926 by Suckling & Haxell's Motor Services, who became Stanford Motors Ltd in 1928. They ran from Stanford church to Shell Haven via 'Coryton' per the timetables, however it would appear that this meant the Haven Hotel. By 1932 the service involved three or four buses for day shift workmen, other weekday journeys for office

The 1930s/40s Campbells service on route 4 is illustrated by this October 1942 Southend area timetable extract. The 11.30am Saturday journey from Pitsea was always advertised as a public journey but it was presumably essentially an empty working. The corresponding morning return, and Mon-Fri afternoon outward, journeys were never advertised. If one takes the timetable at its word, the 5.0pm from Shell Haven ran on Saturdays as well as the 12.0.

The first Eastern National timetable for the 236, from a leaflet produced by EN for the timetable changes of 18th March 1956 on the former Campbells routes. (The routes had all been renumbered in February but the Campbells schedules had continued *pro tem*). In the case of the 4/236 the only significant change was the transfer of the Sunday early morning journeys to the 2C (see 2C timetable, p.94).

The diversion of most 4 journeys via the Shell West Site (originally known as the 'MEC' - Middle East Crude - site) had been effected in 1951 when the new refinery opened. This involved a short diversion off the Manorway into the refinery site and back again. The bus stand at the West Site was by the main refinery office block (grid reference 719825).

The initial 21.8.1955 timetable for the new EN service 242.

92

hours staff, and three return trips for the Shell and LATH-OL three-shift men (5.30am, 1.25pm, and 9.25pm from Stanford-le-Hope; 6.10am, 2.10pm, and 10.10pm from Shell Haven - all seven days a week). On Saturday afternoons there were additional through journeys to Grays, providing a shopping and leisure facility for the inhabitants of Coryton and Shell Haven.

Eastern National took over Stanford Motors in July 1935 and the route became their 35; the initial EN timetable is reproduced here. A reorganisation of EN Grays area services in May 1936 saw the Saturday afternoon Grays journeys considerably reduced, and the addition of weekday journeys to 'Coryton' for Cory's office staff (8.40am from Stanford-le-Hope, 5.0pm Mon- Fri / 1.0pm Sats from Coryton). Unlike Stanford Motors, EN clearly meant by 'Coryton' some point in the village itself, but it is not known exactly where the Coryton terminus was prior to the opening of the new refinery entrance in 1952/3.

The 35 continued, in reduced form, through the war years. After the war most buses ran through to/from Grays. The June 1951 timetable here shows 6-9 weekday buses and 6 Sunday buses to/from Shell Haven, plus the same Coryton journeys as in 1936; any of the Shell Haven journeys could of course also be used by Cory's/ Coryton people simply by walking to the Haven Hotel.

A smaller one-bus operator, Day & Bedingfield of Stanford-le-Hope, also provided one journey a day from 1929 until taken over by the LPTB in 1934. This started from Balmoral Avenue, Southend Road, Stanford-le-Hope, departing 7.15am from there and 5.5pm Mon-Fri / 12.5pm Sats from Shell Haven. D&B ran other journeys from Stanford to Grays and Purfleet. After the LPTB takeover, the D&B operations were worked by EN (being outside the LPTB area, they could not be run by the LPTB themselves). Most journeys were subsumed into the 35 but the Southend Road - Shell Haven journeys became a separate route 59 which lasted until 1941.

In 1951/2 the Grays area services were transferred from Eastern National to London Transport and the 35 became LT Country route 349. The service had to be much enhanced soon afterwards because of the opening of the Vacuum refinery (see the 1955 timetable here). Most buses continued to run to/from Grays. The 349 survived until June 1968, latterly much reduced.

In the late 1940s Westcliff-on-Sea Motor Services began running duplicate journeys from SOUTHEND to Shell Haven on their trunk route 2 (Southend to Grays). These became '2C' in 1951, at which date they consisted of two buses both leaving Victoria Circus at 7.50am, one for the Shell West site and one for Shell Haven, with corresponding return journeys. These were clearly for office hours staff only. Some journeys were extended to Coryton refinery in 1952. Eastern National took over Westcliff in 1955 and the 1956 service is shown here. The 2C continued until May 1973 by which time it was the *last* bus service to Shell Haven / Coryton.

In the heyday of bus use in the 1950s there were over 30 scheduled buses a day to/from Shell Haven or Coryton or both. There were also other buses that did not appear in published timetables.

The bus fares (5d Workmen's Return Corringham to Shell Haven / Coryton in the 1930s, 5½d in 1955) were the

The first Eastern National 35 timetable, October 1935. With very minor exceptions not affecting anyone's travel options, this service is the same as that in the Stanford Motors 1932 registration timetable. Note that one journey in each direction strikes an even more direct blow at the CLR by operating via 'Digby Road' (which presumably meant diverting along Fobbing Road as far as Digby Road, and then back to Corringham). The one journey a week to/from 'Coryton' here had been introduced prior to 1932 and had presumably turned round at the Haven Hotel pre-1935. The logic of this may have been that there were too many people decamping to Grays for the afternoon after Saturday dinner to fit on one bus, so the timetabled relief might as well start from here. The lack of any corresponding return journey may have simply been because people drifted back home at different times in the afternoon and evening.

The last Eastern National timetable for the 35, June 1951. The Coryton workers' journeys are as introduced in 1936 (except the Saturday return journey is now an hour earlier); the Saturday 1.45pm Coryton to Grays had disappeared long before this date. It is fairly certain that several of the journeys in this timetable would have had unadvertised duplicates on a daily basis, as per normal EN practice. Whilst the service is still entirely geared to the needs of workers, it does in fact permit the Coryton or Shell Haven housewife to go to Grays for the morning Mons-Fris.

[The Sunday timetable is omitted for space reasons - the buses running on Sundays were the 5.10am, 7.0am, 1.5pm, 4.10pm, 5.30pm, and 9.8pm to Shell Haven, and the 6.10am, 7.50am (to Grays), 2.10pm, 5.10pm (to Stanford-le-Hope), 6.10pm, and 10.10pm from Shell Haven].

same as the CLR's fares, so there was no financial incentive to stick to the CLR either.

When the new Shell and Vacuum refineries were under construction, the contractors' men were brought in daily by completely separate contract coaches. The contract for the Vacuum construction workers was managed by Victoria Coaches of Leigh-on-Sea, and required 108 vehicles at its peak.

Cory's, Vacuum/Mobil, LATHOL, and Shell, also owned their own buses, principally for internal transport. Cory's are believed to have had two vehicles, hence their ability to replace the CLR trains with a bus in the war years. The Cory's buses were also used to provide a service for Coryton residents to Stanford-le-Hope. This was continued by Mobil who acquired a new Bedford for it in 1966.

London Transport 349 timetable from October 1955. For space reasons, only the Mon-Fri service is shown. There are twice as many journeys here as in the 1951 EN timetable, but LT unlike EN did show duplicates in the published timetables. A new facility is the 7.4am through from Grays to Coryton, with return at 5.35pm, in lieu of the former 5.5pm to Stanford only.

Only LT used 'Thames Haven' as a timing point. This was the entrance to the LATHOL (London & *Thames Haven* Oil Wharves) site. There was a bus stand just inside the gate (grid reference 732827). All bus services passed here although some may have stopped on the Manorway itself.

November 1956 service 2C timetable. The Mon-Fri service now provides a facility for the daytime shift workers at 6.32am, in addition to the previous journeys for office staff. It would seem that at this date the Shell and LATHOL men did not get let out an hour earlier on Fridays as their Mobil colleagues did! Note the varying combinations of West Site / East Site (i.e. Shell Haven) / Coryton served by different journeys.

The Sunday early morning 2C journeys from/to Southend were run because there were no trains early enough on Sundays from Southend for those on early turn (who in the week could go by train to Pitsea to pick up the first 4). Until 1956 this journey ran from Southend to Pitsea only, passengers transferring there to a 4 (Campbell's having successfully 'protected' their route in this way). When EN took over Campbells it was obviously more sensible to run a bus through from Southend to Shell Haven as a 2C. In December 1956 it was extended to Coryton.

The 2C did not reach its peak until 1960 when an additional bus was provided at 8.27am (Mon-Fri) Pitsea to Coryton, and the evening return journey at 5.5pm Mon-Thur / 4.35pm Fri was duplicated with one bus from Coryton and one from East Site.

above RT3636 and Campbell's 1947 Albion LTW 470 stand at the Shell Haven (Shell cottages) terminus in January 1956, a few weeks before the EN takeover of Campbell's routes. The bus stands here, on the west side of the road north of the Shell village (grid reference 737822), were built postwar. It is not known exactly where at Shell Haven buses terminated in the earlier years.
Frank Church

above In the last months of the 349, RT4046 pulls away from the Coryton Mobil Refinery bus stops in summer 1967, passing Eastern National Lodekka 2489 on the 2C. These stands were at grid reference 744823 and from 1960 on buses did an anticlockwise circuit of the staff car park before arriving at them.
Dr J.R. Young

left In February 1967 Mobil purchased two RTLs, 942 and 989, from London Transport for internal works use. The latter is seen being prepared for advertising a works 'Safety Control Programme'.
Mobil

CORRIGENDA and ADDENDA to *THE THAMES HAVEN RAILWAY*

p.6 (upper caption) - should read 'the major reclamations of the *seventeenth* century'.

p.25 (bottom left) - the 21st August 1854 boat train was from *Tilbury*, however the same point applies.

p.40 (r/h column, third para) - should read 'was put in for this in *1918* (4)'.

p.51 upper photo should be credited to Bob Cogger.

p.58 65552 is *J17* class.

p.60 (l/h column, second para) - The working of trains to/from Ripple Lane began in *1973*. These trains were known as 'trippers', and a special bell code 1-5-1 was used for signalling them. The same locos and crews were used on Ripple Lane - West Thurrock and Ripple Lane - Purfleet oil workings.

p.60 bottom left and p.62 map - The new Shell terminal did *not* in the event come into use on the planned date 27.3.1983, owing to delays in commissioning the new Low Street signalling. The new signalling on the branch was belatedly commissioned on 28.4.1983, but this excluded the connections to the new terminal, which were brought into use on 3.5.1983. The first working into the terminal was a light engine for BR testing purposes on 5.5.1983. The first commercial traffic began several days later. (Information from Barry Bridges, then Dagenham Dock Area Inspector).

p.67 (re 1983 resignalling) - The branch was worked by Pilotman from 27.3.1983, when the old signalling was taken out of use, until 28.4.1983, when the new signalling was brought into use.

p.73 The photographer's minder in the middle photograph is Frank Warwick, then a Divisional Freight Inspector at Liverpool Street.

The lines within the 1983 Shell terminal were lifted in 2000.

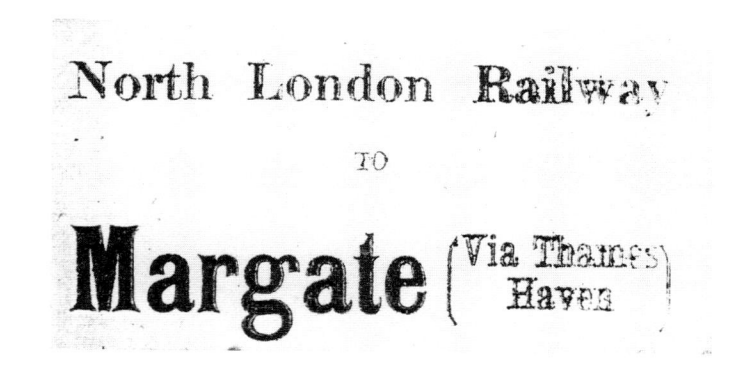

NLR luggage label — *Godfrey Croughton*

Margate to Fenchurch Street single ticket issued on 20th July 1878. — *Godfrey Croughton*

Coryton in 1951 could almost be on some BR country branch line. — *D. Trevor Rowe*

FAREWELL

This May 1948 view must have been taken on a Monday to Friday as the shadows show that it is around 6pm. The timbers under the sleepers in the foreground are the bridge over the Salt Fleet.

Ted Mynett poses during the June 1948 Birmingham Locomotive Club visit.

Joe Moss, courtesy Roger Carpenter